The Other Side

Qazi Nasir Uddin, Ph.D.

authorHOUSE®

AuthorHouse™
1663 Liberty Drive
Bloomington, IN 47403
www.authorhouse.com
Phone: 1-800-839-8640

First published by AuthorHouse   1/20/2011

ISBN: 978-1-4520-7951-6 (sc)
ISBN: 978-1-4520-7950-9 (e)

Printed in the United States of America

This book is printed on acid-free paper.

About the Author

The writer of this book was a faculty member of the University of Chittagong in Bangladesh. He has contributed numerous articles and research papers on literary and social issues and was recognized as a prominent scholar and critic in his country. He came to the United States in 1979 when he was 34 years old. The reason for his coming as he described, "to widen the horizon of my understanding," but he had to do it the hard way unable to bring money from a poor country to a rich country. What he brought with him was a treasure of an ancient culture and civilization hitherto little known to the Western world and a strong determination to understand the Western culture. He decided to keep that treasure with him until it is time to share those with everyone.

After his arrival, while washing dishes in restaurants, attending gas stations, and working as janitors to pay for his stay and study, he kept attending universities to widen his horizon of understanding, and earned an M.A. degree from the University of California, Riverside, and a Ph.D. degree from the State University of New York at Binghamton. He concentrated on the Comparative Literature, which uniquely prepared him to compare and contrast among various cultures and literatures.

He was not involved in any way with American politics and its cultural debates. He is a curious onlooker who honestly and sincerely wanted to express his feelings without trying to be politically correct. That is what makes his essays so thought provoking and unique. It would be very interesting to know what he thinks about American social and cultural values, and its customs and traditions from the other side.

Self-criticism is something we rarely want to do. It is, therefore, necessary to look at us through someone else's eyes. That is why the best

thing to do is to let someone else, preferably an outsider, to take a look at us and criticize us if we really want to know ourselves. To criticize objectively, the critic must be completely detached from the object of criticism, which means that the critic is not going to gain or lose anything by criticizing. In other words, the critic must not have any motivation either to please or displease someone. He or she must not have any intention to be politically correct.

Although it is very difficult to find a critic like that, it is not altogether impossible. It is difficult because the critic not only have to be neutral but also be able to criticize. The critic must have the educational and cultural background to be able to understand the issues to be criticized. Besides the critic must be in a unique situation, which allows him or her to criticize objectively, free from all preconceived notions and stereotyped generalizations. The mind of such a critic must be a tabula rasa, a clean slate.

If we live in a society for a long period, it becomes almost impossible for us to remain detached. We are bound to form an opinion and to take a stand. We must fight for something or against something. This behavior keeps us from becoming a good critic. That is why we need an outsider. But there are not too many outsiders living in the United States who lived in another culture for 34 or more years, were recognized as intellectuals through publications in esteemed journals, participation in seminars and symposiums, and then in the height of their careers, decided to come to the United States.

Foreword

When one side is bright, the other side must be dark. To look at the other side, we have to shed some light on the other side or better be there physically when the sun rises on the other side. We can see pictures of the other side, read books about it, and talk to some people from that side to get some ideas about that side. But, none can be compared to going to the other side and staying there as long as it is necessary to know that side well.

When I was in Bangladesh, once I looked at a globe and drew a straight line from my city to half the way around the world, only to find that I was in Los Angeles. I read books about the United States, watched American movies, and talked to some visitors from the United States to get some knowledge about the state of California and particularly the city of Los Angeles. I was fascinated, enchanted, and excited. I wanted to be there physically to see it clearly.

Unfortunately, there are many who like to see only one aspect of something and refuse to see the other. Considering the other side doesn't necessarily mean that we're surrendering to the values of the other side or rejecting our own values. We do that only to be fair, honest, intelligent, civilized, and cultured. We shouldn't be afraid to look at and consider the other side. If we're afraid, it will prove that we don't have enough confidence, faith, and conviction in our own beliefs and values. Are our values so shaky that if we look at the other side we're going to be converted? If that is the case, it's better to be converted. It doesn't make any sense to live a life with shaky ideals.

I lived in a civilization and culture, which is 2500 years old, and I'd been there for 34 years before I ventured to come to the United States in

1979. When I got myself admitted in a prestigious university, one of my professors greeted me with such words, "Welcome to civilization", as if civilization belongs to the United States only. This is a classic example of an American intellectual's ignorance of the other side of the world. Although I could mention that I was a faculty member of one of the prestigious universities of my country and thereby had some knowledge about world's civilizations, I decided not to say a single word in reply that day and decided to wait for my turn to come. Over the years, I got familiar with American way of life and its culture. Now I think it is my turn to claim that I have a unique advantage to compare and to see the similarities and the differences among different cultures and civilizations.

I studied Comparative Literature in the United States. Over the period of my studies, I was re-educated to think critically and to look at all sides of an issue before making up my mind. I was also advised not to jump to conclusion, so I can compare objectively. But, ironically, I was also advised by one of my professors, "If you want to stay in this country, don't criticize this culture." So, I decided to adhere diligently to that advice for a long time. I appreciated all the nice things about this culture that I could appreciate.

When I first came, I saw a picture of this country, which didn't match, precisely with the picture that I'd created in my mind over a long period of time watching television, reading books, and listening to people. This is why it is almost impossible for someone to know the other side without being there physically. If we want to see what is on the other side of a coin, we have to turn it over. No description is going to match the real thing.

It is not my intention to claim that I am the only one who feels differently and thinks differently. I am sure there are many foreigners and Americans who think exactly the way I do. But we're minorities, and our voices aren't often heard. We don't like to come forward with different opinions. The reason is that we're too often asked to blend in the main stream of American culture, as if it's a crime for someone to see things differently.

This book, therefore, shouldn't be considered as an attempt by an uninformed foreigner to criticize and ridicule or to put down the American culture without really understanding it. This is also not an outcome of cultural shock, as most people would like to think. This is a humble appeal and a request to look at the other side by turning things around. If we do that, we'll be able to think universally and feel ourselves as

universal human beings, completely detached from local color, prejudice, preconceived notion, and stereotyped generalization about things that have profound impact on civilizations and cultures of this universe.

Acknowledgements

The origin of the most of the articles in this book can be traced back to my chitchat at our dinning table with my teenage daughters, Lucina and Poulina. They deserve the credit for provoking, inspiring, and organizing my thoughts often by offering opposing views and sometimes vehemently protesting whatever I had to say to keep them from blending in the main stream of American culture.

When our dinning table chitchat turned into a hotbed of social and cultural debate, my wife Tahmina could not take it any more. She put a curb on my freedom of speech by prohibiting me from talking while eating. Although she often came to my rescue, it was too much for her to endure such a hullabaloo on the dinning table.

I, therefore, decided to write all of my thoughts out, so I don't have to lecture anymore while eating dinner. Thanks to Tahmina for taking away my freedom to speak but not my freedom to write. By the way it took so long to publish this book that by this time Lucina has already earned her Ph.D. and Poulina her M.D degree. However, I still try to keep them from blending in popular American culture.

Contents

Babysitting

Baby-sitting was a term unknown to me when I first came to the United States. When I heard that people are baby sitting or having problem with baby-sitting, I had no idea what they are talking about. One day when I was expressing concern about my deplorable financial situation with one of my friends, he suggested that my wife should do some baby-sitting. When I inquired what baby-sitting is all about, he looked at me in such a way as if he had never heard such a thing in his life, "You really don't know what baby sitting is all about!" he exclaimed. "I have the remotest idea, to be very frank with you", I said. When he explained, it was my turn to be extremely surprised, " You mean mothers leave their babies with someone and go to work!" "That's what exactly it is, and what's so wrong with that anyway", he wondered. "How possibly they could do such a terrible thing to their own children!" It was my turn to be surprised. That's how my understanding of baby-sitting started. The more I thought about it, the more I tried to find justification for it, the more depressed I became. I could see the reason, but I could not find the justification.

In Bangladesh very few mothers go to work. They normally stay home and take care of their children. Especially during the period of their pregnancy and couple of years after the childbirth, they never leave their baby alone even for an hour. Of course some women go to work but well ahead of their scheduled delivery date they stop going to work, and after delivery they wait about couple of months to go back to work. But in that case another female family member such as mother, mother in law, sister, aunt, brother's wife or brother's sister takes care of the baby, no outsiders. Babies always stay in their favorite and familiar own home and see the familiar faces everyday, so they don't seem to mind or get nervous or

scared. Therefore, the system of taking off from work one day before going to the hospital for child birth and going back to work day after child birth, leaving the baby with an outsider, was beyond me. I did not like the idea at all. But then I was told that this was what was American way of life.

The more I contemplated on this issue, I felt mentally disturbed and annoyed. I thought it was not fare to deprive a baby from the loving care of the real mother even for an hour. It appeared very cruel to me. I still believe that the emotional and psychological impact of living children with a babysitter for six to eight hours a day is tremendous, both for the mother and the children. Babies suffer from fear, insecurity, sense of neglect and hopelessness, anger, and frustrations. If you have any doubt in your mind about what I am saying, you have to go back to the time when you were one or two years old. If you can remember, go back to an occasion when your mother left you with someone else for a short period of time to take care of something. I do not know whether it is very difficult for you to remember that, but I can easily go back to that time and can feel the anguish and suffering I had gone through.

If you cannot think about your childhood, think about your children's, if you have any. For example, I have two daughters. My wife and I never have left them with a baby sitter until they were five years old. I remember an incident which is still vivid in my memory and which gives me a tremendous pain when I think about that. My oldest daughter was only 15 months old when my wife was in the hospital to have our second child. I had to go to the hospital to stay with her during the time of childbirth. I, therefore, asked one of my friends to baby-sit my older daughter for that time until I came back approximately after two hours. My friend told me that my daughter cried all the time and did not touch any food or drink while I was gone. I can go on and on giving examples from my own experience and from the recollections of my friends about how they felt or what is the emotion involved in getting abandoned with a babysitter. But I don't think it is necessary.

It is no denying the fact that babies enjoy a sense of security in the presence and in the arms of their parents. If you carry a baby in your lap or on your shoulder and walk through a dense forest and encounter a ferocious tiger, you will be afraid of the tiger, but your bay will not. Babies in the arms of father and mother feel well protected. By dumping our children to a baby sitter, we are depriving them from that sense of security and protection. Those babies, who are being taken care of by baby sitter when grow up and become adult, carry along these feelings of neglect,

hopelessness, insecurity, and lack of protection. It is, therefore, no wonder that in this society we encounter many people who blatantly exhibit such sense of frustration, anger, hopelessness, and lack of protection in their day-to-day life.

I believe that leaving a baby with a baby sitter is the greatest of all kinds of child abuse this civilization have ever seen. In the name of achieving economic freedom and getting even with men, the women of the western world are depriving their children of the most valuable gift of the nature, which may be termed as love, affection, and concern for others. But it is not my intention to put the blame squarely on mothers. It is not mothers' decision alone that results in abandoning babies to baby sitters. Today's fathers are equally playing a greater role in creating a baby-sitting industry in this country. Most of the time irresponsible fathers force mothers with no other alternatives than to seek full time employments and heartlessly dump their babies with strangers. If they had a choice,

I am sure, they would like to stay with their babies at least for couple of years when the children need undivided care and attention of a loving mother, not a paid careless baby sitter.

Ironically, while we are creating unhappy, aggressive, and frustrated human beings by depriving them of the love, care, and affection of their mothers what they so well deserve, we are blaming them subsequently for creating problem in the society by engaging in unsocial, criminal, and violent behavior. We are also spending millions of dollars designing programs to correct many social evils created by such individuals. We should have spent that money in the first place by allowing mothers to stay with their babies at least for two years without being required to go back to their jobs. I think that this society can afford to pay a mother at least for two years to stay home to raise a mentally and physically healthy baby.

Bilingual Education

The United States of America seems to be the only nation in the whole world where a debate is still going on whether bilingual education is appropriate or not. While the federal and state governments are spending millions of dollars for bilingual education, some educators and researchers are not so sure about the effectiveness and purpose of a curriculum emphasizing bilingual education.

What is bilingual education? I examined this concept from various angles to understand what it means and was unable. I often wonder what bilingual has to do with education or education has to do with bilingual for that matter. The implications of intellectual's manipulation of certain words and terms are that once someone can successfully coin a concept, no one tries to examine that coinage to find out its relevance to a particular concept. The reason we do not pay attention to coinage of concepts is that we are always busy debating a concept instead of challenging the concept itself. My intention in this article is to challenge the concept and prove beyond the shadow of a doubt that there is no such thing as bilingual education. The question should be whether there is any such thing as bilingual education, not whether bilingual education

Is good or bad.

A close scrutiny of the term bilingual education will reveal that these words 'bilingual' and 'education' do not go together. Put together they do not have any meaning. First of all, bilingual always refers to human beings. A person who can speak two languages fluently is a bilingual. If bilingual education means the education of a bilingual then it gets very confusing. If someone knows two languages he or she can use one or the other to educate him or herself. For example I am a multilingual person including

5

English, and I used Bengali language in Bangladesh to get educated. When I arrived in the United States I used English to educate myself. I intended to educate myself in American literature. So I took courses in American literature. My textbooks were written in English and my professors delivered lectures in English. I would not feel more comfortable to get a textbook of American literature translated in Bengali and also would not ask for a teacher who speaks Bengali to explain American literature in Bengali. So it is obvious that bilingual education does not apply to people who are already bilingual.

The term, therefore, actually means giving bilingual education to monolingual people. Doesn't it sound contradictory to start with? Why do we need bilingual teachers to teach monolingual students? For example, if a student speaks only Spanish, why do we need a

Bilingual teacher to teach him American history? We need a teacher who speaks only Spanish and a textbook written in Spanish. In this case we are using one language. So what is bilingual education?

The main argument of the proponents of the bilingual education is that the United States of America is a country of immigrants. People from all over the world are coming here every day. Children arriving here from non-English speaking countries often find it difficult to cope with a new language when they enter into American classrooms. It is very insensible on our part not to address that problem. If people are allowed to immigrate to this country, they should be given the opportunity to educate themselves. Not having bilingual education (people use this term without understanding what it means) is equivalent to denying them their basic human rights to receive an education. Some also believe that eventually those students are going to learn English and assimilate in the main stream of American society. Imparting education in their own language will keep them in their classrooms. Gradually they will learn English to the extent that no more bilingual education will be necessary.

First of all, I will examine the feasibility of this proposition. There is no denying the fact that many students come to this country from various linguistic and cultural backgrounds and they need to educate themselves. It is also true that it is very difficult to learn a subject matter using a foreign language. But the solution to this problem does not lie in getting a bilingual teacher and books translated into one's native language. It is not practical because a bilingual classroom may turn into a multilingual classroom with twenty students from twenty different countries. Is it economically feasible to hire one bilingual teacher for one student? Besides,

specific textbooks in translation may not be readily available. On the other hand, it will be extremely difficult to find one teacher with multilingual ability in eight languages (I am an exception).

However, it is not altogether impossible to form a class with a group of students speaking the same language, such as Spanish. Since they do not understand English we are teaching them geography, for example, in Spanish. In that case why should we need bilingual education? We need a teacher who can teach geography using the Spanish language only. But in doing so what are we really trying to achieve? Are the students learning geography in Spanish able to use their knowledge in the United States? Besides, it is going to be very difficult to form one-language bilingual classes in localities with diverse ethnic populations, such as New York, Chicago, Los Angeles, and San Francisco.

Let us pretend that we have a class of all French speaking students. Do we need a teacher for them who is bilingual in English and French? Apparently it looks like a good idea, but the answer to that question is, no. If the students do not understand English, the bilingual teacher will not feel comfortable to explain a concept in English. Besides, why should the teacher do that anyway? Does bilingual education mean teaching a group of students a subject matter using two different languages? Do you have time for that in the same classroom within the same time frame?

From such observations it will be evident that the term bilingual education is a misnomer. It does not carry any meaning whatsoever. Using this banner some educators are doing something completely different. They are grouping together some students with limited

proficiency in English and some with no proficiency at all, and relegating them to a special class with a bilingual teacher to help them out. Their cause is very noble. They want to help those students who have problems with English but want to continue their studies and finish the course to graduate. That I consider a noble effort but the manifestation of that under the banner of bilingual education is very wrong. It is not only wrong but also very dangerous because this innocent looking approach in reality is keeping some students from achieving their goal of learning English and assimilating into this culture.

This segregation of students diminishes their self-esteem and makes them timid and nervous. Furthermore, instead of fostering racial harmony and tolerance in the campus, it creates different groups of students with superiority and inferiority complexes, and hatred and apathy for one another. So in the name of helping them out we are actually doing a great

disservice to them. Is this a conspiracy? Is this another manifestation of racism in the disguise of bilingual education? It is easy to jump to that conclusion, but I don't like to do that. Sometimes an honest and innocent attempt to help a group of people may turn against them.

As soon as we realize that the term bilingual education stands for nothing, we will be able to rearrange things and help those who are really struggling hard to overcome their deficiencies. If the purpose of bilingual education is to help non-English speaking immigrants in the United States, then we have to divide that population into various categories. We have to design curriculum according to their levels of proficiency in English. But the focus must be on teaching English, not any other subject matter. If some one needs to learn a language first, that person should not be sent to a physics class, for example.

I believe that to accommodate all groups of non-English speaking immigrants, we have to design a minimum of four and a maximum of six levels of courses. A placement test will determine who is suited for what level. After successful completion of that course level, students will be eligible to get regular courses. Placing a student in a particular English class and letting the student finish that course will definitely prepare that student mentally and academically to enter into a regular classroom where the medium of instruction is English.

There still remains the probability that even though a student has finished an English course, he or she is not doing well in the subject matter area. To handle that situation, we, of course, need sympathetic and sensitive teachers but not bilingual ones. For example, a teacher may have 33 students out of which 7 students are from 7 different countries. We are not going to ask the teacher to learn their languages to teach them. The teacher should go on teaching as usual using his or her normal method of teaching, but at the same time keep an eye on the non-English speaking students. Because the teacher is sensitive to students from different cultures, he or she wants to make sure that students understand the instructions. If the teacher is sensitive, the teacher will encourage those students to come and see him or her during his or her office hours for extra help.

The more a student listens to a foreign language the more he or she starts understanding it. It is just a matter of sitting in the classroom. When I was a student, once I decided to take a French language course to fulfill a course requirement. I read the course description and found that it would be taught completely in French, meaning no English would be used in the classroom. I sat in there for a full hour, did not understand a single

word the professor said, and got very nervous. At the end of the class I approached him. The professor smiled and said, "I did not expect you to understand anything. That is what language learning is all about. You do not have to understand anything. Just sit down and listen to every single word I say." I did exactly the same thing, and after one month, I felt like many doors and windows were opening for me in a dark room. I started understanding more and more day by day.

The fact is if we want to help non-native speakers of English improve their conversational, reading, and writing ability, we have to put them in a class where only English is used. They may suffer initially but eventually they will start enjoying it. While I am advocating against the bilingual method of learning and teaching, it is not my intention to downplay the importance of being bilingual or multilingual. I can handle eight languages. I am not against learning foreign languages. But, I do not see how the so-called bilingual education can help either to learn a foreign language or to become successful in a foreign country.

The point I am trying to make here is that to learn or to teach a language bilingual approach is not necessary. I have been teaching English as a Second Language for the last ten years. My students are one hundred percent Spanish speakers. Although I learned some Spanish grammar rules and regulation, and words and phrases, that does not make me a bilingual. I explained to my students that they should not expect me to explain lessons in Spanish. I have been successfully teaching them English since 1985. How do I know I was very successful? Once I was Teaching English as a Second Language in a school, which went bankrupt. Students of my class decided not to part from me. They started their own class by renting a small room and rehiring me. That made big news in the Los Angeles Times.

I often encounter such questions as: How do you teach them without using their language? My answer is some of my students do not know their language, meaning they can only speak that language but cannot read and write. How can I use their language to teach them? As you can see, this is a very wrong notion that you have to know someone's language to teach him or her.

I would strongly recommend learning at least two foreign languages besides one's native language. It can be done by requiring knowledge of two foreign languages for high school graduation. Instead of crying for bilingual education, all language lovers must support the idea of making two foreign languages a requirement mandatory for graduation.

By learning a foreign language, one not only acquires that language but also makes oneself familiar with a new culture and new people. One becomes sensitive to the people of other cultures. One develops tolerance and patience for people from other cultures and dispels many preconceived notions and stereotyped generalizations. While bilingual education segregates people and promotes apathy and indifference among people, new language learning brings people together and helps create a new world of living together with mutual respect and understanding.

Boyfriend and Girlfriend

One thing I could not fully comprehend is the annexation and recognition by the United States of a new human relationship known as "boyfriend and girlfriend". In Bangladesh I was used to such kind of family and social relationships as "wife and husband", "father and mother", "brother and sister", "uncle and aunt", "grand father and grand mother", so on and so forth. Just "friend" is also another socially recognized relationship. For example, I could introduce someone as my best friend, brother, sister, father, or mother. I was grew up in an environment of human relationships approved by the society and its culture, where there was no room for another new relationships known as boyfriend or girlfriend.

So when someone in the United States tried to introduce to me a new acquaintance as "my boyfriend" or "my girl friend", I could not understand what that person was talking about. According to our culture, we would claim someone as friend only if he or she is someone outside of the traditional family relationships. It gradually became clear to me that there exist a human relationship in the United States beyond all traditional relationship that I was aware of. I then started pondering on such questions as: How did that happen? When, for the first time, young people started to get into the relationship of boyfriend and girlfriend? What is the purpose of this relationship? Why this society annexed and approved this relationship? Those questions started bothering me until I have

been fully able to comprehend the significance of those terms, boyfriend and girlfriend.

During my close observation and scrutiny, I noticed that boys and girls start getting into that relationship as early as eight years of age. By the time they reach the age of thirteen, most of the boys and girls get involved

in that relationship. If someone for some reason cannot come up with a boyfriend or girlfriend, he or she becomes a subject matter of research, as if it is most normal for human beings to develop that kind of relationship. Perhaps I would also fall into that category if I were born and brought up in the United States and believed that because I don't have a girlfriend there must be something wrong with me. Since I grew up in Bangladesh where there is no such thing as boyfriend and girlfriend, it was an interesting subject matter of investigation for me. It was not to me a normal, natural relationship such as brother or sister or father or mother.

During my research and encounters with people of all walks of life, I found out that this relationship was non-existent in American culture also. Even fifty years ago American society did not recognize any relationship as boyfriend or girlfriend. Could not introduce someone as "my boyfriend" or "my girlfriend". This is a relatively new development in the evolution of the society. How it came along? I started to get the picture. When a society becomes sex oriented, put sex above everything else in life, all members of that society want to feel comfortable and justified in engaging in certain kind of sexual activity which otherwise would be considered wrong, abnormal or harmful. For example, when a man wanted to have an extramarital sexual relationship with a woman, that man did not want the society, the culture, or the religion to tell him that this was wrong, unsocial, or undesirable or against religion. That individual wanted the approval of the society and the society gave him that approval by annexing and endorsing this new relationship boyfriend and girlfriend.

Why was the society so quick in approving this relationship? Because the members of the society found out that this was the most easy and convenient way for man and woman to live together without getting involved in a marriage. Getting involved in a marriage requires thoughtful preparation, commitment, sacrifice, and accepting responsibility, and making adjustment and compromise. Everyone wanted to avoid that. People wanted to have an easy access to sex without getting involved in marriage. Whether this is good or bad that is another question, but I am sure that was the main motivation behind quick approval of this relationship.

It is no denying the fact that sex is one of the most dominating factors of life. But civilization requires that the urge to satisfy sexual desires must be controlled and regulated. That is why the institution of marriage came into being, and the concept of family and child rearing developed. We have become civilized by controlling and regulating our passions and desires

and by taking responsibility for our actions. But civilization once in a while succumbs to assault from our uncivilized and cultured animalistic instincts that inhibit our subconscious mind. The biggest assault on our civilization came when we failed to regulate sex, instead sex started to regulate us.

When sexual desires regulate us, we don't like to think about decency, decorum, privacy, and responsibility or preparation. This is the reason the society is gradually moving away from marriage and promoting such relationships as boyfriend and girlfriend, the requirement for which is less restrictive than the former. Some people argue that such relationship can develop independent of sex. Of course it can, but it is an exception and a rare exception, which has nothing to do with the trend that we have at the present time. Other argues that the existence of this relationship is justified as a prelude to marriage. Before I get involved in such a serious matter as marriage, I have to develop a relationship with someone to know that person well. This argument looks like innocent and reasonable but that does not justify claiming someone as boyfriend or girlfriend.

However, it will be evident from further investigation that this boyfriend and girlfriend relationship did not develop as a preparation for marriage. The fact that 8 to 13 years old boys and girls are claiming one another as boyfriend or girlfriend will provide solid evidence that this concept is not marriage related. A thirteen years old boy does not get a girl friend to prepare for marriage. Once in one of my communication classes I got an opportunity to ask a question: Why do people need a boyfriend or a girlfriend? Many answered: They are checking each other to find out whether they can get married. I nodded in understanding. Then I asked my second question: Why teenagers need boy or girlfriend when they are in high school and not thinking of getting married? A pin drop silence prevailed in the classroom for a moment and then a daring student broke the silence by announcing: to have sex. This time I nodded in understanding too. No matter how hard you try, it will be very difficult to explain a relationship such as a boyfriend or a girl friend without referring to sex. While one can conveniently attribute the reason as preparation for marriage, but one cannot possibly do that when it comes to teenagers. It is difficult to attribute the reason to anything else whatsoever other than to the manifestation of a sexual attraction for each other.

I believe that this relationship among young adults gained momentum with a consent and approval from the parents of the society. Why parents wanted not only to approve but also to encourage such relationship for their children knowing fully well that it might promote teenage pregnancy

and create social problem? Were they out of their mind? Not really so. They just wanted to justify their own sexual behavior. When you don't want to get married but want to have sexual relationship with someone, you have to talk to yourself and to the whole world that their is no harm in doing so. You have to declare that it is a normal human behavior. Also, when father and mother get separated or divorced, and live with their boyfriend and girlfriend, they have to allow their children to do the same thing. When father brings a girlfriend home after divorcing the mother of his children, the father must ask his daughter or son such question as: Who is your boyfriend or girlfriend? Bring him or her home and introduce to me. If they say we don't have any, the father must encourage his children to get one. Otherwise father cannot justify going out with or bringing home in a girl friend. The same thing holds good for the mother too.

After living in this country for so many years, I think I now have a clear picture of what boyfriends or girlfriends are for. The tragic aspect of this whole scenario is this we have a big problem with teenage pregnancy and single parenthood in this society for which our government has to spend billions of dollars designing programs. Unfortunately no one has ever pointed finger to the real reason. People believe that sex education will take care of the problem. They are wrong. The real reason behind having irresponsible father and teenage mother or single mothers is this new relationship that this society created. I am not talking about any values, religion, morality, and philosophy; I am talking about a social problem. The issue at stake is the quality of life being sacrificed to sexual desires.

The Changing Role of Journalism

How would you feel waking up every morning with seven national and local newspapers lying around in your driveway? Probably you would like to get rid of them before they make you very confused. I was only a seventeen years old college student in 1960, so I found myself more confused than anyone else with those newspapers. Yet I thought of collecting those and laying them on a side table in my living room to be able to browse through the headlines quickly. If you thought my family had enough money to subscribe those newspapers or enough time to read them, you got it all wrong. After finishing their education my two elder brothers decided to join the noble profession of journalism. Those newspapers were, therefore, compliments of publishers of newspapers. I considered myself the luckiest person in the world being able to get all the newspapers of the country dropped to my doorstep early in the morning. That is how I developed a love for newspapers and subsequently for the profession of journalism. Once I thought of following my elder brothers footsteps by becoming a journalist but somehow I ended up teaching literature.

But the love and respect I developed for newspapers early in my life stayed with me for a long time, and I could not possibly shake that off for anything else in the whole world. I could not conceive of any other reasons to lose my attraction for newspapers. During the period of my growing up I have seen the intrusion of radio, television, and telephone one by one in my living room but nothing was able to take the place of newspapers. It was almost impossible to conceive of a morning without not only one but also all the newspapers of the country crowding my living room.

The presence of all the newspapers in our living room also elevated our social status in the neighborhood. Our family was considered the

most informed family in that locality. Any one needing any information or confirmation of any event or incidents used to rush to our house and we were very happy to provide all sorts of information that were available to us through newspapers. I still can see that look of respect and admiration that my classmates and neighbors had for me in their eyes. It was than when I first practiced writing in newspapers by sending poems, short stories, and articles in the children and students section of the newspapers.

Also, I felt very proud of myself being known as younger brother of the managing editor and news editor of two local newspapers. Journalists were held in high regard in those days in those countries, next to the teachers. They were always invited in all kind of social, educational, cultural, and political events. It is, therefore, no wonder that I wanted to become a journalist like my brothers. So when after finishing my education I started a career as an instructor in a local college I was not all together happy. I decided to make an adjustment and compromise between these two professions by becoming a staff writer for a national newspaper.

With this background in newspapers, I believe that I am fairly acquainted with the role of a newspaper in shaping up the life an individual and eventually that of a society. At least I know about myself. I can see what role newspapers have played in building my character and my personality. I can easily feel the influence of newspapers in my life. When I contemplate more I can see the influence of newspapers in shaping up my neighbor hood, my community, and finally my country. Those journalist sitting in their office rooms guiding the society and reforming it. In our times most of the journalists did not have cameras and computers, they had only pen, lots of them. I have seen how many my brothers carried.

Now our journalist invariably carry cameras all sorts of them, and laptop computers, and tape recorders, yet how many of our young generation are going to feel that newspapers have any influence on their lives? I doubt it very much. I can guarantee that no teenagers in this culture is going to say that he or she got some influence of news papers in his or her life in any form or manner. I have asked many of my young adult students, do they believe that newspapers have changed their thinking in any form or manner. The answer was obviously no. If a newspaper cannot influence a life, it cannot also influence a neighborhood, a community, and a society as it did and still does in many cultures.

In Indian subcontinent newspapers were responsible in bringing in new ideas, political, social, cultural, and educational. Newspapers inspired people and gave birth to Indian nationalism, which motivated people

to unite against the British rule of India and eventually brought the Independence of India. Newspapers reformed many social and religious customs and traditions. It was the newspapers, which agitated people against the age-old tradition of burning wives alive after the death of their husbands. It were the newspapers which helped in abolishing the popular tradition of compelling wives to pass their lives without getting married after the death of their husbands. It was the newspapers, which fought against the dowry system and brought an end to that practice. It was the newspapers, which created new styles and new genre in literary writings.

I can go on and on giving examples of what were the roles of newspapers in creating and reforming Indian civilization and culture. Can someone write about the role of the newspapers in creating and reforming American civilization and culture? Do American newspapers have any influence on the civilization and culture of this country? To find answer to this question, ask any students of American schools, colleges, and universities whether any newspapers has any influence on his or her way of thinking or does any newspaper have any influence on his or her life. The answer is going to be big no. I would not be surprised if 90 percent of them say they never read a newspaper on regular basis, not to speak of having any influence of newspapers on them. Can any one in this country claim that a newspaper has profoundly contributed in building up his or her character and personality? I doubt it very much. There is a saying in India and Bangladesh that a person is known by the newspapers he or she subscribes. Have you ever heard of any such thing in the United States? We have heard of some books creating an impact on someone and changing a life, but not a newspaper.

I am writing this essay recognizing the influence of newspapers in my life. I am writing this to tell everyone about the contribution of newspapers in shaping up my character, my
personality, and my philosophy of life. If I have not had any influence of newspapers on my life, it would not have been possible for me to write this essay. I wonder whether anyone in the United States can honestly and sincerely claim that he or she has grown up with a profound love and respect for a particular newspapers? I am very interested to hear from them. If someone can come forward writing essays like me recognizing the fact that
he or she owes it to a particular newspaper for the development of his or her personality and intellect; I will take back what I said about American newspapers.

These are some of the serious questions we have to encounter and answer to understand what happened to the newspapers of today in the United States. Today's newspapers do not change any individual or the society. In the United States people changed their newspapers. The designs, layout, and the content of the newspapers are changing to satisfy the demand of the popular culture. The popular culture that prevails in this society is dictating the newspapers. If you turn the pages of any newspaper after reading this essay, you will have no problem in understanding what I am trying to tell you. You will find one fourth of the newspaper filled with advertisement. I am not against advertisement. I fully understand that advertisements are the lifeblood of a newspaper. I have seen the death of many newspapers due to financial trouble. But a real journalist believe that it is better to die than to sacrifice his or her professional ethics.

However, I have no problem with filling up the pages of newspapers with as many advertisements as possible. But I don't like to see pornographic advertisements in the disguise of advertising bras, brassieres, and underwear newspapers nowadays are displaying naked women's bodies on their pages. In other words newspapers are yielding to the demand of perverted individuals and satisfying their animal instincts. Instead of changing the obnoxious behavior of some spoiled human beings, newspapers are changing for those people. Newspapers are shaping those people up to satisfy popular demand, and cater to the cheap sentiments of some people.

In other cultures newspapers have respect for themselves. They have a sense of decency and decorum. They do not sacrifice their quality, integrity, and philosophy for money. They do not print obscene advertisements to stay in business. Ironically in many countries newspapers cannot stay in business if they sacrifice their quality. For example, if a publisher of a newspaper in Bangladesh starts publishing tasteless pornographic materials in the name of advertisement, the circulation of that newspaper will drop. People are not going to buy that newspaper any more and eventually it is going to close its door. It is not so in the United States. The more pornographic materials it inserts, the more popular it becomes.

Did all the newspaper always play this role of entertaining people in the United States? I don't think so. If we look back to 50 years from now, we will find that American newspapers were not that different from the newspapers of the rest of the world. Traditionally newspapers all over the world were instrumental in shaping up politics, culture, and literature of a country. While newspapers in many countries are still shaping up politics, literature, and culture of many nations, in the United States the

last vintages of such role of newspaper can be found confined to the area of politics only. Newspapers in the United States definitely have something to do with politics. They play a very important role in organizing public opinion. Politicians are dependent on the newspapers. They need help from newspapers unless they get rich enough to own one. When a political party or an individual politician becomes owner of a newspaper, journalists working for that newspaper lose their freedom. They are not any freer to write what they believe. They must sacrifice their personal philosophy and ideologies if they want to work for that particular newspaper. In rare occasions, they might find themselves very lucky if they don't see any conflict between their philosophy and owner's philosophy.

So it is unlikely for any journalist in the United States to have an independent philosophy where money play a big role in politics, where only rich people can afford to engage in politics. The politician must be rich or must have connection with rich people, which mean that they must be guided by the vested interest of rich people. In such a situation it is almost impossible for a journalist to maintain his or her integrity of character. So journalist does not create newspaper, the politicians or the rich people do. When I made my above statement that the last vintages of the role of newspapers can be found in the area of politics it is outwardly true, but inherently not.

It will now be evident that the popular American culture that I talked about before influences the newspapers of this country, but it cannot influence the political philosophy of a newspaper. The political philosophy is controlled and dominated by the business magnets and their puppet politicians. On the contrary, in Bangladesh the newspapers create politicians. Some old newspapers are considered as huge institutions. Politicians need their endorsement to stay in politics. Money cannot buy journalist in Bangladesh. Everyone knows that. Most of the prestigious newspapers in Bangladesh came into existence by the effort of prominent intellectuals of the country. Business people had nothing to do with it.

A capitalist cannot start a newspaper business in Bangladesh only because he or she has money. To start a newspaper business, one must have solid educational, cultural, and intellectual background. If some one, with money, but without the background mentioned above, wants to own a news paper that person will have a very difficult time in finding journalist working for them. That owner will only find some journalist willing to work if he or she signs a contract specifically mentioning that as an owner he will have no control over the opinion of the editors or over their

philosophies and ideologies. Owners will control the finances only not the philosophy of the paper. I don't believe this is so in the United States.

Once a prominent newspaper in Bangladesh with a distinct ideology went bankrupt. A capitalist wanted to buy that newspaper with a condition that the paper must sacrifice its rigid ideological standing and make some compromised by being flexible. The owner refuses to do that. Money cannot by everything in Bangladesh.

Let me draw her a good analogy from my own experience to make this point very clear to my reader. Once I started a college in a locality in Bangladesh, which felt the need for a college, but had no resources with which to begin. I arranged public meetings, advertised my project in the newspapers, raised funds, bought lands, and constructed a building. When I had done all of these with the help of the local people, a prominent businessman locally known as sowdagar came with the offer of huge amount of money to build the college but with one condition. His name should be added to the existing name of the college. I refused. I told him that he could donate money for a noble cause without asking anything in return. It is up to us to decide whether we would like to recognize his contribution by adding his name to our college. We do not accept any donation with any condition attached. My governing body fully endorsed my viewpoint. This is what is Bangladesh. Money cannot buy a college or a newspaper in that country.

History of Becoming Uncivilized

Back in the late 1950s after graduating from high school, when I first went to college, I came upon an essay entitled "What Civilization is Not" by Clive Bell. That was required reading for my English class. The pace of learning was a slow and relaxing one in those days and in those countries in the far eastern part of Indian sub continent now known as Bangladesh. No panic, no pressure, no research to match your courses with specific job requirements. My parents told me to go to college not to find a job, but to get some knowledge and to become a perfect human being. I was in college with the intention to get some knowledge. I was there to know myself, know the world, to know the history of human beings, and the history of civilizations.

It never occurred to me that I was seriously in pursuit of knowledge, instead I felt that knowledge was coming to me without knocking on the door, as I left the door of my mind open to receive it. It was very surprising for me, therefore, to realize one day that there was a precious moment in my life when I realized that I had really learned something, right then and there, which had dramatically and drastically changed my thinking process forever.

Clive Bell's essay was one of those rare articles, which I still remember and will cherish for a long time to come. The point he was trying to make was that we think that we are civilized contrasted with those people who lived in caves and killed animals to satisfy their hunger. Bell proves that this notion of civilization is not true. In his article he mentioned a prehistoric tribe that used to make loud noises and announcements before eating each meal, as an indication of invitation to people who might possibly be hungry. Bell poses a serious question: Would you consider

them uncivilized only because they lived in caves and just killed a bison for dinner that night?

The reason we consider cave dwellers and animal hunters as savages and uncivilized is that we confuse the connotation of civilization with that of material progress, advancement in science and technology, building of skyscrapers, and highways. We believe those are the signs of civilization. Some would even refuse to admit that they are confused when they talk about technological advancement and civilization. These terms are synonymous to them. So, they cannot think of civilization without the existence of highways, airplanes, and skyscrapers. Another reason why most of us believe that material progress is synonymous to civilization is that we have been taught that we are gradually becoming civilized. Our schools, colleges and universities are teaching courses entitled "History of Civilization" which normally traces the progress that human beings have been able to make in changing their living conditions over a period of time. According to that theory, when we leave a cave and build a house, we become civilized. When we change an old occupation for a new one, we become civilized, so on and so forth. History of civilization basically establishes the notion that civilization is a progression from an uncivilized status of human being to a civilized one meaning improved and enlightened.

No one has argued with this concept of civilization although Clive Bell had tried to explain that what we thought was civilization was actually not. The reason Bell's definition was not paid attention to was simple. Who wants to confess that we are gradually becoming uncivilized? However, Bell had only initiated the discussion by bringing to the forefront the question: Can those cave dwellers be really termed as uncivilized considering their behavior such as waiting for hungry people to share food with and distributing food to the needy people? To find the answer to that question, we have to understand what the real connotation of the term civilization is.

As I understand it, the basic traits of civilization lies on the fact that civilized people have respect for themselves and for others. Civilized people are not selfish. They manifest love, care, and sympathy for fellow human beings. We would not call a person civilized only because that person wears expensive clothes, drives a luxurious car, and lives in a huge mansion. We would call him or her civilized only if he or she behaves nicely with people. Similarly, if we find a rich and famous person engaged in a behavior which we consider inappropriate social conduct, we call him or her uncultured

or uncivilized although that person might possess several billion dollars and a Ph.D. degree.

From such an observation it will be evident that civilization has a different connotation than material progress, progress of human beings in controlling the natural forces and improving their conditions of living. While the history of human beings is a progression in knowledge, science, and technology, history of civilization can be considered as a regression in love, concern and sympathy. It is not my intention to prove that every single human being is becoming uncivilized day by day. The fact I am trying to establish is that if a person can gradually become civilized (acquire certain qualities to be termed as civilized), another person can also gradually become uncivilized (earn certain characteristics to be termed as uncultured or uncivilized).

If civilization reveals certain inner qualities of human beings as generally agreed upon, building of cities, roads, and machines cannot be the manifestations of those qualities. We might live in a perfectly built city but we can gradually become uncivilized. Ironically when our buildings can continue to go up and up to touch the sky, our inner qualities can keep on deteriorating and go down and down to touch the ground.

It appears to me that once upon a time our houses were small, roads were narrow, but our minds were broad. We were civilized and cultured at that time. As our houses started to grow bigger and taller, roads started widening, the relationships between human beings also started widening and continually we started to become uncivilized.

Now that I have been able to clarify that material and technological progress of a nation has nothing to do with the improvement of the inner qualities of its citizen, we cannot indiscriminately claim that we are civilized. Before claiming that we are the most civilized people in the whole world, we have to take an assessment of our inner qualities and find out whether they are still intact and developing, or we are losing them. We have to look at our behavior and ask ourselves such questions: Does our behavior qualify or justify us to claim that we are civilized?

Those of us who are trying to write books entitled, "History of Civilization", have to realize that the history we are trying to write is not history of civilization at all. Those books may be called history of human progress in arts, science, literature, sculpture, and architecture. But culmination of progress in those areas never equals civilization. Civilization does not manifest itself in those items alone.

If we really want to write a history of civilization in the true sense of

the term, we have to trace the manifestation of human beings' unselfish love, concern, and respect for fellow human beings beginning from the pre-historic days. Unfortunately no one has ever attempted to write that history. Is that because it is a tremendous task? Maybe it is, but it is not the only reason for not writing.

In such an attempt of tracking down human being's love, concern, and respect for one another as revealed in their behavior, we might find out that those qualities are gradually disappearing. Although we came out of the caves and are living in air conditioned, well-carpeted houses with nice views of surrounding skyscrapers, we have little knowledge of who is living next door. In such a situation one would be tempted to change the title of his or her book from, "History of Civilization" to "History of Becoming Uncivilized". I believe that is the reason why no one wants to write that history.

Date Rape?

There is an apparent contradiction between these two terms, "Date" and "Rape". Yet these two words somehow got entangled and found a place in American dictionary as a new word to pay attention to. I was familiar with term 'Rape' and knew what it meant. I was also familiar with the American meaning of 'Date' and knew exactly what it meant. From my knowledge and understanding of these two terms, I never thought they could be put together to create a new word and a new problem for this society.

First my understanding of rape was to apply physical force and to intimidate some one to engage in sexual activity. Rape involves violence and aggressive behavior. According to my understanding, rapists aren't normal human beings; they are mentally sick people, perverted. They don't date people to rape them. They look for an opportunity. They are same as criminals who rob banks and mugs people. Their victims are not their acquaintances. They don't go to make friendship first with someone and then rob him or her. Their victims are completely unknown to them. There are of course some people who rob people pretending to be a friend. Those people are known as con artists. Rapist does not come under this category because raping involves more than just taking money from someone. Besides rape involves brutal physical assault and con artists cannot afford to do that for obvious reasons.

Now, the dictionary meaning of 'Date' is a social engagement with a person of the opposite sex, or may be same sex in case of gay and lesbian relationships. From this definition of the term it will be evident that this is a social engagement, not a business one. If it were a business engagement, we would not call it a Date anyway. We would call it an appointment. When it comes down to social engagement between opposite sexes there

must be a reason behind it. Most people will immediately find the reason as such that this is a social engagement to know each other well as a prelude to getting married or living together. This approach seems innocent.

There are many people in this society who do not believe in marriage. They just want to live together. They need to use this 'Dating' method to choose their partners too. This is understandable. But then there are other people who do not want to get married or live together. When those people 'Date' what are their reasons? Of course they 'Date' to find someone to have sexual pleasure. If you are out there 'Dating' people only to change sexual partners and have fun, it will be very difficult for you to tell your 'Date' not to touch you. In such a case you have to explain to your new 'Date' that you 'Date' people only to find the right person to have sex with and you don't think that your present 'Date' is the right person. You will be insulting your new 'Date', hurt his or her feeling. Besides it might appear meaningless because your new 'Date' may say something like this: Oh, come on. We are not going to get married or living together anyway. This is just for a moment's pleasure. You don't have to like me to spend only one night with me. After this I will be out of your life if you so desire. If you get raped in such a situation, think about

your contribution to it. Didn't you create this problem for yourself in the first place? My point is if someone 'Dates' only for sex that person cannot complain about Date rape. If you do not like someone at the first sight, do not make that social engagement. That means do not make a 'Date' and go out with that person. If you agree to a 'Date' you are virtually giving consent, and after giving consent do not complain that my 'Date' raped me. No one will understand your situation because after you agree to a 'Date' there is no rape. It is that plain and simple. Date rape does not apply in your situation.

Now, if you 'Date' to select a person with whom you intend to get married or live together without getting married, I do not understand how you can get raped. First of all, if you decide to get married you won't like to give your 'Date' an impression that you are just up to having some temporary fun. No, of course, not. You will do your best to convince your 'Date' that you are looking for a serious relationship such as marriage. If your 'Date' do not like the idea, too bad. You will just pull the plug because you are serious. You do not want to fool around with people any more. You don't have any time for that. If your 'Date' is also willing to consider you as husband or wife only then this 'Dating' affair can go on until both of you come upon certain point of understanding.

In such a situation sex do not come to picture. No. I don't think so. No one thinks about sex when they think about marriage. Especially in the United States, where premarital sex is commonplace, it is out of the question. In Bangladesh where premarital sex is impossible, people get sex and family together in a marriage. The fact is you do not go out with someone who is only looking for your body when you get ready for marriage. If you have a feeling that the person you are 'Dating', thinking about the possibility of getting married, is only after your body, you do not continue the relationship for your own benefit. Think about it seriously. You cannot keep someone married to you only by your body. You have to have something else in you besides your body, which can go a long way pleasing and satisfying your partner. Your body alone does not have that ability.

As soon as you get a hint that this relationship is not heading towards your goal, you stop. That means you avoid the situation of being raped. Send a clear message to your 'Date' that this is not what you are looking for. Don't try to change someone's mind or behavior. It is very difficult to change someone else's mind, attitude or behavior. Change yours so you won't be raped. It does not make a whole lot of sense to complain about it as such, "I love you so much. I was looking forward to a beautiful family life with you. How could you do this to me? Now I realize that you never loved me. You were after my body. You are an animal." Lamenting like this won't change a thing. Animals don't turn into human beings after listening to a nice lecture. So, in such a case also Date rape does not hold good. If you complain, I was dating him only to get married but he raped me one day, no one will understand what are you talking about. You have to ask yourself a question: Did I contribute to create this situation in some form or other? The same thing can be said if you 'Date' someone to live together. Living together means a long-term relationship similar to marriage without any religious constrains and social obligations. I was 'Dating' him only to find out whether we can live together but he raped me one day, does not hold good either. Does not make sense to many people.

Now we are left with only that kind of ëDateí, which has nothing to do with sex, getting married, and living together. This kind of 'Dating' seems very innocent. Especially young adults get involved in such activity. Young people such as high school, college, and university students go out on 'Dates' in this country. At this stage no one is talking about getting married or living together or having sex. Just getting out on dates seems so innocent in this culture that this has got family recognition and approval.

The only expressed concern from the family is that you have to attain a certain age of adulthood to be able to go out on 'Dates'. Some very liberal families allow even 13 and 14 years old boys and girls to go out on 'Dates'. But when they do so the families also express their concern that teenage girls may get pregnant and often set a curfew how late at night they can stay out as if it is difficult to have sex during the time frame they are allowed to stay out by themselves.

When you as parents express your concern about your daughter getting pregnant, you are recognizing the fact that, no matter how hard you try to justify this Dating of young boys and girls as innocent, you cannot remain one hundred percent sure and satisfied with that notion. If you were honest with yourself you will never find innocence behind young boys and girls' going out on 'Dates'. Going out on 'Dates' on the part of young adults can have only one significance, which is to get sexual pleasure, not necessarily the ultimate one. So the purpose is sexual pleasure, but young boys and girls are setting a limit to the extent of that pleasure by abstaining themselves from getting the ultimate pleasure. You know what I mean. This is what gives them a sense of innocence. If confronted they talk like this: Yes, we go out on dates. We are just friends. He is my boyfriend. I like him very much. We hang out together. We enjoy each other. But that does not mean that we sleep together. There is nothing going on in this relation ship. We are innocent.

Well, when there is so many thing going on, you argue that there is nothing going on only because you abstained yourself from getting the ultimate pleasure. But one day your boy friend might lose control and it is not very unlikely when he is very young and restless. My theory is that if your intimate relationship with your boy friend prompts him to rape you one day that cannot be termed as a rape in the true sense of the term. Why? Because both partners have contributed in creating such a situation when one could not stay within the limit any more. The feeling is: I could not take the 'no' anymore; I had to go for it. Therefore, in spite of the partnerís objection one proceeds to get the ultimate satisfaction and exerts some kind of force. Then you complain about rape without realizing that you are also a part of it. In fact you have created this rape. What I am trying to say here is this that the true significance of rapes reveals itself when the victim and the aggressor are not known to each other.

At this point some of my readers may jump to attack this observation by arguing that no matter how you try to justify it, using force to have sexual satisfaction, whether by an unknown assailant or a friend, constitutes a

rape. But the fact remains that to rape is to violate someone. This sense of violation does not come from a friend whom you see every day, touch, hug, and kiss. Besides the tone and manner of objection differs in relation to force from a stranger and force from a friend. Think about it.

If you are being attacked by a stranger, you will most probably try to scream frantically and try to get away if possible. Of course, you would try to hurt the assailant with anything that you can get hold of unless the rapist places a knife on your throat. But incase of a friend you will only say: Please, please, don't do it. I thought you were nice sensible person, etc., etc.

Why do you do that? Because at that time you did not want that to happen. But it happened anyway. You feel guilty about it. But you don't want to blame yourself. This is not your fault. It is a basic human nature that people don't want to take responsibility for their own actions. For my failure to do something, I blame someone or something else. It is not my fault that I failed the test. The teacher was so boring that I could not learn anything. My Date raped me. It is not my fault. I said no, but he didn't listen to me. He is an animal. This kind of excuse does not seem very forceful to anyone. Although you do not want to see your part in it, every body can see what your contribution was, and how did that happen.

I, therefore, would like to say that to accuse someone of raping you, your contribution must be zero. You must not have any relation to that person whatsoever. That is what must be termed as real rape, real violation when a stranger jump on you from nowhere. A person you socialize with, familiar with is your own creation. You are partly responsible for creating a rapist in him. You are responsible for regulating his emotions, sentiments, feelings, and behavior. That is why I don't believe that the words 'Date' and 'Rape' can coexist.

Drugs: Demand and Distribution

As long as we have demand for a commodity, the supply will be abundant. This is the principle of economics. There is no way to get around it. Demand creates and increases the supply, but a lack or decrease of supply does not necessarily decrease the demand. If we destroy the source of supply, the demand will not automatically go away; instead, demand will create a new source of supply.

This is what is going on in the United States when it comes to drugs. Everyone knows that getting hooked on drugs is dangerous. It ruins a life, yet drug addiction among teenagers and young adults of this country is increasing at an alarming rate. Nothing seems to work. Our government has tried and is still trying everything humanly possible to arrest the progress of drug addiction among teenagers, but is not successful. Our government even went to foreign countries to search for the source of production and distribution centers of drugs and was able to successfully eliminate some of them, but the problem still remains. If one source gets destroyed, another pops up somewhere else. It is a very difficult situation.

So, instead of wasting our valuable time, energy, and money on locating and destroying the sources of distribution, we have to concentrate on the sources of demand. Unfortunately nothing substantial has been done so far to find the sources of demand, meaning the reason behind the demand for drugs. Instead of looking for the reasons for a high demand for drugs, we are coming up with slogans such as, "Say no to drugs," as if it is that simple. As if a slogan coming from outside has more motivational power than a slogan that comes from the inside of an individual, "Say yes to drugs".

When I say inside, I refer to a person's strong desire to have drugs. The only thing that can prevent someone from doing something wrong is that

person's will power. Can a slogan promote that will power? If slogans had that power, this world would be a better place to live. We hear so many slogans every day (obviously they come from politicians, religious leaders, and social reformers), but do we listen to them and act accordingly? Do not we hear every day that all men are created equal, and terrorists are enemies of peace? Do we change our behavior only by paying attention to those slogans and sermons? No, we do not. That is why when we really mean to do something about getting rid of a dangerous habit, we go for professional help. We go to psychiatrists who try to develop and enhance our will power. If only slogans could develop our will power, we would not have to go to those counselors and spend our hard earned money.

Counselors do not start with "Say no to drugs". They do not draw a picture of your bleak future in front of your eyes while mentioning the dangerous effects of drugs. How do I know? No, I have not been there, but some of my best friends are in the profession of counseling. During our casual conversations, I was able to figure out what kind of counseling they really do. Besides, those of you who have already received counseling and were able to get rid of your bad habits know what I am talking about. It is not as simple as, "Just say no to drugs". Therefore, when I hear this slogan often I react by uttering to myself, "well give them a reason not to say yes to drugs". I believe that all drug addicts utter this to themselves when they listen to this slogan.

We have to understand that when we need strong will power to abstain from doing something wrong, we equally need strong willpower to get into a bad habit knowing fully well that it is going to destroy our lives. Those people who commit suicide, develop a strong will power to destroy their lives. To do something good for me, I need strong will power. Similarly, to do something bad for me I also need strong will power.

The demand for drugs lies in the strong will power of a person to have drugs. I am not speaking of the people who are already addicted. I am thinking about those who are entering everyday into this world of drug abusers. Did not they hear a hundred times that using drugs is dangerous? Why do they still start using drugs? Why do they develop a strong will power to have drugs? If we really want to know the answer to this question, we have to look at our family lives where we develop our personality.

Being aware that drugs and self-destruction are synonymous, it takes a lot of will power to indulge oneself in that self-destructive behavior. Everyone knows that destructive behavior and attitude is the product of a negative environment. A person who does not see anything positive in his

or her environment or upbringing turns out a very negative person. Let me explain in detail what I mean by a negative environment.

After a child comes into this world, if that child is denied the natural love and affection of both the parents, that child is supposed to develop a negative attitude towards life. A child develops a positive attitude when he or she gets profound love and care from his or her parents. If both father and mother stay with a child, the child develops in himself a sense of security and fulfillment. On the other hand, if the child is born with a single mother, and left with a baby sitter for the most part of his or her childhood, that child tends to develop a sense of insecurity, frustration, despair, and hopelessness. The big problem here is that the child, as he or she grows up, can compare his or her situation with others from the environment and if that child finds examples of other children living peacefully in a healthy family environment, feels very lonely and deceived.

It is a psychologically proven and established fact that human beings become depressed, destructive, and pessimistic out of a sense of loneliness and meaninglessness of life. Lack of love and affection from father and mother, from brothers and sisters, from uncles and aunts, from grandmother and grandfather creates a vacuum in a child's mind. Those family members mentioned above are supposed to play definite positive role models for a child. The most important factor in shaping a child's attitudes towards his or her life is her father and mother. If a child is allowed to lose respect for his or her father and mother, the child finds no reason to develop respect for any other human being, any other values, or any other slogans.

Even if a child comes from a family with all of the above members present and the father and mother fail to provide a definite positive role model, the child is bound to suffer from the syndrome of a negative attitude toward life, and may engage in self-destructive behavior. I, therefore, firmly believe that it is possible to develop a strong will power, meaning strong desire for a child to engage in anti-social, anti-establishment, and anti-normal activities when the father and mother cannot become a positive role model for their children. Human beings' strong urges for drugs, sex addiction, alcohol addiction, and desire to become a criminal, a serial killer, and a rapist come out of a negative attitude towards life. I am sure no one is going to argue with me about this. No one would like to debate that there are also some positive aspects in those kinds of activities.

Now, my point is if those are considered negative aspects of human behavior, how can they come from a positive environment of a family life? Is not it inconceivable? At this point some of my readers and parents might

protest vehemently, "Do not blame the parents always. We, parents, have never engaged ourselves in antisocial activities, never touched any drugs, and are confident that we have been able to provide a positive role model for our children. Yet some of them somehow got hooked on drugs. It is none of our fault. " Well, if not, then whose fault is it? Do you believe that aliens abducted them and made them drug addicts in an effort to destroy the human civilization?

So the obvious answer is peer pressure. It is their friends who are responsible for destroying their lives. Let me tell you something about this. Once we had a family discussion about this subject at our dining table. I wanted to know from my two teenage daughters what is the meaning of the term "peer pressure". To my surprise both of them replied at the same time, "There is no such thing as peer pressure". To my profound surprise and satisfaction they explained to me that it is impossible for any of their friends to put pressure on them to do certain things, which they believe, are wrong. "Why dad? Why do you think I am going to listen to my friends' advice and act accordingly?" For discussions sake I wanted to know, "Then why do some parents blame it on peer pressure when it comes to drugs?" My eldest daughter replied, "It is only to shift responsibility. No parents want to admit that it is because of them their children are doing drugs". My wife and I were very happy and thrilled and felt very proud of us. We knew that we have been able to play a positive role model for our daughters.

When we as parents believe that we are innocent, and we are doing everything possible for our children. Maybe we are not doing that the right way. Only by abstaining from using drugs or not becoming alcohol addicts, we cannot establish the parenthood. We have to be involved in every aspect of their lives. The most important thing is we have to make sacrifices for our children and when we can do that, our children develop respect for us. In that case their friends do not become very important for them. We parents become very important in their lives. Their lives revolve around us. They enjoy themselves feeling secure and well protected. When that happens, peer pressure becomes irrelevant. That is why when you start blaming it on peer pressure, I feel sorry for you, parents. In that case you announce to the whole world that friends of your children are more important to your children than you! You do not have any control or influence on your children. Their friends have tremendous influence on them. Would not you feel ashamed of yourself when you talk about peer pressure?

Therefore, when you are looking for the source of drugs in foreign lands, you are doing the wrong thing. You have to look for the source of demand, if you really want to do something about it. Where is the source of demand? It is in every family in the United States. By destroying our family structures, by not being responsible parents, by not sacrificing our pleasure for the sake of our children, we are increasing that demand day by day. We are creating children in this society with negative attitudes towards life. We failed to provide positive role models in front of them to follow. When we parents fail to fulfill their demands, friends and drugs come to the rescue.

So, the cry "say no to drugs" will be a cry in the wilderness as long as you have to depend on your babysitter or a nanny for the upbringing of your children. If your own life, your profession, your enjoyment becomes more important than your children, you will have no influence on their lives. When you cannot take care of them, gang leaders will extend their inviting hands towards your children. You children will find security, protection, fun, and a sense of belonging being a gang member, and eventually a drug addict or a criminal.

My slogan is: deteriorating family life and irresponsible parents are creating a demand for drugs in our children. We have to destroy that source of demand if we want to get rid of drugs. If we destroy the demand, the distribution will naturally diminish. This is the only way to deal with the drug problem.

Addressing Dressing Up

Why are you dressed up today? Confronted by such question, I was often puzzled and confused. My thinking was, "I am dressed up because I am in public. I always dress up when I come out of my house, unless I go to catch fish or play something. I even change my dress inside my house when I come out of my bedroom and go to the living room." Although I felt a strong desire in me to shout out all those words, I often restrained myself from giving such an answer. Instead I just said, "I enjoy dressing up whenever I can, don't you".

This is one of the most perplexing cultural confrontations that bothered me and still bothering me. Dressing up in public is considered the most appropriate thing to do in Bangladesh. First of all, we have clearly and distinctly two different concepts of dressing, indoor and outdoor. Certain kinds of dresses are appropriate for indoors and certain kinds of dresses are appropriate for outdoors. It is unthinkable for a person in Bangladesh to come out of the house wearing indoor dress. Besides I have never heard of such words as "dressing up" or "dressing down" in our culture. We have only one word in our dictionary, which is called "dressing". For example, we are going to watch a movie in a movie theater and it is getting late. My wife is not ready yet. I can only inquire, "Are you dressed yet". The absence of the word "up" has a great significance with respect to dressing in our culture. Which means that there is no room in our system for dressing down.

Therefore, it never appeared to me that sometimes I can dress down if I wanted to before I arrived in the United States and was asked such question, "Why are you dressed up?" I realized that according to this culture, you must have a reason to be dressed up, an special occasion such

as a graduation ceremony, marriage reception, going to church, going to a party, etc. Most of the time you are supposed to dress casual, ordinary. This was very difficult for me to comprehend and accept because my culture taught me to be always in my best attire. I must always look perfect whenever I come out of my house for whatever reasons. Only exception was when I needed any special outfit to do a special job.

I have never seen anyone in Bangladesh dressing down just for dressing down. Everyone always wanted to dress up. Why would people like to dress down? It was beyond me. You would like to look your best, won't you? That was my understanding. So when I first saw people in the United States roaming around in all public places almost naked, I was shocked. I could not believe my eyes. I was given the impression throughout my upbringing that getting dressed is the most valuable gift of this civilization. Savage cave dwellers did not know how to dress. They were naked. Gradually they learned to dress. First, they felt the necessity of dressing during the winter season to get protection from cold. But then they were not satisfied only by protecting themselves from cold, they wanted to look good. That is how fashion came along. The history of civilization is also a history of evolution of fashion. That was my understanding.

When I was in high school, one of my teachers told me something like this: History repeats itself. When I asked for explanation, he told me that we have made wonderful progress. Our buildings are trying to reach the sky. One day we will get tired of it and would like to go back to the cave, and start it all over again. When I started watching almost naked people roaming shamelessly everywhere in the United States, I wondered, "Am I seeing an example of that?" May be the United States has reached that point when it must go back to the original. May be we still have a long way ahead of us when similar thing will happen in Bangladesh.

However, it was very difficult for me to look at those people everywhere wearing distasteful, weird, and absurd kind of dresses. I was appalled when I saw young people going everywhere from grocery store to the university library wearing something in summer, which we call underwear in Bangladesh. Isn't it awful? Don't they have any shame? I talked to myself. I could not check my temptation to inquire about that, so I asked one of my Bangladeshi friends: How come people walk around in public in this country wearing only their underwear? My Bangladeshi friend explained to me that what we call underwear in Bangladesh are actually called "shorts" in the United States. They of course wear underwear with that

short. I was not satisfied with that answer. I wondered, do two underwear makes one short?

Being a member of the male it was very embarrassing for me to look at female wearing such thing as short which appeared nothing but an underwear. But those who were wearing underwear did not seem to be a bit concerned about it. Their gestures and postures were so normal that one would imagine that it was the most normal out fit for them to wear. They are not doing something out of the ordinary. So how can I blame them? I couldn't associate any desire on their part of being sexually explicit or provocative with the wearing of shorts. They are wearing shorts very innocently without any intentions associated with it.

But one thing kept bothering me throughout all those years of my schooling in the East and West coast of the United States. Universities seems to be the perfect environment which many students would like to use to experiment with their weird desires, whims, and caprices. In Bangladeshi culture university, schools, and colleges are considered sacred places equivalent to church, synagogue, temple, and mosque. People go there to concentrate on learning. Students bring to the universities a highly motivated and concentrated mind. In that mind there cannot be any place for experiment with dress or any abnormal behavior. Universities in the United States are well built and well kept. They are gorgeous to look at. The entire serenity of the atmosphere surrounding the campus is very uplifting for the enrichment of the mind.

I always wondered American universities are perfect places for learning. Ironically, when I look at the dress students are wearing, the way they are interacting with one other, appears to be not supportive of creating a learning environment. For example, when I see students wearing underwear (shorts!) entering a well carpeted, well furnished, air conditioned classrooms, I often think, if this civilization can decorate a classroom so beautifully, why the same civilization fails to decorate a student's body beautifully, so a university student looks like a university student, engaged in the pursuit of knowledge?

I think this is a contrast. I do not want to see a smelly street bum wearing wrinkled T-shirt and jeans with holes inside a beautifully decorated room. It does not match. I have seen poor people coming out of dilapidated mud and bamboo made cottages in Bangladesh, half naked and starved. Those people are agricultural workers, day labor. They have hardly enough money to buy food not to speak of decent dresses. Men wear something

like under wear and often go naked from waist and up during summer. They belong there and perfectly match with their environment.

In Bangladesh educated and sophisticated people dress to reveal their personality, to command respect, and to look beautiful or handsome. In the United States very few people dress for those reasons. Here people wear dresses to reveal their bodies, to become sexy, and to look ugly. Let me give you a reason why I said ugly. I have never seen a desire among young men and women in the United States to dress beautifully. If you dress beautifully you are being stared at. So you end up dressing weirdly to blend in.

Another problem is dressing beautifully and looking sexy has become synonymous in the United States. In Bangladesh these two terms carry completely different connotations. Beautifully dressed people are never considered sexy in Bangladesh. To call someone sexy is to insult that person. It is believed that only the prostitutes desire to be called sexy. On the other hand, people get happy in the United States if you call them sexy; they accept it as a compliment. Most of the Americans do not realize that while their dresses can inspire respect for them in people, similarly their dresses can also provoke sexual desire in people. If I have any respect for myself or if I want to inspire any respect for myself in people, I would like to be beautiful or handsome, not sexy. I do not understand why a civilized and cultured person would like to see himself or herself as a sex object. Unfortunately, people do not realize this in the United States, and they get very happy to hear that they look sexy.

I have heard young men and women complimenting one another in such words as "you look sexy today in this dress" as I have mentioned earlier in another essay "Sexual Harassment". The reply they get is "Thank you". If a male student said this to a female student in Bangladesh, the male student would probably get a slap instead of a thank you. Further, if the female student decided to complain about it to the administration the male student might be expelled from the university. As we can see, these two cultures have completely different outlook on what to wear, how to wear, and why to wear a dress. Which one is proper and which one is improper, it is up to the reader of this essay to decide.

Another striking difference between dressing up in the United States and Bangladesh is that in Bangladeshi culture we dress up as we grow up. I was supposed to wear certain kinds of dress when I was one to five years old. Between five and ten, another and between ten and fifteen yet another, so on and so forth. Which means that children's dresses are not appropriate

for adults. But in the United States, I have seen people wearing same kind of dress irrespective of their ages. For example, I have seen a 40 years old woman wearing a dress, which is designed exclusively for the use of 5 to 10 years old in Bangladesh.

In psychology I have studied that human beings have two different kinds of ages, one is chronological and the other is mental. As time passes by every one grows older. After twenty years from my date of birth I am twenty years old. I can't change this fact. This is my chronological age. However, it does not necessarily mean that I am mentally twenty years old. Mentally I may only be ten years old. I believe that most of the Americans do not grow up mentally. That might be the reason why they do not want to dress up like adults should.

Amazingly, Americans require people to wear appropriate attire when they go to do specific jobs, go to a place of worship, go out to dinner, or enter into a hospital to visit a patient. They even require people to wear appropriate clothing to ride a bus, a train, or an airplane. But they do not require their children to dress appropriately when they go to school. Why they let their children dress as they wish when they go to school? Is school a less sophisticated place than all of the above? Any society must have a norm, a standard, and a conception about what constitutes appropriate attire. Decent and cultured people have no confusion about that. I believe I don't have to define what I mean when I say appropriate attire.

But when it comes to school, this conception does not seem to work. Is it very difficult to define what is appropriate to wear in a school and what is not? School going children are not ready yet to conform to the norms and standards of the society. Unless they see any example or are introduced to those standards, they would like to experiment with the clothes they wear just out of curiosity or to stand out of the crowd without realizing the adverse effect of such behavior. It is, therefore, necessary to show them what is ëappropriateí and what is not in a learning environment. I believe that introducing uniforms is a right step toward achieving that goal. Americans have been too careless about this aspect of their culture for too long, resulting in a deterioration of the educational atmosphere in schools. Schools are sacred seats of learning where we send our children to learn some knowledge and skills to be able to do a job and to become a decent human being as well. It is, therefore, necessary to ensure that an appropriate environment of teaching and learning prevails in our schools.

If requiring young learners to wear uniforms helps promote that environment, I would, definitely, support the idea of introducing uniforms

in our schools as we do in Bangladesh. I believe that uniforms help the creation of a serene and sublime atmosphere of learning by promoting a sense of unity and togetherness among young learners. It also helps develop a team spirit, which is absolutely necessary for success in professional life. School is a place to concentrate on learning. It should not be turned into a dress exhibition. If we turn our schools into dress exhibitions, we will only provide a means of distraction rather than concentration. Also, a school should not be a place to experiment with weird sizes, bizarre color combinations, and brand names. If students pay too much attention to what they wear, they will not be able to pay attention to what they learn. If students compete with one another for excellence in dressing up, there will be less competition to achieve excellence in academic areas. Uniforms, definitely, will prevent students from wearing inappropriate attire in a learning environment.

Of course, what is appropriate for the beach or for a picnic is not appropriate for an office or a school. In the name of protecting our freedom of expression, or right to choose, some social and liberal political leaders are unwittingly encouraging our children to dress as they like. As a consequence many children are polluting the atmosphere of learning environment by wearing sex provoking dresses in our schools. This should stop. Uniforms will certainly put an end to that practice. It will also stop those spoiled kids of the so-called rich and famous who go to school only to socialize by wearing the most extravagant clothing just out of the factory. Another good aspect of uniforms is that it will put an end to the practice of wearing gang association signifying attire in schools, because there will be no way of maintaining group identity in the midst of uniforms.

A lawmaker has recently introduced a bill to the California Senate, which will allow women to wear slacks to work not skirts. Women rights groups in California who are supporting this bill contend that some employers are requiring women to wear skirts which results in showing their legs and they do not want to do that. I was very confused! If female employees do not want to show their legs, why don't they wear long skirts as their grandmothers used to do even when working in the field? What's wrong with long skirts? No body is telling them to wear short skirts. Employers are only demanding their female employees to wear skirts. They did not define the shortness or length of skirts, did they? So the question must be whether some employees are requiring their female workers to wear short skirts. If they do, they must also define what is considered short.

If some employers maintain a dress code specifying the length of skirts, I think that should be considered utterly disgusting. Women should not be forced to show their legs to satisfy the erratic sexual pleasure of some sick men who cannot see anything else in women other than sex. Women are only sex objects to them. If women have any respect for themselves, if they have any personality, they cannot surrender to this animal instinct and lust of some nasty men. Men should look at women with respect and admiration not as sex objects, especially in work places. So, I can see why some women are trying to create a law allowing them to wear slacks. They have respect for themselves and they don't want to reduce themselves merely to sex objects. In fact no decent and cultured person would like to see him or herself only as an object of sexual pleasure. It is indeed very disgraceful for this civilization and culture.

But the problem is exposing legs has become a part and parcel of women's dress in the western world. It is not very difficult to understand when and how it started. Once upon a time a patriarchal society had decided to quench its perverted sexual pleasure by forcing women to expose their legs. Being economically slave to a male dominated society women had no other choice but to surrender to this humiliation and insult. Unfortunately, over the lapse of time this has become normal, and our women have totally forgotten the humiliation and harassment associated with keeping their leg exposed. It is amazing that someone has been able to recognize the insult and has decided to do some thing about it. But I am very concerned that this bill will face a strong opposition from those women who have lost all self-respect. Not only do they show their legs but they also enjoy showing almost everything in the name of wearing short shorts.

Very recently a civil right conscious lady in New York City demanded that it was her constitutional right to ride topless in city's subways. The authority has to grant her wish. In the face of such movement and strong desire on the part of some women in the United States to expose their bodies in public, I think it will be a tough to convince everyone that exposing legs is nothing but surrendering to the nasty perverted pleasure of some men. If the women of the western world do not feel the insult in exposing their legs, men will continue this kind of sexual harassment of women as long as they wish.

The idea to put some clothes on is the most wonderful gift of this civilization as I mentioned earlier. The necessity arose to protect us from exposure to extreme cold or hot climate conditions. Gradually we developed

a sense of shyness and wanted to cover our body as the civilization progressed. Subsequently we also wanted to look beautiful. Nowadays civilized people all over the world wear clothes to reveal their personality and character, not to expose their body and become sexy. Individuals with character and dignity hate to look sexy because it diminishes their sense of decency and decorum. Americans need to learn that lesson one more time.

Entertaining Students:
The American Methodology

The word "teacher" had a different connotation 50 years ago in the United States and all over the world as well. While the connotation of that term has drastically changed in the United States over the span of half a century, it has not changed equally in all parts of the world. Some civilizations have been able to retain that connotation unchanged until today. Bangladesh is one of them.

What was the connotation of the term "teacher" 50 years ago in the United States or all over the world? Teacher was at that time considered a person who not only teaches a subject matter but also touches a life and changes it forever. Changing the life was the job of a teacher in those days. People who decided to come to this noble profession were dedicated individuals. They enjoyed shaping up a life, and they had a profound impact on the lives of their students. Teachers were role models. Teachers in those days, therefore, had enough freedom to adopt strategies to change the lives of their students without any interference. Society and families were happy and content by entrusting the teachers with the responsibility of shaping up the lives of their children.

Everything was moving smoothly until that time when society started developing new philosophies of leading a life in this world, and started dictating the teacher what to teach and what not to teach, and how to teach and how not to teach. Under pressure, teachers gave up their roles as shapers of someone's life; rather they became instructors only to teach students certain skills so they can do a job. Nowadays students go to school, as if, to buy a skill, not to develop any qualities that make one a

decent human being. So schools, colleges, and universities have become shopping centers and students become customers, teachers salespersons. Do the customers have to have respect for a salesperson or the salesperson has to have respect for the customer? Evidently respect for education, educators, and educational institutions have disappeared.

Although this is what exactly happened in the United States, it is not so in the rest of the world. It is true that a Far East Asian country like Bangladesh has gone through many changes, but the society or the individual did not challenge the basic values that once were attributed to education, educators, and educational institutions.

I was born and brought up in an atmosphere where traditionally teachers were held in high esteem. Teaching was considered the most respectable profession one could have. I grew up respecting my teachers. We used to touch the feet of our teachers as a gesture of respect. We felt like doing that spontaneously although we were not required to. Teachers were great people. When I finished my education and became a teacher myself, I got used to getting respect from my students. They looked upon me as their guardian angel when I was only 22 years old and fresh from the university and the youngest faculty member of a college.

Although students may be older than the teacher, no one ever shows disrespect to the teacher. In fact no one ever uses the first name of a teacher in Bangladesh whether the environment is a school, a college, or a university. No students can enter or leave a classroom without the permission of the teacher. No one can engage in side conversation in the presence of a teacher. Imagine each classroom as a place of worship, as if you were in a church, a synagogue, a temple, or a mosque praying to god.

So it was very difficult for me to adjust when I first entered into a university classroom to receive further education in 1979. I have been able to convince myself that I have to adjust and compromise. I am in a foreign land. It was not for me to criticize their way of life. But when I became a teacher in the United States, it was not very easy for me to adjust and compromise considering my teaching background. Students here were not ready to clear up the hallway pushing themselves all the way to the wall, instead they were almost about to push me out of their way when I was about to enter a classroom. First I thought of taking it easy and blending in. But then I talked to myself, "This is not what teachers are for. Students are not going to direct me how to teach them, I am going to decide how to teach them. That is why I am a teacher and they are students."

I tried to keep up with my conviction and beliefs. I was not ready to give up the role of an ideal teacher no matter what. When I first started teaching in the United States in 1985, I have been reprimanded on several occasions by my supervisor for not adopting the American method of entertaining students in the classroom. I was termed as a boring teacher. On one occasion three of my students stormed out of my class and complained to my supervisor about my poor performance. The next day I got the following memo, "I will not tolerate your inappropriate conduct of the classes assigned to you. You must improve your methodology immediately. Otherwise you will be fired". When I asked the chairperson of my department to define "inappropriate conduct", he told me that according to my students I was a very boring teacher. Later under cross examination of a disciplinary committee the students involved revealed that I was good teacher but not an entertaining one. Subsequently they came back to my class and developed a profound respect for me. A few days later after the meeting of the disciplinary committee, I was given a copy of the recommendation of the committee, which read, "This committee was pretty disappointed with the attitude of the students. It was appropriate for 11 years old, not young adults. Dr. Uddin is very kind, soft-spoken, and gentle. Certainly too gentle for hoodlums. He has been counseled in American methodology. His good qualities outweigh his passive ones."

That is how I struggled to maintain the integrity of my character as a teacher and eventually that paid off in an incident. Lately I was teaching part time English as a Second Language in a school in southern California. The school went bankrupt and closed its doors. But my students were not ready to give up. They revived their own class by renting a small room and rehiring me. Was this the reward of being a boring teacher? They could not pay me anything substantially but that was not what I was looking for. So I announced that I would teach this class free until I finish the course that I started. I believe that an ideal teacher should be able to inspire real love and respect for him in his students. After the news appeared in the Los Angeles Times, someone wrote in a letter to the editor,"Uddin set an example of an ideal teacher that is rare in this age. I consider him a hero and bow my head in respect for him." Another letter appeared in the Ventura Country Star, which read, "Of course, we need immigrant like Dr. Uddin in this country. We have something to learn from people like him."

It is not to say that American teachers have failed to maintain the integrity of their characters as a teacher. But it has become a tendency in the United States to put the blame on the teacher, if a student drops out of

that teacher's class. The teacher is not good, doesn't know how to motivate students, and doesn't know how to keep students in his or her class. The teacher is boring, not entertaining. The teacher doesn't know how to make his or her class interesting. Finally, it's the teacher's fault if the dropout rate for a period of time is higher for a particular teacher compared to other teachers. The teacher takes the blame, suffers humiliation, and sometimes even loses his or her job.

The situation is completely different in Bangladesh. It is impossible for a student to storm out of a class. In my student and teaching life, I have never seen a student storming out of teacher's class complaining about the performance of the teacher. I have seen teachers storming out of a classroom being annoyed with the students. In such a situation students of that class get reprimanded by the principal not the teacher. It is considered students responsibility to keep a teacher in the classroom not the other way around. Bangladesh believes that students' dropout or storming out has nothing to do with teachers. No matter how excellent, inspiring, and entertaining the teacher is, students are going to drop out of his or her class anyway if they have to or decide to. It is absolutely impossible for a teacher to eliminate the dropout phenomenon. In contrast, the teacher in the United States has to bear the burden of the blame, accuse him or herself for not being able to do a good job of keeping every single student in his or her class intact.

Why is it so in the United States? Why does everyone like to point fingers at the teacher in this country? Why does the teacher have to take the responsibility for the students' decision to drop out? It is not very difficult to find the answer to that question. The notion that if a particular student drops out of a teacher's class it's because of that teacher, gains momentum when the student who dropped out also substantiates this assumption that if he or she had a good teacher, he or she could somehow continue and finish his or her course. Eventually, administration of an educational institution and parents join in accusing the teacher, often citing student's comment as a valid ground for that accusation. While in Bangladesh as soon as a student starts accusing the teacher he becomes a laughing stock. No one pays attention to him.

Let me explain why students like to blame teachers when they drop out. Blaming others for one's misfortune is a basic human nature, and students are nothing but human beings. If something goes terribly wrong with them, if they make a big mistake in their lives, if they fail to accomplish something, they would like to seek a reason for such failures outside

of themselves. They would like to find something to put the blame on because they don't want to confess that it's their fault. To confess that I am responsible for my own problem takes courage and strength. Most of us don't have that courage and strength. So we attribute our failures to such thing as, "If only I had a good teacher, If only I had a few more days to study, if only I could get some cooperation from my friend or husband or wife. If I had a babysitter, if I didn't get laid off, if my wife didn't get pregnant, if I didn't get divorced or separated," so on and so forth. These kinds of contemplations culminate in such a conclusion, "I am not responsible for my failure, someone else or something else is." So when students blame a teacher for their misfortunes, they're not doing anything new. They are just acting as another human being, not taking responsibility for their own actions.

Now, why does administration, very enthusiastically, join in blaming teachers instead of blaming the student? Because by doing so they can smoothly run their administration. If they can always accuse teachers that teachers are not doing a good job, teachers will be intimidated, submissive, and non demanding. There will be no complains and no demands for pay raises. When a teacher is afraid of losing his or her job, how can he or she ask for a tenure, better position, promotions, and a raise? Besides, the administrators are also human beings. Why should they take the responsibility when they could shift it squarely to others? While this is exactly what is happening in the United States' educational institutions, I am not ignoring the fact that there are educational institutions where we can still find a harmonious cooperation between the administration and the faculty, although this is not the normal practice.

I should also mention here that this tendency on the part of the administration to put down teachers is very detrimental toward the professional development of a teacher. Instead of telling the teachers that they are not doing a good job, if the administration could, once in a while, tell them that they are doing an excellent job, they could turn a mediocre or even bad teacher into an excellent one. If I always here that I am good for nothing, I get depressed, suffer from an inferiority complex, and eventually think of changing my profession. While the administrators could create excellent teachers only by appreciating a teacher, they are driving away many promising teachers from this noble profession. This thing never happens in Bangladesh. Administrators of academic institutions in Bangladesh have profound respect for the teachers.

American parents, obviously, wouldn't like to blame themselves for

their children's failure in school. It is all school's fault. Parents don't immediately point fingers at the teacher (most of them don't even know the names of the teachers of their children), they point fingers at the schools in general, signifying that our schools are not doing a good job. Now, what constitutes an educational institution? Of course teachers, administrators, students, and parents. But who wants to hear that definition of a school? It never appears to anyone that without a congenial relationship among parents, students, teachers, and administrators, a school cannot function smoothly. When parents blame the school, they destroy the very concept of an educational institution. When administrators blame the teacher, they also do the same thing. And when the teachers' turn comes, they cannot conveniently blame anyone, poor teachers!

This is a danger sign for the progress of any educational system in any social condition. Once you start blaming others for your misfortune, you won't try to change your attitude toward life. You will be asking others to change for you. Now, which one is more difficult, changing others or changing you? Of course changing others is a very difficult task since we don't have any control over someone else's life. It should, therefore, be considered almost absurd to change someone else's life. Still we try to do that when we blame others for our failures. We can only try to change us, not others. So when a student blames a teacher, the student is simply announcing that the teacher has to change for me, I am not going to change for the teacher. With that attitude it is impossible to learn something. The question is: Can you have a personalized teacher? A teacher that is particularly suited to teach you alone? Also, if you don't get one, do you decide not to learn? Isn't it ridiculous to think like that? If you don't like a particular teacher, you might think of changing that teacher and going to another teacher. If you can't find a teacher in a school that you like, you might as well think of changing the school. But you don't think of giving up learning altogether, do you? That is why I believe those who drop out do it for some other reasons, not because they had a bad teacher. However, they blame the teacher anyway to console themselves and also to find a convenient excuse to account for their failures. Who wants to confess that he or she is a failure because he or she didn't take something very seriously?

Passionate students take their job of learning so seriously that instead of blaming their instructors they force their instructors to change. This might seem strange but this is possible. This means challenging a teacher to come up with strategies to teach a very demanding and aggressive learner.

When there are active learners, the teacher cannot be passive. This is to say that when a student demonstrates a positive attitude, he or she sees everything positive around him or her. On the other hand, if they have a negative attitude everything turns negative. The point I am trying to make here is that if I am a serious student, I never think of dropping out or storming out. I can learn from anybody, anyone. Anyone can teach me when I am a serious learner. That is what I call a positive attitude.

When I am emphasizing the fact that teachers are not to blame for students' failure, I am not denying the fact that there are good teachers and bad teachers, as there are good human beings and bad human beings. But just because there are bad human beings, no one decides to drop out of this world and go to heaven. Of course not all teachers are excellent. Some teachers are so excellent that students don't want to part from them. On the contrary, some teachers are so boring that students hate to go to their classes. But they tell themselves that they have to live with it until they finish their course. They never think of giving up or dropping out. The same as no one decides to leave this world just because some human beings are bad.

Unfortunately this society is doing a great disservice to the process of teaching and learning by not emphasizing the fact that it is the negative attitude of the learners and the indifference on the part of the society that is the main cause for students dropping out of schools. It is not the school, not the teacher, but those out there who think, "if only the teacher wasn't so boring". To ask for entertainment to be able to learn is childish. Until and unless we change this childish attitude, the drop out rates from our schools will not decrease. If we want to keep students in our classrooms, we have to tell them to be serious and positive instead of telling the teacher to be an entertainer. The students must be prepared to adapt to a teacher.

I would like to make here the following suggestions, which, I believe, will help to retain students in their respective programs or course of studies:

1. The admission office must administer a placement test to accurately place a student in a class exactly where he or she belongs. Most of the cases of dropouts occur when students feel stranded in their own classrooms, not being able to comprehend the subject matter that is being taught.

2. In an effort to increase enrollment, administrators must not tell the students that the school has excellent teachers, rather tell them that no one can teach them unless they're prepared to teach themselves. Learning isn't

buying something from a fancy department store. Knowledge cannot be delivered to you only because you have money.

3. Adult students shouldn't be treated just as another student, rather as colleagues or friends. We must show respect to adult students. If we try to amuse or entertain them, they'll feel insulted as if we don't have any respect for their intelligence.

4. Married students must get one hundred percent help and cooperation from their respective spouses to continue their education. Before we admit any married student, we should ask them to go home and talk to their spouses about the benefit of continuing studies and get their full approval. It is almost impossible for married students to stay in school without the approval and cooperation of their spouses.

5. If the prospective student holds a steady job, the student must get wholehearted cooperation and help from his or her boss. Before we admit a student, we must tell our prospective student to work out a flexible work schedule with his or her boss, around his or her school schedule. Without the support of the employer, it's very difficult for anyone to continue to work and study.

6. If the prospective students are single mothers or single fathers, tell them to make a steady and reliable source of babysitting before they even think of coming to school. If possible, suggest an alternate source of babysitting such as preschools or day care centers for our students. Admission offices must not indiscriminately admit students without prior consideration of their personal lives and related problems.

7. If the student is a single adult, try to get some information about his or her social, economic, educational, and family backgrounds. If you decide the student is from a disadvantaged background, try to address that issue as positively as possible. For example, before admitting a gang member to our school, we should remind our student about the sacrifices he or she has to make to be able to benefit form an educational institution. It is useless to encourage someone to achieve something without addressing the real problem a person is confronting.

8. If the prospective student is a young adult, try to gather some information about the student's parents. Find out whether they are married, living together, separated or divorced. It is a good idea to get approval from both parents. Also, persuade them to believe that without their help and cooperation, it won't be possible for their kids to succeed in school.

9. Admissions personnel must be able to determine whether a prospective student is a drug or alcohol addict before recommending that student for

admission. We are not suggesting such students should not be admitted, but it should be recorded in student's confidential file so appropriate measures can be taken for possible remedial steps or counseling.

10. Appropriate measures must also be taken to accommodate students whose native language is not English. Again, placement offices must determine the efficiency level in English of a student before placing him or her in any intensive language orientation or ESL programs.

11. Students coming from another country must receive proper orientation and counseling, so they can overcome their initial feelings of loneliness and cultural shocks and can adjust appropriately to their new environments.

12. Sexual Orientation (homosexual or lesbian), religious beliefs, ethnic, cultural, and economic background of prospective candidates for admissions must also be ascertained; not for the intention of discrimination but for the purpose of assisting a student toward a

smooth transition to an educational environment.

These are the some of the most important factors that should be taken into consideration before any student gets enrolled in any educational programs in the United States. As it will be evident, it is impossible for a teacher to check into those aspects of a student's life without any help and cooperation from the school administration, parents, and society as a whole. Besides teaching in the classrooms, teachers have to prepare lesson plans, quizzes, and tests; correct papers, read new books, professional journals, do research and publications. The teacher must stay up to date in the continually changing world of gathering new knowledge and information. It is, therefore, not fair to dump the problem of the society to an individual teacher, and then blame him or her for not being able to keep a student in the classroom.

It should be the concerted effort of the school administrations, parents, spouses, and friends of learners that would keep a learner in a classroom. No matter how hard a teacher tries, the above-mentioned factors will always drive a student away from a classroom and the unfortunate teacher will get the blame as usual.

Finally, the most important factor that influences the dropout phenomenon is lack of respect for the educational institution in general and for teachers in particular. In this society the term 'Education' has lost its real meaning and significance as I mentioned earlier. Education has become synonymous to training. Students nowadays go to schools to get some training to be able to do a particular job and earn a living. They do

not go to school to get educated. Once upon a time educated persons were considered cultured, enlightened, ethical, and knowledgeable. Therefore, teachers were regarded with high esteem considering the fact that they were entrusted with the sublime responsibility of changing human behavior and bringing out the best of a human being. Teachers in the United States are no longer required to do that. They are now told to strictly adhere to the subject matter without expressing any concern about the proper or improper behavior of their students.

Making Eye Contact

I do not remember making frequent eye contacts with my parents, my teachers, an elderly person, or any respectable person. According to our culture making frequent eye contacts with a person who can command and demand respect from me is considered showing disrespect or ignoring that person's authority. I was born and brought up within that cultural environment where people do not look at people when they talk to one another if they are not equal in status. Age, money, education, and job can be taken into consideration in determining the status of a person. I do not remember looking directly to my father or mother's eyes constantly. I also do not remember looking at the eyes of my teachers continuously. It is not that they did not like me or I did not like them. Not making eye contact was considered a very normal thing to do and I never thought otherwise about it.

Now that I have been far away from my country for a long time and living in a country where not making eye contact in conversation is considered an abnormal behavior, I can clearly see how misunderstandings can occur if you do not have cultural awareness of different nations of this world. Not making eye contact in the United States is not only considered as an abnormal behavior but it could also mean that you are ignoring or showing disrespect to someone. It took me a while to get this message and set things straight to my advantage. In the mean time, I suffered tremendous losses for not being able to look straightly at the eyes of my teachers and bosses in the United States when I was talking to them.

First of all, this bad habit kept me from getting hired. In job interviews, I never made eye contacts with the members of the search committee in an honest endeavor to show respect to them, but it backfired. This is the

United States, not Bangladesh. Therefore, it cost me many jobs without my realization that this is what is the reason. When I started working in the United States, I got fired on many occasions. No one told me that they are firing me because I do not make eye contacts. Maybe it did not appear to them also. They thought there was something wrong with me. I was just not normal to them. Maybe they wondered why that guy acted so strangely. If they had any idea about the culture of Bangladesh, they would know exactly what was wrong with me. They would be sympathetic to my situation. They would feel like giving me some advice even. Instead they thought that I was the most unfriendly person in the whole world. Maybe I did not like to work with them. Maybe I was very indifferent to my environment.

When sometimes I sit face to face with myself and contemplate about my struggle for existence and survival, I feel that all those negative feelings that I was responsible for generating among people stemmed from my bad habit of not making eye contacts with my listeners. This is a very bad habit that I brought from Bangladesh, which I was not aware of until that time when I started writing my dissertation on the reception of Rabindranath Tagore in the United States and Britain.

When Tagore won the Nobel Prize for literature for his splendid collection of devotional poems "Gitanjali", he was invited to the United States by some prestigious universities to give lectures on his philosophy. While doing my research one day I came upon a criticism of Tagore's speech in an American daily newspaper, which stated that Tagore ignored his American audience. I was wondering how possibly Tagore could ignore his American audience when he was an invited guest speaker. What could be his motive or reason for ignoring American audience when addressing them? Then suddenly the question dawned on me, "Did Tagore make eye contact with his audience?" Most probably not!

I have rarely seen prominent philosophers, writers, or religious leaders making eye contact with their audience in Bangladesh or in India. In those countries it is still considered normal behavior. Also, Bangladeshi speakers never smile when they face the audience. You would see a somber and very serious expression on their faces. They start talking looking over the heads of the audience, often staring at the ceiling or out the window. In fact they do not interact with their audience, and do not create a friendly atmosphere. Most probably Tagore's body language did not impress the critic in question who decided that Tagore ignored his audience. What Tagore did was he did not make any eye contact with his audience.

I received my schooling in an environment where teachers stood in one place delivering knowledge through lectures, sometimes explaining concepts on the blackboard depending on the subject matter. For example, teachers had to use blackboards if it was a math or grammar class. Other than that we had nothing to see but to listen and take notes. You keep your eyes fixed on the teacher but you even do not get a feeling that the teacher is directly looking at you, unless the teacher decides to ask you a question. Eye contact is a rare phenomenon in our culture. I still visualize most of the faces of my college and university professors delivering lecturers, teaching us but not looking at us. They seldom left their desks to mingle with their students. They rarely walked around the classroom to check who is doing what. Sometimes I felt like thinking about my teachers as aliens coming from outer space to impart knowledge upon us. Still today I hesitate to think of my teachers as human beings with flesh and blood. So it was perfectly all right for them if they failed to make eye contact with me.

With that background, when I entered into the American classroom to receive education from American teachers, you can imagine the extent of my surprise and astonishment. I had some theoretical knowledge about the teacher-student relationship in American culture, but the real picture did not even come closer to that picture. The biggest surprise of my life was to hear the teacher being addressed by the students using the teacher's first name. Gradually I tried to blend in but it was not easy. Finally, I was able to understand one thing that making eye contact is the outcome of the friendliness that existed between the teacher and the students.

I often found myself critical of many aspects of the American culture, but I have been able to develop a love for this eye contact business. First I thought it started out of necessity. As soon as I realized that not making eye contact was costing me my jobs, I thought of correcting that problem by making as much eye contact as possible with my bosses and my coworkers. Pretty soon this new effort on my part started to pay off. I was able to communicate better and found myself more relaxed and more acceptable by my coworkers and my bosses. Eventually I learned more about the importance of making eye contact when I was asked to teach a course in communication. In the textbook of that course there was a complete section on what eye contact can do for making effective communication. Of course, everyone knows the contribution of eye contact in developing a romantic relationship, but I am not talking about that kind of relationship. I am talking about strict business relationships where eye contact has its definite contribution.

I believe that face-to-face communication does not take place in the absence of eye contact. Now I cannot even think of talking to someone without looking at that person. I do not have any first hand knowledge about any other Asian culture except Bangladesh, India, and Pakistan, but I think that most of the Asian countries have a problem with making eye contact. I have written to my friends in Bangladesh explaining the importance of making eye contact and its special implication in the field of communication. My friends agreed with me that we do really have a problem in our culture regarding making eye contact. We must get rid of that bad habit if we really want to make progress in the area of communication. If we want to develop a harmonious and congenial atmosphere among people working together or learning together, we have to start looking at one another instead of looking out the window, or to the floor or to the ceiling for that matter.

We have to learn that looking directly at someone's eyes should not be construed as an indication of disrespect or disobedience. Nor is it an attempt to become friendly with a person who does not want to be friendly. No one is going to lose any self-respect by letting someone else make eye contact. The United States opened my eyes to this essential aspect of human relationships. Now I can see people more clearly, can converse with them confidently, and can also read someone's mind quickly.

But one thing I still need to work on is to try to make eye contact with my wife. I often keep my eyes glued to television screen, a newspaper, or a book while conversing with her. The reason I forget to look at her while talking is not that she is not beautiful. My friends believe that I married the most beautiful woman in the whole world. To tell you the truth I enjoyed such remarks and still feel good about my wife's appearance, and of course I love her very much. But making eye contact! It just does not happen normally, and believe it or not it look like she does not mind all whether I make eye contact with her or not. It does not bother her at all. This is what is known as cultural characteristic of a country.

Personal Freedom

If we believe that our death is the end of everything, it gives us immense freedom to do whatever pleases us. If we further believe that we are only responsible for ourselves, and no one cares for us and we do not have to care for anyone, it also gives us freedom to do whatever we want to do. On the other hand, if we do not believe that death is the end of everything or we believe that we are not only responsible for ourselves, some other people care about us or depend on us, we don't have that kind of freedom to do what we want to do.

I, therefore, believe that it is easier for someone to engage in criminal activity who believes that death is the end of everything and nobody cares for him or her or he or she has to care for no one. I am not saying that those people who believe in this philosophy are all criminals. What I am saying is this: All criminals must necessarily have this philosophy of life.

Can someone choose a career of crime who believes that there is an existence after death? Can someone engage in criminal activity who believes that someone cares for him or her and he or she has to care for that person? During my childhood, I read in a religious book that once upon a time there was a robber and murderer who turned a saint. How did that happen? One day he was about to kill and rob someone who stopped him by asking a question: Do you have a family that you take care of? "Yes, I do," the robber replied, "I have my wife and three children." "Do they approve what you do for living," the victim wanted to know. "Yes, why? Of course, I do this for them anyway," replied the robber. "Don't be so sure, go home and find out, I want to know before you kill me. Tie me up to this tree." So the robber did exactly what the man told him to do. When

he came back he started crying. His family members do not want to share his sin, he confessed. From that day he changed.

The relationship human beings develop among themselves by means of a family life creates a sense of sharing and caring. When you care for someone and find out that person does not approve your behavior, you either have to give up that relationship or change your behavior. There is no other way in between. If you care so much for someone that you do not want to break the relationship, then you change your behavior. That is why I believe that people who do really care for someone, such as a father, mother, brother, sister, or sons and daughters cannot become criminals, unless the whole family agrees to let a member of the family become a criminal, agreeing that they will jointly share the consequence of his or her crime. We are with you, and we will share your sin, we will go to hell with you.

This is very unlikely to happen. I have never seen a whole family living together endorsing the criminal act of one of its members. Therefore, we often find that those individuals who are caught committing heinous crimes, such as robbing banks, killing people, molesting children, and raping do not come out of nice families where father, mother, and children live together. It is absolutely impossible for a person who was raised in a perfect family atmosphere with love and care from both parents to become a serial killer, for example. We have not seen one so far. If we do, it will be a matter of research for the prominent psychologists of the country. Again, I am not saying that if we do not come out of a good family environment or if we decide not to have a family life, we are going to be a criminal. But criminals are most often going to come out of that environment.

There are two groups of people in this world. One group believes that life exists after death. Death is not the end of life. After death we exist in another form. This belief may exist independent of religion. Many religions believe that we have an existence after death, but that does not mean that some people cannot conceive of that possibility although they do not follow any religion. Religious people, of course, believe in the existence of life after death. Buddhist and Hindus believe that soul not only can exist independent of body but also can enter into another body. That means after a person's death his or her soul can come back in another body and live another life in this world. Muslims believe that soul exists after death and God is going to revive them on the Day of Judgment with their bodies and send them to heaven or hell. Jews and Christians have similar beliefs.

Whether we have faith in one of those religions or not, still we

can believe in the existence of soul after death. This belief comes from contemplation and concentration independent of religion. In our dreams when we travel to various places we can feel our existence outside of our body, as if we got a chance to get out when our body is resting. This is not very incomprehensible. Therefore, many people can actually comprehend a separate existence of their soul apart from their body.

What kind of impact does that belief have on our behavior? If you believe that someone's soul will exist even if you destroy that person's body, you will be very afraid to destroy that body. You will not feel free to kill someone if you believe that by killing someone you are not really killing that person. You are transforming that person into a greater invisible power, which can come after you to take revenge. Is not it very scary? This belief will keep you from killing someone.

That is why I said that it is very difficult for a person to become a criminal or a killer if that person believes in the existence of life after death. At this point someone might think, well this belief might be a deterrent for the killer, but all other criminals are not killers. How to keep, for example, a bank robber from robbing a bank with that belief? Those who decide to rob a bank are very aware of potential danger. They have no concern for their own lives or other's lives. They know very well that they may get shot and die in the act of committing a robbery. So they get ready to shoot first if they see any possibility of getting shot. All criminals are potential killers. There is no such crime that does not require killing, instantly or consequently.

Besides, since criminals do not care for anybody and believe that nobody cares for them, they feel free to take any risk including death when they engage in a criminal act such as hijacking a car. Therefore, my assertion remains valid that violent crime will drastically reduce if people start caring about one another through family relationship, and also start thinking that there is an existence of ourselves after our death.

Why are these two ideas very difficult for most of us to accept? First of all these ideas can also be found, as I have already mentioned, in various religions. There exists a perpetual animosity between science and religion. People believe that if you believe in science you cannot believe in religion. But even if we are able to alienate these two ideas from religion and can establish that the existence of soul can scientifically be proven and caring people with family lives cannot commit crimes, still some people are not going to like those ideas because they restrict individual freedom, freedom to do whatever pleases them. Unfortunately most of us do not realize that

we cannot enjoy our freedom without paying a price for it. This price we are paying in upholding this philosophy of carelessness and no existence after death is promoting more crime and criminals. They are thriving under this philosophy of life.

We cannot on the one hand ask for less crime and criminals and on the other hand promote a philosophy of freedom, freedom from all bondage of religion, morality, and spirituality. You cannot at the same time say that you do not believe in the existence of life after death and on the other hand ask for less crime and criminals. It is a very difficult situation. You may be a decent individual. You hate crimes and criminals and never think of engaging in criminal acts. But just because you have a philosophy of life that all criminals must have, you are promoting their cause. If through scientific research you can establish beyond the shadow of a doubt that there really is no such thing as God, and there really is no such thing as existence of life after death. There is only one life to live, and when you die, that is it. You are here only to take care of yourself. This life is only for your enjoyment, and you do not have to worry about anything else. Feel free to do whatever you want to do with it. Then do you see the implications of these messages for those out there who want to kill and rob people? Having this philosophy of life, do you believe that crime will decrease?

Now, you might think, well there are irresponsible people out there, and I cannot give up my philosophy of life only because that philosophy might promote crime. But the problem remains that you are not only concerned about crime, you might one day become a victim of a crime. So, you cannot relax by having a philosophy, which does not guarantee your safety. We have to start preaching coexistence and mutual respect. You have to shout, "Wait a minute. Just because there is no God, just because there is no existence after death, you cannot create chaos and confusion in the society by robbing and killing people. To enjoy life, you have to have a life. If we start killing each other, very soon there will be no life left to enjoy. Therefore, we have to come to terms.

Coming to terms means going back to square one. That is talking about mutual respect, talking about sharing and caring. But these feelings must come from within and from following examples. For example, if someone is being born out of wedlock, if the father or mother abandons their kids, if someone has never seen such a relationship as husband and wife, father and mother, brother and sister how to teach that person the basic principles of human relationships? How to promote a sense of sharing

and caring in that person? How to teach that person what is respect, who has never seen an example of respect? How to tell that person to show respect for someone or his or her property?

Ask the law enforcement to take care of them? Can law enforcement solve the problem of the society? Can any law hold good when there is no moral support behind that law? Who decides what is good and what is bad? Law enforcement does not write the code of conduct. They are only responsible for enforcing those codes. Ironically if the society turns bad things into good things and vice versa then the law enforcement will have to start accusing the citizens for doing something good. If we declare that starting tomorrow it is going to be all right to kill someone if you feel like killing that person, then the law enforcement will have no job of accusing someone of committing a crime. Murdering people will be legalized in this country.

There is no such thing as enjoying your individual freedom when you have to live with other people in an environment, which is prone to crime and criminals. You will be under constant threat of murder and violence. While you can cherish a material philosophy of atheism and carelessness at the same time you will have no peace of mind. You will always have to be on guard of your life and property. In other words, you will have to live in self-imprisonment. You have to barricade yourself from potential danger. You have to lock your door at night. Is this the freedom you want? Freedom of living under constant threat.

On the other hand if we are able to develop mutual respect and tolerance, if we start loving each other, if we start sharing and caring for one another, if we start taking responsibility for our own actions, we will be able to enjoy real freedom, freedom from worry and anxiety. I believe that kind of freedom is freedom in the true sense of the term. Therefore, those who are seeking freedom from the traditional norms and values of the society by propagating such philosophy as death is the end of life, and I stand for my own pleasure without any concern for any one else, cannot get the essence of real freedom. Real freedom is a sense of security and peace of mind, which can only be achieved in a society with minimum crime.

Unfortunately, no other democratic nations in the entire world are so paranoid as Americans about losing their individual freedom to an authority known as government. In an attempt to secure and protect individual's freedom, Americans most often sacrifice some traditional values and norms that keep the society and its people together. Americans

are afraid that strict adherence to traditional values might take away their freedom to choose any life style or to express themselves as they wish. For example, Americans believe that traditional respect for the flag of a nation can restrict individual's freedom of expression. So they prefer showing disrespect to the flag by burning it as a means of making a political statement.

This too much craving for freedom to do whatever pleases them to do is taking a great toll on the sustenance of the society by destroying the senses of decency, decorum, and respect for other's opinion and feelings. Those who are after enjoying individual freedom often forget that they cannot have their freedom when they have no respect for someone else's freedom. Living in a society means having respect for one another and coming to a compromise in the event of a clash of ideas or ideologies. In the name of your freedom, you cannot impose your ideas on someone else. You cannot require some one to change his or her way of life only because it does not conform to yours. Living together entirely depends on making adjustments and compromises. Most Americans seem not to comprehend this simple fact of life. They often claim, "This is my life. I have every right to live my life the way I want to live it. No one can dictate my life. Leave me alone. Let me live my life." When they say this it sounds very appropriate. But the inherent defect of such a statement is this that it is removing an individual from the society, from any relationships with other people.

If we want to maintain a relationship with someone, we cannot make the above statement. Making a statement like this is nothing but imprisoning ourselves. We become a prisoner of a self made prison. We close all the doors to any relationship whatsoever. Ironically, our effort to enjoy freedom turns into losing freedom. To enjoy freedom and a normal and healthy life, we have to have a social, emotional, and romantic relationship. Those relationships cannot be achieved by declaring to the entire world that this is my life, and I would like to enjoy it the way I wish. If this is my life, and I only care for my own satisfaction, how am I going to get someone to stay with me? Don't I have to have respect and concern for my partner's satisfaction also?

The word personal freedom is meaningless. We are sacrificing our values only to protect something which cannot be protected in the first place or protection of which becomes undesirable. People sometimes confuse self-esteem and personality with personal freedom. To have respect for you and to have a desire to stand out of the crowed are good qualities and are

expected of all cultured and sophisticated human beings. But personal freedom in the sense of freedom to express oneself in any form or manner without regard and concern for others is very detrimental to the welfare and progress of a society. Personal freedom has meaning only in relation to the society, not independent of the society.

A Country of Human Beings

I always wondered, could there be a country, which may safely be called a country of human beings? This utopian country has always been in my dream since I left my homeland in search of a country where I can improve the quality of my life. Along with improving the quality of my life, I also wanted to improve the condition of my living by staying in a country which may plainly and simply be called a country of civilized people, not only a country of Hindu or Muslim, Buddhist or Christian, White or Black. Just a country where people are recognized and honored simply because they are human beings not a member of majority, not a member of a particular religion, ethnic, or cultural groups.

This contemplation has always bothered me that I cannot be happy only by improving the quality of my life. I would also like to feel important as a human being. I do not want people to look at me and give me a look as if I don't belong here. Also, I did not like to encounter such question as: Where are you from? I often thought of answering such question sarcastically: I am from another planet, an alien. Just decided to check it out here how you, human beings, are doing. Instead, I just said, "I am from Bangladesh". I wondered whether that made any sense to anyone who never heard of a country known as Bangladesh.

Is there going to be a time when it will make no sense to ask such a question as, ìWhere are you from?î, because the obvious answer will be: I am from this planet earth unless I look like an alien. You are also from the same planet, are not you? This innocent looking question makes a wide gap between you and me. That is why I wanted to have a country where no such silly question will be asked any more.

This vast universe is inhabited by people of all colors, shapes, religions,

ethnicities, and races. But anywhere you go, you will find supremacy of a group of people over the other. People always glorify the point of difference between them and divide themselves into majority and minority. The majority always tries to dominate the minority and the minority lives their lives timidly recognizing themselves as second-class citizens. That is why I wanted to have a country where there will be no name calling as majority or minority. This notion will carry no meaning in my imaginary land where everyone will be recognized just as human beings irrespective of their differences.

Bangladesh was a part of India before 1947. When I was born, India was under the British rule and they ruled it for more than 200 years. Before leaving India the British divided the country in two parts creating two countries, India and Pakistan, on the basis of Jinnah's two-nation theory. Both Jinnah and Gandhi, two national leaders of India, fought for the independence of India. The Hindu majority areas became India and the Muslim majority became Pakistan. I have seen how Hindus and Muslims killed each other in communal riots. I have seen how people had to flee their own homeland and migrate to Pakistan or India for fear of their lives.

Subsequently, those people were termed refugees by their host countries and had to live miserable lives. When I was a child it was very difficult for me to understand why people have to hate one another so much only because they belong to different religion. When I grew up and read the history of British rule in India, I knew how it started. In fact the British created this hatred between Hindus and Muslims. It was there policy to divide and rule. They decided to incite Hindus against Muslims and Muslims against Hindus. Let them kill one another. We don't have to kill them, and we can rule this country forever. That was the policy of British administration. That's what I figured out from my reading of history and events.

To come to this conclusion, I compared the British rule of India with the Muslim rule of India. As I mentioned, the British ruled India for 200 years but the Muslims rule India for 700 years. There were no riots between Hindus and Muslims when Muslims were the rulers. Hindus and Muslims lived peacefully and there were harmonious relationship among them. We never heard of any persecution of Hindus by the Muslims before the British came to this country. If the Muslim rulers and their minority citizens were thinking of killing the entire majority Hindus for those 700 hundred years, there wouldn't be any Hindu left in that subcontinent. Nor did the

Muslims tried to annihilate Hindu culture, literature, or languages. The Muslim rulers had profound respect for all religions and cultures.

I firmly believe that India under Muslim rule was a country of human beings. People of India were not too much conscious about their religious differences at that time. They did not like to kill one another. But as soon as the British took over, everything changed dramatically. I could go on and on to show how the British rule had succeeded in planting the seed of hatred between Hindus and Muslims in India, but this is not the purpose of this essay.

Living in a small country known as Bangladesh, which was first created as East Pakistan, I have seen how politics had exploited the religious sentiments of the innocent and honest people of the villages. Bangladesh could be a perfect example of a country of human being, not Hindus' or Muslims' considering the honesty and sincerity of the people. Unfortunately corrupt politicians always try to use religion to achieve political advantages, a legacy they inherited from the British administrators of India.

The reason it is very difficult to find a country of only human beings is that people all over the world like to group together according to their own cultural and religious affinity. There is nothing wrong with that if politicians do not come to teach us to hate each other and to blame one another for our misfortunes. Where there is no politics, religion does not bring any difference among people. Religion by itself does not teach, inspire, or provoke hatred among people of different religions. I believe that Hindus do not hate Muslims or Muslims do not hate Hindus, Protestants do not hate Catholics or Catholic do not hate Protestants, Jews do not hate Muslims and Muslims do not hate Jews.

Politicians teach us to hate one another to gain some political advantages. If you can remove politics from people's lives, you will be amazed to find how people of different religions live together respecting and enjoying each other.

If you do not understand what I am talking about, I will give you a concrete example from my own experience. You have heard about riots in India. Hindus and Muslims from time to time start killing one another. But when the Muslims and Hindus from India come to the United States and started living together, they become good friends. They live like family members. I have some Hindu friends from India living in this country whom I consider my best friends. It never bothered them or me that we are from different religion and cultures. The reason is we are now detached from that environment where politics dominates people's lives. Where

politicians create hatred among people to engage one against the other only to rip political benefit. I often thought the politicians are number one enemy of the human beings. I have not seen a politician who has never used a group of people against the other.

We hate criminals but we do not hate politicians. We respect them and support them and make them our leaders. I think they are the main roadblocks that we don't have a country, which we can call a country of human beings. As long as there are politicians in this world there will always be hatred among people because it is politician's job to create that hatred. It is a politician who takes advantage of this fact that some one is Hindu and some one is Muslim, some one is Buddhist and some one is Christian, someone is Black and someone is White. Politicians tell us that one is creating problems for the other. Politician takes sides pretending to be the savior of the cause of a particular group of people thereby creating rifts and divisions among people.

In my utopian country there will be no politicians. The politicians will be looked down upon as criminals. There will be no such thing as politics. It will be considered as a bad word. The dictionary will define this term as a science that provoke hatred among human beings. A politician is a person who engages in such activities as telling lies, giving false hope, and using one against the other. Politicians create disturbances in the smooth functioning of the government. They are the greatest enemy of the society and human beings in general. I am thinking of a country where instead of glorifying politicians and making them our leaders, we could glorify teachers, engineers, scientists, and physicians and make them our leaders. We need these people in a country, which will be known as country of human beings.

Our leaders will be selected from the group of people mentioned above. They will be nominated by the people and subsequently given a test to qualify for leadership and to qualify for performing a particular task. We don't need demagogues. Our leaders will not be those people who can stand behind a podium and shout for hours together giving false promises. We need people with real working knowledge. There will be no public meetings, no lobbying, no caucuses, and no debates. People nominated and selected through the test will directly hold certain offices and administer the country according to the guidelines laid down in the constitution of the country.

I don't know whether this will happen in my life time, but I will very much like to see a country declaring itself as a country of human being.

From now on there will be no politics, no political parties, no majority or minority, no black or white. You don't have to be born here to be citizen or to qualify for the position of the president of the country. It is not a country of a particular group of people but it is everyone's country. To immigrate to this country the only qualification you need is to become a human being, yes, and a human being in the true sense of the term, not a racist.

Welcome to this country if you can really want to become a human being by getting rid if all kinds of bias, prejudices, and superiority or inferiority complexes and get along with everyone to create a great race of only human beings.

Freedom of Speech

Since the Supreme Court of the United States interpreted the meaning of freedom of speech as freedom of expression, we entered into a whole new area of controversy. If the Supreme Court interpreted the meaning of freedom of speech as freedom of expression through verbal language (words) or nonverbal language (body language), we would have no problem today in making political statement in a civilized manner. Supreme court decided that freedom of speech could extend to freedom of expression. But expression of what? If the Supreme Court said freedom of expression means to express one's opinion or criticism of the government's policy, we would have no misunderstanding about this constitutional provision. Instead the judges of the Supreme Court decided that it could extend to expression of anger or frustration in such a form as starting a fire by burning such a sacred thing as a flag of a country. So freedom of speech now can manifest itself in burning a flag to make a political statement.

I understand that the word speech has a relationship to the word expression. We express ourselves through speech. We can also express our anger, frustration or criticism through speech meaning language. If for any physical handicap situation such as being deaf and dumb, we are unable to use verbal language, we can use nonverbal language such as gestures and postures to express our consent or dissent. I think when the founding fathers of this nation decided to use the word speech they were very careful even two hundred years ago. Two hundred years ago we had dictionaries and word expression was there in those dictionaries. Why they decided not to use the word expression but speech if they had expression in mind? Because they wanted to make it clear that we should have the freedom to express ourselves, our anger, frustration, and criticism, but we have to use

language or speech, and in exceptional cases nonverbal language when we are handicapped, as a means of expression. We cannot use any other means. If they had any idea that in the future some judges of the Supreme Court will interpret the speech as such that we can express ourselves by whatever means we deem appropriate, they would of course define what they mean by speech.

I firmly believe that the writers of the constitution had no doubt in their mind what speech meant. It was impossible for them to believe that some might have another definition for the word speech. I have been teaching linguistics, philology, and phonetics for a long time. I have gone through the process of learning eight foreign languages. I am still teaching parts of speech everyday in my English grammar classes. To tell you the truth, I tried very hard to find another meaning for speech other than my language in all major languages of the world but were unable. I don't really understand how supreme court judges can decide that the meaning of speech can be extended to expression of anger in the form ofë burning something whether it is a flag or not. It is beyond me how burning and speech can be synonymous.

Speech is a most valuable gift of this civilization. When our cave dweller ancestors were speechless they used to express their joy, anger, frustration, and intention through meaningful sound and gesture and posture. It was quite appropriate for a prehistoric cave dweller speechless or languageless man or woman to set a fire in a house or a piece of cloth to express his or her anger. The gift of civilization is that we don't do that any more. We express our anger by shouting (using language), and more civilized and cultured people do not shout at all, they write letters of complaint. They use language, the written form of it. To say that we can express ourselves by burning a flag is to deny the progression of modern civilization and to ignore a wonderful gift of civilization known as speech. When we have speech, why do we have to burn something? I wonder when Gregory Johnson burned a flag at the 1984 Republican National Convention. Was he speechless like our cave dweller ancestors?

Let us think about another consequence of letting people burn something instead of using speech. Burning involves physical destruction. By speech we cannot physically destroy anything. Of course we can hurt someone's feelings by our speech, but we cannot physically destroy that person. We cannot eliminate that person from this world. If today I allow you the freedom of burning a piece of cloth, thinking that it is merely a small piece of cloth not considering its symbolical context, tomorrow how

can I prevent you from burning a warehouse or a manufacturing plant where flags are stored and produced? Your frustration and anger can be so intense that you want to get rid of a large number of flags to make a big statement. How can I prevent you the next day from blowing up a federal government building with 170 people inside it?

There is no such thing as a small fire and a big fire when it comes to anger. If my anger can take the form of expressing itself in a small fire, that small fire can get out of my control and turn into a huge one. This small fire can get out of control because when I am angry, I myself am out of control. So it is not a good idea to start a fire specially when I am angry. What happens if Timothy McVeigh argues that he only exercised his first amendment right when he was expressing his anger on that Oklahoma federal building?

Everyone is going to say that this is absurd. Burning of a flag cannot be equated to blowing up a federal government office with 170 people inside it. But if today my anger can find a way to express itself in small fire, tomorrow it may be tempted to burn a house.

Besides if freedom of speech can be interpreted as freedom to burn a flag to make a political statement then why not burn a book because someone does not like the ideas expressed in that book? How about burning some pages of the American Constitution itself because someone does not like some provisions of that constitution? And gradually, how about burning that IRS office because it taxes us exorbitantly? I know at this point my readers are thinking: Well, you cannot destroy life and property in the name of freedom of speech. Burning a flag is not destroying life or property, it is just a piece of cloth and there is no victim and, therefore, relatively harmless. We cannot let you inflict harm on individual's life and property to exercise your freedom.

Well, then flags come in different sizes and different prices. Supreme Court has to specify up to what sizes of flags could be burnt which won't fall under the category of destruction of property. Think how ridiculous it is going to be in such an effort to justify a flag burning. Not only that, supreme court will also have to determine what else can be burnt when people want to make political statements. The Supreme Court also needs to tell us we can burn this and that but not these or those. It is going to be really confusing out there.

As we can see, freedom of speech can be interpreted as freedom of expression, but freedom of expression by the means of language only (speech) not by any other means. It is so clear to me, but I don't understand

why it was not that clear to our honorable judges or to our lawmakers who still could not decide what is the true meaning of the term "Freedom of Speech".

Some people believe that we have to understand the freedom of speech in its wider sense. In that sense it means freedom to protest against government and that protest can take many forms and shapes. We do not only protest by giving speeches in a meeting or writing in newspapers, we stage demonstration against government in various ways such as calling a general strike, by noncooperation, by holding rallies and processions, and by picketing. As long as expression of protests are non-violent and victimless there is nothing wrong in adopting those methods. Flag burning is one of them. Making this act illegal may result in similar protest illegal and the government may turn to dictatorship instead of democratic. Supporters of burning flag are paranoid that by stopping burning of the flag the government can take away their rights to protest one by one.

The main flaw of this argument is this that while on the one hand this is advocating nonviolent protest, it is opening up a door to resort to violence on the other. As I have explained earlier, afire is a fire no matter how small it is and it has the potential to start the big one. Secondly this argument is trying to get its support from the first amendment of the constitution. The advocates of such interpretation of first amendment are wrong. They cannot change the meaning of speech to fit their own explanation of speech. If they want to protest against the government by burning a flag, by burning an effigy, a house or setting fire on the federal government offices, they should amend the constitution allowing them to do so. They have to change the constitution as such: Henceforth freedom of speech shall not confine to freedom of expression of anger only by burning a flag, it will extend to freedom of expression by starting a fire not resulting in human casualty and destruction of property.

Let's change the constitution to that effect and let's every one carry a matchbox in our pockets so we can instantly start a fire when we want to make a political statement. Why not? This is easier than sitting down with pen and paper and organizing our arguments against the government. Besides these is what democracy is all about, getting angry and losing temper and striking someone with bullets, starting a riot, and burn a city. We have every right to do that in a free society. Our freedom is very precious. But one thing I don't understand is that why every time we have to go back to the Constitution and take out a word or a phrase out of context to justify our action? Can't we justify our action with out the support of

the Constitution? Why are we so dependent on the Constitution? Why in our every step we have to ask for support from the Constitution even if we have to distort it for that matter?

If we are so sure that we are right, why can't we sometimes say that the Constitution is wrong. It was written two hundred years ago. Some of its provisions cannot be applied to today's circumstances. If we are brave enough, we should be able to say something like that once in a while. Freedom of expression may also apply to freedom from depending on the Constitution. The point is, if we have respect for some Constitutional provisions, let's stick to those. If we don't have respect for some other provisions of the Constitution, let's also speak against them. But let us not distort the Constitutional provisions by bringing out a new interpretation whether it make any sense or not. I, therefore, do not believe in the Supreme Court judgesí interpretation of freedom of speech as freedom of expression resulting in burning a flag.

Homeless or Hopeless?

I have never encountered the word homeless in Bangladesh. Bangladesh is a very poor country. When you live in the United States, Bangladesh looks even poorer. Therefore, when I say I have never encountered such a word as homeless, everyone might get very surprised. Of course, there are many poor people in Bangladesh, but they are simply known as poor or beggars, not homeless. The poor and the beggars are not homeless either because they live in makeshift homes, a dilapidated home but home after all. Being poor or beggar does not necessarily mean that those people do not have a home to live. Most of the people in Bangladesh live in some kind of homes although those homes may be falling apart. People love their home, and poor people do not like to be termed as homeless.

In big cities some people like to live in parks, under the bridges, or in an condemned or abandoned buildings. They are known as vagabonds and worthless people not as homeless. Therefore, when I was first introduced to this word "homeless", my reaction was that it must refer to a life style deliberately chosen by some individuals. It has nothing to do with poverty. Some people do not like to live in homes. They want to live outside as if they got sick and tired of living in a home. They are not less in anything only less in homes. That is why they are homeless. This interpretation made sense to me at that time. The United States being one of the richest countries in the whole world it was impossible for me to think of some people as poor, so poor that they can not afford to provide a roof over their heads.

Subsequently, I learned that this word is synonymous to poor people in American context. Every country must have some poor people, no matter how rich the country may be. So the United States has poor people

and they don't have homes. Some people are, therefore, very sympathetic to their situation. Homeless people also beg, so they are also beggars. It is no denying the fact that they are poor people. Politicians and social reformers always talk about doing something to alleviate the sufferings of homelessness. They blame their government for not taking care of these people.

At that time, I started wondering how such a rich country can produce such a group of people so poor that they have to beg for food and cannot even provide a roof over their head? What's wrong with this system? Then I compared my own situation with respect of being poor and homeless in the United States to understand the homeless issue. I came from the poorest country to the richest country, and I could not bring a home with me. So when I landed in the United States with only $10 dollars in my pocket, I was not only poor but also homeless. I was looking for food and shelter at the same time. I had to spend only one night at the Los Angeles International Airport sitting in a chair waiting for the sun to rise. When I faced a new world, not only I managed to earn my own food but also was able to find a roof over my head. I was homeless just for one day!

Therefore, you cannot blame me if I don't understand what money has to do with becoming homeless in the United States. What homelessness has to do with becoming poor as we always like to assume. Some become very sympathetic and talk about homeless people as poor and helpless as if for lack of money they cannot provide a home for themselves. If homeless people only needed homes it would be easy for the government of the United States to provide homes for them. But the homeless people preferred not to use those homes. They preferred living outside under the open sky.

The problem of homelessness is in no way connected with poverty. Money cannot solve this problem. This problem can only be handled if you do not call this people "homeless" but identify them as "hopeless". I firmly believe that people become homeless when they become hopeless. When an individual finds no reason for his or her existence in a society, he or she loses all respect for traditional norms, decency, and decorum and becomes homeless. When some people cannot lean on their past to relax, cannot enjoy their present life, and don't see anything happening in the future, they abandon all hopes. First they become hopeless and eventually become homeless. When people become hopeless they lose all notions of time: present, past, and future and live in a huge vacuum.

Those of us who live in homes time flows for us. Day comes after

night and night changes into day. We have a notion of the past and can look forward to the future. That is what I call the flow of time. But time is static and some times appears terribly static for some human beings on earth who suffer from an acute sense of nothingness of their existence, who live in a large vacuum of emptiness in and around them and cannot come out of it. If they could come out of it, most probably they could pass their time and even feel that time is passing very rapidly. They would feel like making good use of their time like the rest of us and would feel like looking forward to a bright future. Unfortunately they cannot do that and become hopeless and eventually homeless.

The complexity of human life in this hostile universe creates a sense of nothingness in some people's lives. They find no way to shake it off to proceed towards a new beginning or to search for a new meaning of life. Then they want to pass their lives with this feeling of nothingness. Ironically, one cannot pass his or her life by nourishing and nurturing a single feeling that life is meaningless. If someone wants to do that, he or she will find that time is not passing for him or her. When that happens people become utterly hopeless and subsequently homeless.

As it will be apparent, those people who are homeless have a mental condition. They are mentally sick. Most of them have mental sickness, which needs treatment. They are not out of their homes, they are out of their minds. To categories them as homeless is, therefore, a big mistake because in doing so they get mixed up with poor people. This is of course a wrong diagnosis, and a wrong diagnosis will not cure a disease. I am one hundred percent sure and certain that a check of all the homeless people by a psychiatrist will reveal this fact that all of them are mentally ill. This is especially so in the United States.

Compared to the United States homeless people of Bangladesh will rarely be found as mentally ill. People in Bangladesh are homeless because poverty has driven them out of their homes. Once upon a time they had a small home in a small village. They had a piece of land to grow food, a pond to grow fish, and some cattle to raise. They suffered through the generations of exploitations by the greedy and jealous landowners, natural calamities like cyclone, flood, draught, and epidemic. To add to the problem, during the turn of the century the industrial revolution shattered the peace and tranquility of the once peaceful hearth and home of the poor peasants. They were forced to leave their homes with the members of their families. They flocked together around big cities to survive. Some of

them found a new life in the dean and bustle of a new environment. Some slipped through the crack to become homeless.

I have no doubt in my mind that the root cause of their homelessness was poverty, not mental condition. It is, therefore, justified to think of them as poor and helpless people who need help to get back on their feet. While Bangladesh can solve its homelessness problem only by money, the United States cannot solve that problem that way. As I tried to trace back the root cause of homelessness in Bangladesh, we have to do the same thing in respect of the United States. We have to find the reason behind some people's turning to homeless. To become homeless in an affluent society, one has to take enough of abuse and neglect from that society. The factors that drive people towards homelessness varies from society to society.

In the United States some people started to discard their homes due to the disintegration of the traditional family life, values, norms, and ideals, not because of poverty. Some people started to hate their homes. They lost all interest and comfort of living in a home. They developed a new philosophy of life. They started to revolt against establishment. Home is an establishment, so they wanted to destroy their homes. There was an attempt to alienate oneself from the society and find a new meaning of life in mysticism. The hippies of 60s bear testimony to such an observation. This eagerness of some angry young people to break the tradition and norms does not evolve out of economic crises. Rather its origin may be traced to affluence.

People sometimes get bored and tired of getting too much of something and come to point when they cannot take that comfort any more. They look for drastic change. At that point some people decide to become homeless only to break the monotone of a secured and comfortable life. Some others decide to leave their homes as a manifestation of their anguish and hatred that they accumulated over a long period of time because of the abuse they received from their respective families and neighborhood. They lost all attraction for their homes. They talked to themselves in such way, "I have lived in homes, home sucks. If this is what home is all about, I don't want this home. From now I do not have a home."

If proper research is conducted to unearth the root cause of homelessness in the United States, it will be apparent that poverty did not generate the problem of homelessness in this country. A further investigation will reveal the fact that in both cases a group of people wanted to revolt against the system. Obviously they did not see any hope for them in a home life in a traditional setting with a nuclear family. Those who developed an

alternative philosophy of satisfying the purpose of life by using psychedelic drug or alienating from the society obviously did not see any hope in the traditional family life. Therefore, these people can be categorized as hopeless people, they are not really homeless.

If we call them homeless, it looks like they wanted to live in homes but because of the economic disparity of the society they have been deprived of living in a home. We must do something for them, they need our help and attention. But the truth is far from this as I tried to analyze in this essay. Hopelessness is a mental condition. Hopeless people live in a vacuum. Money cannot fill that up. Allocating money in federal budget to solve this problem of homelessness will not do any good.

I Love You

Among many other surprises, one of the pleasant surprises of my life was to hear such expression from parents to their children, "I love you." While I started thinking about that, I further noticed that to finish a conversation over telephone American parents rarely miss this expression, "I love you." First I thought this is something wonderful in American culture compared to Bangladeshi culture where my parents never told me out loud that they love me. I was, therefore, pleasantly surprised when I heard that, but alas, that feeling did not last long.

In Bangladesh the sentence, "I love you," is only being used in cases of romantic relationships. During my college and university life, I remember hearing the use of this sentence among male and female classmates. In our culture we consider this expression of emotions as very superficial and temporary because when you really get deeply involved with some one, you do not utter those three words any more. You just look at each other. You communicate non-verbally with your eyes. You want to express this emotion to your lover: There are no such words in the whole world, which can express my feeling for you. In such a situation you do not feel like using the sentence, "I love you".

It was, therefore, very amazing for me when I started hearing these words all around me in the United States. I asked myself a question: Do these people really love one another so much that they can't help it announcing aloud? It gradually become clear to me that there are other reasons to say these word so frequently than to express a sincere feeling of genuine affection and true love for someone. This society must use these words to circumvent certain kind of guilty feelings. What are those guilty feelings? Let me explain.

The reason my parents never told me, "I love you", was that it was so obvious that if they told me, a question would follow, "why are you telling me that daddy or mommy?" In our culture people get married not to get separated or divorced, they get married to stay together for the rest of their lives. The prime consideration for getting married is to start a family life. No one ever thinks of getting separated or divorced in the near future. Once married husband and wife become one entity. One's destiny becomes other's destiny. They might both work but they don't keep track of their income separately. The don't maintain separate bank accounts. In other words two lives become one. There is no 'you' and ëlí, there is always 'we'. They make decision together and they look forward to a beautiful future when children will come illuminating their small house. When children come they become father and mother not husband and wife any more. There names changes to Karim's father or Runu's mother. They become known by their children. I have seen how my fathers and mother's lives revolved around me and my brothers and sisters. How many sleepless nights they passed taking care of us. They did not want anything for them. Our pleasure was their pleasure. After all these, did they have to tell us that they love us?

Now let me talk about the United States. People get married in this culture to get separated and divorced. Why they get married in the first place? It is beyond me. I heard a radio talk show host the other day providing statistics that the average marriages last for a maximum period of seven years in the United States. If you want to get separated or divorced you can find hundreds of reasons. On the other hand, if you want to stay together you do not have to find any reason whatsoever.

In this culture people get married for all other conceivable reasons other than to start a family life and to look forward to smiling children illuminating their houses. I have no doubt in my mind that married couple's lives do not revolve around their children in this culture. They have some other priorities in their lives. They can heartlessly dump their children to a babysitter to go to a party and dance. They justify this dumping when they go to work. But there are some other things they have to do without any justification whatsoever; for example, going on a vacation by themselves leaving the children behind. Since they do not make any sacrifices for their children, their love and affection for their

children are not so obvious as it is in Bangladesh. They are well aware that their children may be in doubt about their feelings for them.

When the father and mother announce to a three years old, "Honey,

we have to go to a party to night. Susan (baby sitter) is going to take care of you. We are going to drop you to her house now." Then the child feels hopeless, frustrated, and scared. The child starts to think: Is there someone or something more important than I am to my parents? Parents can also see that question in their children's eyes. To compensate for that and to circumvent the guilty feeling, they have to say, "I love you". Since 'love' of parents is not obvious to the children, parents have to announce it out loud.

Do you think that your children get very happy when they hear those three words? No, they do not. That does not change anything. The question still remains in your child's mind: "If you love me so much as you say daddy, why do not you cancel your party to night and stay with me? But they never utter that question. They suffer mentally. I cannot remember any social event in my life where I went by myself leaving my wife and children behind unless it is strictly work or business related. They are part and parcel of my life and I cannot imagine my existence without their presence. Same with my wife. If someone invited us and we knew children were not welcome, we politely refused to accept that invitation. Now my daughters go to high school. They have their own friends. Sometimes they do not enjoy going with us whenever we go to some place. Sometimes they say, "Why don't you go to someplace by yourself, mom and dad and live us alone. Don't you think we are grown up and take care of ourselves?" When they say this we really feel like going to some place. We tried sometimes but that trip turned out dull and monotonous. We enjoy ourselves best when we are all together surrounded by our children.

Fathers and mothers in the United States never realize that their children love to see them living together. They love both father and mother jointly, not separately. They naturally believe that it is normal for their father and mother to live in the same room not only in the same house, sleep on the same bad and eat on the same dinning table and relax on the same couch. They feel good when they see mommy loves and takes care of daddy and daddy loves mommy and takes care of her. They feel proud of themselves. They believe that this is for them that this thing is happening. They get a sense of fulfillment, safety, and security.

0In such a situation, it is useless to go to them and explain: Although your mommy and I do not live together any more but it has nothing to do with you. I love you very much. So does your mommy. They listen to this explanation intently, try to understand its meaning but do not understand anything: But it does not make any sense to me. I don't like to be loved

separately by my mother and father. I am a human being. I am not a toy that you can like and dislike me. What about my feelings? I want to love you too , my dad, but I can't when I see you don't love my mommy any more. I lose all respect for you. I want to love you my Mommy, but I can't when you don't love my daddy. I want both of you to love each other. Because you are my daddy and my mommy. That makes me happy. When I see you don't live together, it breaks my heart. I feel frustrated, defeated. I feel I could not bridge the gap between you two. No matter how hard you try to convince me both of you love me separately that does not lessen my pain.

I don't think that I am making those up when I speak for a child's response. If you have any doubt about what goes on in a child's mind when parents come up with the idea of getting separated or divorced, you can go back to your past and put yourself in that time frame when one day your parents came to talk about getting separated or divorced. If you are one of those lucky kids whose parents never got separated or divorced, find out by asking your friends' kids or a school's counselor. They will be able to give you a clear picture about what goes on in the minds of the children when their parents file for a divorce. I think getting divorced and separated on the face of the children is the worst form of child abuse this civilization has ever seen.

The massage parents send to their children by getting separated or divorced is that you are not the most important thing in my life. I have a life to live, and I want to live it up to the fullest of my satisfaction. The true meaning of that satisfaction becomes apparent when father brings a girlfriend at home and mother brings a boyfriend at home and introduces to their children. Children get the message that sex is more powerful and more important than love, affection, and concern for one's own children. A child's emotion, safety, and sense of security have no room in a world where sexual desires proclaim its supremacy above anything else. Under such a situation how can parents demand respect from their children? And how can they ask their children not to pay too much importance to sex? Not to become frustrated and to say no to drugs? That is how children grow up with a sense of frustration and absurdity of their existence. They lose all respect for their parents and any norms and ideals or the values of the society. They feel defeated and cheated. No matter how hard you shout, "I love you", "I love you", it will never make any sense to them.

Love for Guns

Some people love guns very much, so they come up with justifications to have one. It is obvious that if they did not love guns they would not take the trouble of finding so many reasons to have guns. Rather than examining the justifications, I decided to find out why people want guns so much. There are many people who cannot even think of living a life without having a gun around. They are nice law abiding citizens. They have no criminal records and they never may not have any. They only love guns and they enjoy guns. They use guns for recreational purposes, such as hunting, target shooting, etc. Of course they are not thinking of using their guns for any other purpose than recreation.

There are another group of people who love to have a gun because they always feel insecure.. They feel that they need a gun to protect their lives and properties if the situation warrants. They feel empty and helpless in the absence of a gun. If the necessity makes them love guns, we should also call it a kind of love. It is ,therefore, obvious that both the above-mentioned groups must support guns. When the question of gun control comes, they are not going to support it anyway. They cannot even think of government taking away their rights to have guns, or standing in their way to easily access a gun.

Now, another group of people believe that we have a problem in this society because of the easy availability of guns. They present statistics to establish the fact that guns are dangerous to have either in your house or in personal possession. When you believe that you can protect your life or the lives of your loved ones, you virtually end up destroying your life or your loved ones lives accidentally or frantically. So they hate guns, not

the question of loving a gun. They want the government to control guns strictly, especially ban all sorts of assault weapons.

Those who are in favor of controlling guns further believe that easy access to guns helps the lunatics become mass murderers, and helps criminals kill people indiscriminately when they want and wish. This debate is going on and on, and there seems to be no end to it. I often wonder, is it very difficult to decide whether guns are good or bad? Why cannot our law makers come to a conclusion such as: don't blame it on guns, people kill people, or let's get rid of all guns, we don't need them anyway. Why are our lawmakers wasting our valuable time and money deliberating on this issue over a long period of time, and coming up with no conclusion?

I think, I have the answer to this question. Through my deep concentration and contemplation, I have fund that average Americans have a profound love and respect for guns. They have developed this love and respect over a long period of time. This is not peculiar to this country. Human beings have developed this love and fascination for deadly weapons since the prehistoric times. The cave dwellers first made weapons out of stones to protect their lives from ferocious animals and to hunt for food. Eventually they started to refine weapons to achieve more accuracy and efficiency. Weapons were essential part of their lives. Weapons were invented to serve a definite purpose, out of a necessity, not as a means of recreation.

The need for having guns to procure food or to protect lives from ferocious animals gradually disappeared. Human knowledge progressed in such areas as agriculture and domestication of animals. Although they did not need it, some people could not get rid of their old friend guns. So, innocently, they thought of using them for recreational purposes, such as, hunting and target shooting. So far it looks all right.

The problem started when some people started looking at weapons as power, as a means of intimidating another tribe or a group of people and to dominate over them. This is how guns created various units of human habitats or territories known as village, city, state, and country. This is how guns also created social outlaws subsequently termed as criminals who wanted to defy the authorities created by guns. In a sense, the manifestation of power through guns helped create our governments around the world. Guns have become an integral and essential part of the all political entity that we have been able to create so far.

When guns give us power and power gives us a country, the existence

of a country depends on guns. In such a situation it is almost impossible not to fall in love with power or guns. If on the one hand we justify or glorify the role of guns to protect our freedom as a nation, on the other hand we cannot downplay the importance of feeling powerful in our individual lives by having a gun. We only surrender our gun to an organization, which we call a country and ask that organization to become more powerful every day by inventing more powerful and destructive weapons, so we can achieve absolute supremacy over other nations.

The point is, we do not hate physical or brutal power, we love it. Our love for physical and brutal strength manifests itself in our attempt to create more sophisticated weapons and more destructive power. This trend is not peculiar to the United States. Any nation in this world can develop such a desire to become powerful and gain absolute supremacy. That is why the arms race is still going on, and we are spending billions of dollars to achieve supremacy.

Asking people to get rid of guns should be supported by asking all nations of the world to get rid of their weapons and armed forces. It is a double standard to keep guns in government levels and than to eliminate guns in individual levels. The governmental love affair with guns must come to an end to do away with individuals' love for guns.

We brag about doing away with the era of kingship and entering into the era of democracy. The main thrust of democracy is to recognize and respect the power of the people, not he power of the gun. It will be very difficult to establish the power of the people in the presence of the power of the gun. Those who believe that democracy can be secured or restored through the power of guns are totally wrong. The use of power only provokes use of power by the opponents.

Democracy thrives in an atmosphere where there is no threat of application of power. Democracy gains momentum in a society, which believes that the pen is mightier than the sword. This is what civilization is all about. Power of a gun can give us a country but cannot give us civilization. Our respect of scholarship, sense of decency, decorum, and love for reason not force made us civilized. Civilization has no other connotation as I have explained in my previous essays.

Human beings' progression from the love of a brute physical force to the power of knowledge is the history of civilization. Human being became civilized by giving up their love and respect for physical power and by starting to show love and respect for the power of knowledge. We created so many codes of conduct, religion, law, regulation, and constitution, so

that the reign of reason can prevail over the reign of terror. We created many organizations and entrusted them with power to control the outlaws, and to lead a peaceful, good ,and productive life in this universe.

Asking to possess a gun at this juncture of our civilization is to deny this progression of human being from a brutal status to a civilized status. It is to announce that I have not changed one bit. I have not grown up. I still have that love for brutal physical power. It is in my blood. I inherited it from my cave dweller ancestors, maybe genetically. I could not develop a respect for knowledge and scholarship. The sword is mightier than the pen to me. Some people have a very difficult time handling a pen but they can easily handle a gun. I am one of them. Give me a gun. Would you feel proud of yourself if you could not handle a pen? Think about it before you ask for a gun.

Those people who support guns should, therefore, think twice about what they are announcing to the whole world. They are basically saying: we still love guns, we enjoy guns, we are not growing up, and we are still uncivilized. Ironically these people are not ashamed of not growing up. They do not ask for any help. They think it is all right not to grow up, not to become civilized. To trace the progression of the human mind from a crude, brute, and uncivilized status to a refined and cultured status, you don't have to explore the history of civilization of thousands of years. If you are twenty-five years old, just think about your mental evolution.

When I was in high school, I always liked to read detective novels. Private detectives inspired my imagination. I thought about them as great people with an uncanny ability to solve mysterious murder cases. They were my heroes. Another thing I liked was the revolver they carried concealed. I always dreamed of becoming a private detective with a shinny revolver in my pocket. As days went by and I went to college and university to educate myself, that desire gradually disappeared. After finishing my education, I never felt like becoming a detective with a handgun in my pocket. Now I cannot even think of owning a gun. I enjoy having all different kinds of pens in my pocket and drawers, but not a single gun anywhere near my sight. This is an example how people grow up.

I, therefore, do not understand why people should get together in an organization what they call the National Rifle Association only to announce that they don't want to grow up, they don't want to change. They want to worship brutal force and deadly weapons. They want to remain uncultured, uncivilized. Why?

Making a Living

We call it earning a livelihood in Bangladesh. They call it making a living in the United States. Whether you earn a livelihood or make a living, you do the same thing. Earn some money, enough to buy food, clothes, shelter, and pay for health care, education, transportation, and entertainment. While providing those necessities of life is possible in the United States by working hard, it is not possible in Bangladesh, no matter how hard you work for it. Here is another big difference between Bangladesh and the United States. In the United States if you are a human being and are able to work, that is what it takes to make a living and sometimes a comfortable living. You do not have to go to school and learn a skill to be able to make a living. You can just grow up and start working in a restaurant, gas station, car repair shop, and agricultural fields. The money you will be able to make will provide for your food, clothing, basic housing, normal health care, transportation, and even entertainment. If you get married or enter in to a relationship with some one and decide to combine your resources together, you can even own a house and go on vacation once a year.

What I described above is a daydream for Bangladeshi people. The money Bangladeshi ordinary workers earn in a month to support themselves or their loved ones can only provide for one third of the cost of living. Where the rest of the money comes from? No one has a definite answer for that question. There are very few people whose earnings from their jobs provide the basic necessities of their lives. The fact is there is no balance between the money you earn and the cost of your living. I don't understand how I can prepare a balanced budget showing my monthly salary as $3000 and my monthly expenses as $9000. Everyone knows that it is impossible to support a life or a family's life depending only on the

money one makes from his or her job, but then you don't have a choice. Part time jobs are not easily available in a country like Bangladesh.

Another social tradition that adds to the problem is that certain kinds of job are for certain kinds of people in Bangladesh. Even if I want, I will not be allowed or welcome to do a job that is not my line of work. For example, if I am a teacher, I am not suppose to work in a restaurant, a gas satiation, or in a agricultural field. People are being respected in Bangladesh according to the work they do. You are looked down upon by the society because you do an odd job. Your friends will not invite you to parties. They will be ashamed to admit that you are one of their friends. So, who would like to be boycotted and condemned by doing an odd job?

Sometimes some brave people want to break the tradition. For example a college professor decides to be a cab driver in his or her spare time. If something like that happens, it makes a big news. It is not that some people do not care for the approval of the society and do whatever pleases them to do, but their numbers are very limited. Besides various kinds of job are also not readily available in Bangladesh. Therefore, you end up doing only one job and getting a fixed amount of money every month whether you like it or not. To make up for the money they need, some people resort to illegal means. They accept bribes, steal public money by preparing false vouchers of expenditure. They explore all possible means to make money from illegal or unethical sources.

Others who do not like to do that often go hungry, live in substandard living conditions, borrow money from friends, get groceries on credit, and in case of emergency get an advance against their salary if possible. They often cannot pay their debt on time and suffer humiliation. They are considered good for nothing by their friends, relatives, and even by their own family members. They cannot get proper treatment when they get sick. If their condition becomes serious, they end up in public hospitals, but the irony is that they seldom come back home from those hospitals fully recovered. In most cases they do not come home at all. Their loved ones shed one or two drops of tears. They leave this world almost unwept, unhonored, and unsung. How do I know all of this? Because my father was the one who ended up like that.

On the other hand, there are some people in Bangladesh who can afford to send their loved ones to the United States for treatment. They spends million of dollars in foreign currency. They have connections with high-level government officials, and any one can quickly establish that connection if he or she has money. So rich people from Bangladesh come

to the United States even with minor health problem, take advantage of the most recent development in health care, go back home and live happily there after.

In addition, there is another social tradition that cripples Bangladeshi's ability to breath freely which is the tradition of living together as a joint family. It is all right for the family members to stay together until a child grows eighteen years old or more. That was what I used to think when I was there. But not all are used to think like me. The fathers and mothers, although can hardly make enough money to support a joint family, are unwilling to see their kids moving out of the family homes before they finish their education, get a job, and get married. Sometimes even after their kids get married and start their own lives, parents prefer them to stay in the family home if they can manage to arrange an extra room.

This strong sense of family togetherness has its merits and demerits. While it helps promote a sense of security and unity, and strives to upheld some family values, members of this joint family often lose their individual freedom of movement. Besides joint financing of a family often creates an atmosphere of lack of direction and responsibility. No one knows who is responsible for what. It often creates confusions and misunderstanding among the family members when all earning members cannot contribute equally either towards finances or other obligations pertaining to the day-to-day life of a family.

Sometimes this joint family concepts ends up in making only one individual as the head of the household because of his or her major contribution. It might also make one person responsible for the maintenance of a huge joint family consisting of more than 15 members. When I was there I often thought there must be a better way than this. The family structure of the United States provided me with that answer.

One thing I admire very much about American family structure is individual responsibility. As soon as children reach the age of eighteen or even before that, they try to make it on their own. They do not necessarily drop out of school to do that. What they don't like is to hang around their parents and depend on them one hundred percent for their sustenance. Of course parents are always willing to help and are concerned about their children's well being, but they enjoy their kids preparing for a career and at the same time earning some money to subsidize the cost.

Not only children but also husband and wife don't want to be dependent on each other. Both of them want to be independent. They want to be able to make equal contribution to the family in some form or other. But it

is not so in Bangladesh where wives traditionally have no responsibility regarding financing the family. It is considered husband's responsibility to provide for the wife and the children. So when a man wants to get married in Bangladesh, the first question he has to answer to himself or to the parents of the bride: Does he have a solid job or what is the source of his income? Does he have the ability to support his wife?

As it is understood and accepted, wife's place is only at home in Bangladesh. Changes are taking place now here and there slowly. Some wives are coming out of their kitchen and finding jobs suitable for them, but the society is still very rigid about what kind of jobs are good for them and what are not. They do not have enough freedom to move in the job market. To add to the problem, they are often kept from receiving higher education and preparing them from getting better training.

There was a time when getting training to serve as a nurse in hospitals was considered a very degrading jobs for respectable women. I know it because my eldest sister was there during 1950s. My father was criticized by his friends because after graduating from high school my sister went to the capital city of Dhaka to receive a specialized training to have a career as Lady Health Visitor. After receiving the training she was appointed as Director of Maternity and Child Welfare Center, a medical clinic designed specially to take care of childbirth including prenatal and post natal care. Only because lady health visitor sounded like a nurse, so people thought she became a nurse and that's what a women from a respectable family should not do.

This is what is Bangladesh. My intention is not to put down my motherland because I do not live there any more. If I did not care I would not have written this essay. I believe that if you do not come out of your country, you cannot see it clearly. You have to look at your country from a distance to find out what is going wrong. My intention is to point finger to the wrong thing we do. My intention is to remove the fog of orthodoxy, meaningless social rituals and customs that are looming large on the horizon of the entire country and destroying it. When I was under that fog, I could not see clearly what direction I was heading towards. After I moved out it was possible for me to see that country in its entirety detached from emotions, sentiments, bias, prejudice, and preconceived notions. I found myself in a unique situation to asses the real problem and suggest solutions to those problems.

Coming to a foreign country from one's own often does not prepare

someone to be critical and to see things differently. It depends on an individual's status in his or her own country. Your ability to understand and comprehend the problem of your own country, your entire educational and social background enables you to think critically about your own country. The main point I am trying to make in this essay is that, also making a living in Bangladesh is difficult still people won't like to get rid of their bad habit of hatred for some kinds of profession. It is difficult to make a living in Bangladesh even if you do not limit yourself to a particular profession. There is no such job in Bangladesh that can provide you with exactly the amount of money that you need to write checks for utilities, buy food, pay for clothing, health care, education, housing , and transportation. I have not seen any job like that since I left Bangladesh in 1979.

I went back in 1991 to visit my family and friends. I have not seen any remarkable change in twelve years. If twelve rears of a country can be wasted, how many twelve years will it take to set things straight? We should realize that solution to the problems mentioned above does not lie on changing the government. Also solution does not lie in calling in a general strike and closing down schools, colleges, and universities. If someone asks me the question as to how to solve the problem of Bangladesh, I will say that we have to close down the traditional way of living our lives, and open up new doors so fresh air can pour in and we can breath deeply and say to ourselves: This is not what I came to this world for. I am not going to take it anymore. I am not going to listen to the stupid politicians and dictators anymore. No one can change my life only I can change my life.

The above-mentioned solutions to our problem may seem very vague and sentimental or even emotional, but what else someone can do when no concrete solution is visible? What I am thinking is, people have to wake up. Wake up to the call of their own selves, inner personality, not to the call of the politicians to violently over through the government. Yes, we can over through the government. We have done that many times in the short history of Bangladesh, but nothing has changed. A new government came and a new set of people got rich. Nothing happened to the lives of the vast majority.

The slogan Bangladeshi people must learn to utter is this; we don't want to change the government. We don't want any revolution any more. We don't want a general strike. We don't want to close down everything. We want to help our government and by helping our government, we will change our lives. We would cooperate one hundred percent with our government. If we do change our government we will change it for the

better. If the Bangladeshi people really want to make a living, they should make their government work for them. They should let a system run the country. Let the system change the government when time comes, not the military or the politicians.

Man Eaters of Kumayun

Making an argument against capital punishment is easy. We can say it is inhuman, brutal, uncivilized, and cruel. Also, you can argue that by supporting capital punishment this society and the government are becoming killers. Killers are most of the time termed as lunatics, criminals, uncultured rouges, outlaws, stubborn, and uncivilized people. It is appropriate only for people of those categories mentioned above to become killers. But by arguing against capital punishment, no body is really sympathizing with the killer or supporting killing. What they are saying is this: Because these people are killers, we the people who consider ourselves as cultured and civilized should not indulge ourselves in killing in the name of capital punishment.

Opponent of capital punishment further believe that taking away the life of a killer does not help stop killing. It never served as a deterrent, nor will it serve as a deterrent in the future. Capital punishment was prevalent in ancient societies. Since then it has been continuing until today, but for that matter killing has not stopped. No matter how many killers you put away by killing, new killers will emerge from the society. So something else should have to be done to minimize killing although elimination of killing of human beings by human beings may not be altogether possible.

But what are the steps to be taken to stop this incident of killing a human being by another, or killing many people over a long period of time by one individual that we call a serial killer? If someone is caught red handed of killing, or someone is found guilty of a murder beyond the shadow of a doubt, what kind of punishment would be appropriate if not capital punishment? Can a killer be rehabilitated in the society? These

are the questions need to be answered before deciding on whether capital punishment is appropriate or not.

Unfortunately, it is very difficult to find reasonable answers to these questions. First of all, people do not kill people for only one reason. Second, there is not only one kind of killers. Some are professional killers. They kill ruthlessly and indiscriminately. They kill in the act of committing a crime. If someone gets into their way when they are committing a crime, they decide to eliminate that person. There are other kinds of killers who kill people because they want to take revenge. Someone did something terrible to them, which makes them so angry that they resort to killing. Some people kill because they are considered mentally sick.

Whatever the reasons are if someone committed only one murder in his or her lifetime that would receive a completely different treatment. We would find only one category of killer in this society who killed only one person at one time and only once in his or her lifetime. We could look at that incident as an accident. In such a case killing a human being by another human being would be a big news, just like a big earthquake or a plane crash, which rarely happens. Everybody would be surprised and shocked. The question would be, how a human being could kill another human being? We would be interested in listening to psychologistsí research and explanations of that murder and would be willing to know exactly under what circumstances that terrible thing happened. In that case it would be possible to devise ways and means to prevent the recurrence of that kind of circumstances that lead to a murder.

Also, in that case no one would be in a big hurry to put the murderer to death because this kind of incidents happens rarely. When a plane crashes no one suggest to do away with air travel altogether. Similarly just because somebody killed a person in his or her lifetime, we would not rush to take his or her life. Psychologist would like to save that person's life to conduct experiment and research, although, sometimes I think, no matter what if it is found beyond the shadow of a doubt that a person killed another person that person should be put to death.

Now the problem in this society is this that many killing are not just happening accidentally or rarely. Most of the time when a person is found guilty of a murder it appears that person has the potential to kill. Going through that individualís background we can easily come to the conclusion that it is possible for a person of that nature to commit a murder. May be this is his or her first murder but this type of people can commit a murder.

If he or she did not get caught, may be he or she would end up committing more murders and eventually would become a serial killer.

On the other hand, it is not unlikely that sometimes we might find a killer who has no potential to kill in his or her background. Everyone might become absolutely surprised by thinking about the reason. It might come as a shock and disbelief. In that case it might seem as an accident, which we usually term as "on the spur of the moment". These two kind of killers need to be looked at, examined, and treated very differently. But the incidents of ìon the spur of the momentî killing are not too many in this country. As I have already mentioned, in most of the cases of killing we can see why it happened and who can kill. We are not surprised any more. In this society murder has become commonplace and everyday many people are getting killed. It is no more a surprise or a big news.

The reason I am always mentioning murder can be surprising big news is that I was born and brought up in a society where murder was always big and surprising news. It was not a common day-to-day event to be found in the pages of newspapers. When the news of murder of someone appeared in Bangladesh the entire nation got terrified as if that was something least expected in a civilized society. But it is not a nerve shattering news in the United States any more. It is not the least expected news item, but the but the most expected one. I would like to through a challenge to anyone to find a single day in the United States of America when no murder took place. Even if you find a single murder-less day by an odd chance, it will be quickly compensated by three or more murders in the previous or subsequent days. Therefore, it does not give anyone any consolation that in a particular day no murder took place in this country.

When this is what actually happening and when we really don't want that to happen, we cannot just ignore the fact that something must be done to minimize the incident of killing to that level when we could think of killing of human beings by human beings as rare, not an everyday event. To achieve that objective of reducing murders, I believe that convicted murderers should be clearly and distinctly put into two categories. One who has the potential to commit a murder, and one who does not have the potential to commit a murder but did it on the spur of the moment. It might seem a very difficult and confusing job but in fact it is not. To find out who has the potential to kill and who does not, we only have to look at those who have committed only one murder.

Those who have committed two or more could be immediately put to the category of potential murderers and should immediately be removed

to the maximum-security prison and be executed without any delay. Those who committed only one murder should be scrutinized then and each situation should be evaluated very seriously to determine who committed a murder on the spur of the moment and who committed it cold blood. Those who committed a murder deliberately and cold blooded should immediately be removed from the society and placed in a remote Pacific Ocean island to spend the rest of their lives.

Now we have only a small number of killer who killed on the spur of the moment or because they were mentally unstable or became temporarily insane. They should stay in the prison also for the rest of their lives, but they don't have to be removed to a remote island. These are the prices one should pay for taking someone's life. Life is very precious. No one should even consider taking that away from another person, no matter what. There should not be any compromise or adjustment if we really want to reduce and eventually eliminate this disgrace of human civilization. It might appear that I am oversimplifying the issue by suggesting a quick solution to this problem. I have a very valid scientific reason for suggesting annihilation of serial killers and potential serial killers.

Tigers are abundant in Bangladesh and India. I was brought up with a fear of tiger. My mother used to warn me, of course to protect me from all source of danger, if you go out at night a tiger might catch you. When I was a high school student I still believed that human beings are natural prey of tigers and tigers like to eat human flesh very much until that they when I checked out a book from school's library entitled Man Eaters of Kumayun by Jim Corbett. That was the first time when I learned that human beings are not the favorite food that a tiger is looking for when it gets hungry. Some tigers become man-eaters when they grow old and cannot catch other animals or when a tiger gets injured such as loosing some teeth. But the problem is once a tiger starts eating human beings it becomes man eater and don't like to eat anything else but human beings. So all tigers are not man-eaters some tigers are and that is the reason they have to be destroyed.

I tried to draw an analogy between man eating tigers and serial killers and found that my theory works. Serial killers of human beings are nothing but Man Eaters of kumayun. Once a tiger becomes man-eater and starts terrorizing a village, the only solution to that problem was to identify and isolate that tiger and positively confirm that it is the man-eater and eliminate it. To do that difficult job Jim Corbett risked his life. He followed the trail of the tiger and its victim just after a killing was reported. He was

able to kill the man-eater and save a village from the terror and nightmare of living with a man-eater. Corbett never indiscriminately killed tigers. He killed only the man-eaters.

If we want to have a terror free society, if we want to get rid of the nightmare of living with serial killers, we have to do what Jim Corbett has done. In this case the only difference is our target will be some human being who are actually man-eaters of kumayun in disguise of human beings.

Oklahoma Bombing

The United States is known all over the world as the father of modern democracy. People of the rest of the world have profound respect for the democratic system that prevails in this country. In the history of the United States, no government has ever been thrown out of power violently by the opposition party or by the army. That image of the United States has recently been shattered at home and abroad, not because of the Oklahoma bombing but due to the fear of their own government as expressed by some politicians, Radio, TV talk show hosts, newspaper columnists, and by a support for a militia movement following the bombing.

Whether the bombing has anything to do with the militia movement is completely a different issue. We have not concluded that yet. But worrying that militia might have something to do with this bombing, some journalists jumped to find an excuse for such an act on the part of militia. They believe that federal government is encroaching on individuals' freedom. So there are valid reasons for Americans to be afraid of the federal government and start supporting the militia movement as a means of keeping the federal government under check. This kind of interpretation serves the purpose of promoting violence against the government, which is, obviously, undemocratic.

The United States has never supported terrorism, no matter what the reasons. Why, then, this sudden shift in some peoples' thinking? It is nothing but a paranoia about losing their individual freedom. It is very disturbing to note that when a tragedy of that magnitude struck the nation, instead of condemning the act of violence and empathizing with the victims' families, some people are paranoid about losing their personal freedom and making a hero out of the militia by asking them to come

forward on radio and TV programs as champions of the cause of protecting individuals' freedom against the federal government. It is reported that encouraged by talk show hosts, some even went to the extent of suggesting to shoot federal agents in the head in case they wear bullet proof vests. This is not what is called democratic spirit. The Constitution of the United States provided for a well-regulated militia for the security of a free state. Militia must be formed by the state and must be regulated by the state to ensure freedom of the state, not to secure the freedom of individuals. United States armed forces have nothing to do with guaranteeing individuals' freedom. Similarly, a state's militia has nothing to do with securing freedom of people by resorting to terrorism. It may secure the political freedom of the state from federal intervention, if it ever happens.

In a democracy peoples' freedom do not come from the barrel of the guns, people organize against their government and change the government peacefully by their power to vote. Democracy does not allow individuals to take the law in their own hands. If we do not like some federal regulations that restrict our personal freedom, we should fight through our elected representatives to change those regulations. We should not get afraid of the government and start organizing a militia movement to over through the government violently, should we?

Is Pen Mightier Than the Sword?

During the period of my growing up in Bangladesh I was taught by my parents and teachers that the pen is mightier than the sword. My teachers used to say this often when they had an opportunity. It was not that I did not understand the inherent significance of this statement, but I always enjoyed asking some silly questions to my teachers just for the fun of it. So I was looking for an occasion for the teachers to say that one more time and I did not have to wait too long. "Is the pen mightier than a gun also," I wanted to know timidly. That made my teacher so angry that he thundered,î Yes, the pen is even mightier than an atom bomb." At that time we were very close to the impact of an atom bomb on our lives. It was just after five years from the dropping of atom bombs on Hiroshima and Nagasaki. What an atom bomb can do was still fresh in everyone's mind. So the whole class kept silent for a moment, and I felt guilty for disrupting the class. That was the last time I made fun with this statement with a teacher.

But that thunderous voice of my teacher still has a resonance in my ears. I remember developing a strong and profound respect for pen from that day. If I accidently dropped my pen, I got into the habit of picking it up gently and hold it to my hart and forehead and kiss it couple of times as a gesture of respect. I learned that method of showing respect from religious teachings. Subsequently that habit of showing respect extended to all kind of textbooks, writing papers, and pencils. From that very day I had developed a strong conviction that knowledge is power. Civilized and intellectual people's powers come from knowledge, not from the possession of any weapons or physical strength. I grew up with that notion in Bangladesh and devoted myself whole-heartedly to the pursuit

of knowledge. I engaged myself in reading books, newspapers, listening to radio talks. We did not have any television or telephone in our house or in our neighborhood. Although I regretted about it at that time, now I think how fortunate I was to be born in a country where children could not afford to watch television and talk with friends over telephone for hours together.

I did not feel like building my body or learning karate. I did not feel like excelling in any sports other than just to participate and have some fun. Of course, I wanted to play sports and sometimes wanted to be the winner but never thought of having a career in sports. It was always in my mind that knowledge is power, nothing else. You grow up the way your parents and teachers want you to grow up. If my teachers had not told me that the pen is mightier than the sword, if my parents had not told me that I have to respect books, I would not have developed that respect for knowledge. But before you give an advice you have to believe in that advice yourself. My teachers and my parents had profound respect for books and pens not for sports and guns. If you have profound respect for sports and guns, you probably won't be able to say something like, "the pen is mightier than the sword," with assertion and conviction for your children to believe that. If you keep a handgun in your drawers and feel up your garage with baseball bats, you certainly won't be able to send a message to your children that, "the pen is mightier than the sword," Instead the message you will be sending is, "the baseball bat is mightier than the pen," and your children will understand how true it is by looking at a pen and a baseball bat. Your children will also feel that a handgun is more powerful than a book if that book does not come with hard cover and fat enough to resist a bullet.

That is what actually happened in the United States of America. It has been a long time that the high school students of this country heard such word from their teachers that the pen is mightier than the sword. This phrase has become very old fashioned. How do I know that? Have I gone to high school in the United States of America? When my two daughters were high school students, once I asked them, "Did any of your teachers ever told you that the pen is mightier than the sword." The answer was no. I told them to report to me if ever they come upon such a phrase in their school. It never happened. On the other hand, they have always been advised to go to physical fitness program and excel in sports. When they expressed their intention to get the highest education they could possibly get from a university, they were discouraged, "Do you think you really

want to do that? It is a terrible waste of your youth and energy. There are many shortcuts in making a good living nowadays. If you want to get rich and famous quickly there are ways and means for that too." If you think I am making those up you can talk to my daughters to find out whether I am telling the truth. Those are the words their counselors actually uttered when they asked for advise.

If we do not teach our children that knowledge is power instead of teaching that physical strength is power, how can we expect them to develop respect for knowledge and scholarship? If they do not develop respect for scholarship, how can we expect them to develop respect for educational institutions or for teachers? If the students find out that their playgrounds are becoming larger and larger everyday, more money is being spent in gymnasium and sports related paraphernalia, what kind of message they are going to get? It will be apparent that the main object of an educational institution is to prepare the body of a learner not the mind.

Is not this what is actually going on nowadays? Is there any conspiracy? Are there some people at the helm of the affairs who do not won't our children to grow up with love and respect for knowledge. If not, why? Those questions kept bothering me for a long time. On the contrary, in Bangladesh people always down play the importance of games and sports. We always get advice like this: Do not waste your valuable time in engaging in games and sports, concentrate on learning, and acquire knowledge. Knowledge is power. We accepted this as an axiom, no question asked. No one ever thought of challenging this in Bangladesh.

So I was living a peaceful life believing that the pen is mightier than the sword until I arrived in the United States. Now my daughters coming from schools every day challenge me that you have to excel in sports, not only academically, to get accepted in prestigious universities. That's what their counselors told them. I argued with them that even if it was so, I don't understand why a prestigious university should do that. Physical fitness or skills in playing sports has nothing to do with acquiring knowledge. No one agrees that physically fit people or skilled sports men and women are academically brilliant. It is the other way around. Normally those who are physically strong are not found academically strong. So, what's the point here? Why a prestigious university should prefer someone who is equally strong in sports and academic subjects?

Well. some people at this point may come up with this argument that a sound mind resides in a sound body. If your body is not sound, you cannot have sound mind. There is no problem with that. To have a sound body

we don't have to excel in competitive sports. We can be health conscious by eating good food and exercising and participating is sports. I am using the word participate to make a distinction between participation and concentration. If you concentrate on sports, you cannot concentrate on academic subjects.

As a matter of fact, it is very hard to find a rational excuse for emphasizing the importance of sports and physical strength. It is better to admit that those who pay too much attention to sports and physical fitness, do not normally become very brilliant academically. Besides, really cultured, sophisticated, and intellectual people do not pay too much attention to physical power and games and sports.

We have come a long way from Stone Age to this modern civilization. Some people do not seem to realize that. They got entangled in time and space. Time is not moving for them. They are of course growing up chronologically but not mentally. Long time ago our cave dweller ancestors used to hunt animals with some kind of weapons they made out of stones. They used the same stone to start up a fire to barn meat and eat. Some people still enjoy hunting and barbecuing. Therefore, I believe that this is genetic. Although we don't have to go hunting and barbecuing but we do that because of the active gene that has been transmitted to us from generation to generation. There is no shame in admitting this fact but to try to justify that behavior is very embarrassing. We might possess some primitive urges in us because of the inheritance of the genes, but human civilization is nothing but a constant struggle to over power the influence of those primitive genes and be civilized. I do not see any reason to be proud of possessing certain characteristics of the cave dwellers. We can recreate the past to have fun once in a while but not to the extent of becoming a cannibal!

The reason I am bringing this up here is I have seen some responsible educated people bragging about their habits they inherited from their prehistoric ancestors. In a conference of National Rifle Association a prominent senator of the United States' Congress was bragging about his hobby of hunting and explaining to everyone how a rifle has become an essential and integral part of his life. Now he even cannot think of his existence without the presence of rifle by his side and he cherished in stating many anecdotes related to his hobby of hunting.

Civilization started when cave dwellers found a way to domesticate animals for food and learned how to grow food, which now we call agriculture. It was then when hunting for animals, eating grass or tree

leaves ceased. That is what civilization is all about. At this juncture of civilization to show affection for hunting and barbecuing are nothing short of a nostalgia for that remote past. There is nothing to brag about it. Therefore, justifying keeping a gun to kill wild animals in the name of sports is nothing but ignoring the progress of civilization and identifying oneself as uncivilized and uncultured. It is just like saying: I want to go back to the cave where I came from. I want to hunt for animals and burn their meat to satisfy my primitive hunger.

Through the evolutions of millions of years, we have gradually abandoned weapons and learned how to make a pen and how to symbolize our words into alphabet. That is what refinement and sophistication is all about. To put down some one in Bangladesh people often say, he or she does not even know how to hold a pen. What do you expect of him or her? In the United States it appears that people are not ashamed of not being able to hold their pen right, they are ashamed of not being able to hold their swords (guns) right. People in this culture have little respect for pen although they have profound respect for swords (guns). It is, therefore, no wonder that my daughters never heard this phrase in school.

Physical Education

Is the United States the only country in the entire world where physical education and athletics have become an integral and essential part of educational institutions? In other countries educational institutions concentrate on academic education only. That means schools, colleges, and universities are there for imparting education in academic subjects such as English, Mathematics, History, Philosophy, Chemistry, or Biology, etc. While in the United States most of the academic institutions brag about their football and basketball teams.

For example, in Bangladesh schools, colleges, and universities do not maintain any football teams. There is no such thing as football scholarship. In Bangladesh people believe that educational institutions are for teaching academic subjects only. They have nothing to do with sports. But things are very different here in the United States.

While in Bangladesh people do not believe that it is school's job to take care of or to promote sports, it is not to say that Bangladeshi people do not like sports. Bangladeshi people like physical education to get in shape and they enjoy watching sports, but they simply do not want to believe that schools have anything do with it. On the contrary, the school, college, and university in Bangladesh discourage their students to get too involved in physical education and sports, thinking that students should concentrate on academic subjects. They should not pay too much attention to extra academic activities. Bangladeshi educational institutions allow their students to engage in sports but limit this engagement drastically by expelling students from classes in the event of students' obtaining poor academic grades. Bangladeshi universities do not aspire for good athletics, they aspire for good scholars.

Why is it so? Why the United States value sports so much and Bangladesh ignore sports that much? The answer to that question can be found in the cultural analysis of the two nations. In Bangladesh there prevails a culture where intellectuals are glorified, honored and respected. In Bangladesh people respect professors, doctors, engineers, social, political, and religious leaders. No one cares about the people who are in entertainment business, in sports, and in physical fitness programs. There is no such thing as a nationally known football player. Very few people remember the names of football player and movie stars. People enjoy their acts but do not want to establish any contact or relationship with them. They don't get any respect from people in general. Basically, we can say that they are being ignored by the general populace.

So when there is no social recognition but a social apathy for players, who would aspire for a career as a football player or a movie star? Besides, in Bangladesh entertainments are sharply divided into two categories: refined entertainment and cheap entertainment. Cheap entertainment has no room in radio and television programs. In Bangladesh people know the difference between humor and farce. People like to be entertained, they like to laugh, but they want to do that without sacrificing any quality. It is unthinkable for a Bangladeshi TV talk show host to invite a prostitute, a burglar, or a serial killer to his or her show. Similarly it is unthinkable for TV talk show hosts to invite football players or film stars to interview him or her. The reason such a thing is not going to happen in Bangladesh is that Bangladesh people do not want to hear the life story of those people. They are simply not interested in those kind of story.

When I say that Bangladeshi people do not want to hear about the life of a soccer player, does it mean that they do not like sports? They like to watch the soccer game in the stadium but they are not interested in a single player by itself. It is also true that some consider watching game and movie is actually wasting time and engaging oneself in relishing in cheap entertainment. They feel guilty of spending their valuable time by watching a game or a movie. But the same person might go to watch a game anyway thinking that life is monotonous and we have to take a break from this monotone and relax once in a while.

Under such a state of mind no one can develop a sense of enthusiasm or respect about games or players. People cannot think of asking a player for an autograph. There is no such thing as baseball cards collection. Players have no social recognition merely as a player. Therefore, there is no

career as a football player. Athletes are not well known as football player, baseball player, or basketball player. There are players in Bangladesh and they are good players but they have a different profession. A player may be a teacher, a lawyer, a doctor, an engineer, or simply an office worker. This is to say that Mr. so and so is an English teacher of so and so college and he plays football for so and so team. The significance of this is that the sports have not turned into a business. No business owner owns any football team in Bangladesh and players are not workers. There are clubs or associations where players get together and become members. They can get an allowance for playing in a particular team being member of a particular club. But there is no labor dispute, no salary, and no employee employer relationship. A sport is not an industry, and it is not a business.

Coming from a culture like that you will never understand what a sport has to do with academic institutions. You will never understand why school students have to participate in physical education or cross-country. Why school have to have huge gymnasiums, racetracks, football, basket ball stadiums when classrooms, lecturer halls, libraries, and dormitories are shrinking day by day. I, therefore, always wondered why does not this country start schools, colleges, and universities only for physical education and athletics. Then the students could fully concentrate on engaging in different kind of physical and sports related activities. There can be department of football, department of basketball, department of baseball, so on and so forth. There can also be department of figure skating, department of hockey, department of swimming. Students could receive B.A., M.A., and Ph.D. degrees in those areas and then apply for a job as professional players. They could also get a career as faculty members on those universities.

Regular academic institutions should not get involved in sports business by maintaining a team and hiring coaches to teach students and then earn some money. If the administration of a regular university gets involved in sports, they cannot concentrate on teaching and research involving academic subjects such as language, literature, physics, and chemistry. A regular school should not be termed as outstanding because it has an outstanding football team. It is a disgrace for a university, which is designed to impart higher education to become famous only because it has a good football team. Integrating games and sports in academic curriculum in the name of physical education and requiring students to take a physical education course to graduate is grossly unfair.

I have two teenage high school going daughters who have been receiving outstanding grades in all academic subjects. One day they came home complaining about having to participate in P.E. or cross-country. I wanted to know what happens if they decide not to participate in physical education. "Well then we don't get a grade and our GPA is going to suffer," they replied. I thought this is not fair. They are getting straight A's and now if they don't participate they will get a bad grade. I, therefore, told them to participate anyway. If this is the system in this country, we cannot do anything about it. I told them just to find out some kind of physical activity that was not too much demanding or strenuous, which is not going to take a great deal of time and energy and which was not going to interfere with their academic concentration.

Approaching this problem with such a compromising attitude I felt good about myself and thought that I have taken care of a problem easily and I could relax, but I was mistaken. My daughters are going to finish high school, so they are getting ready for the

college. The issue came up when we were talking about sending them to prestigious universities. I told them that to get accepted by those universities they have to be extraordinarily brilliant. They have to have straight A pluses in all subjects. At this point both of them stopped me to tell me that I was all wrong. Only academic excellence won't qualify them for acceptance at the IVY League universities, they must also excel in sports.

I vehemently objected, arguing with them that excellence in sports will not enhance the possibility of their acceptance. But then my voice was a lonely one. They had already been told by their counselors at school that it was really the case. I got corrected by my daughters that everyone knew that simple fact, and I was the only one who didn't know that. Although I stopped arguing with them and that time, I was not fully convinced. I hoped that they were wrong, but then I talked to some of my American colleagues who agreed with me that this should not be the case.

I then started talking to myself: If that is the case in the United States then I have to live with it, but no one is going to convince me that it is absolutely necessary to equally excel in sports and academic subjects to be accepted by a prestigious university. That is not what universities should be looking for. When I was talking to myself this compromising idea came to my mind: why not open separate universities for sports only? It's not a bad idea. If we give so much importance to sports, if we want to concentrate

on bodybuilding instead of mind building let's go for it. Let's open up a University of Physical Education and Sports and leave those regular universities alone and let them concentrate on teaching those who believe that mind is more powerful than the body.

A Political Disease

Disease had no role to play in politics. To my knowledge no one has ever used a disease to gain political advantage or wanted to be politically correct when referring to a disease. Politicians have used all sorts of thing to gain advantages in politics. They used religion, ethics, morality, and entertainment industry. They used gun control, domestic violence, child abuse, drug abuse, abortions, same sex marriage, etc. But none has ever used a highly contagious disease such as leprosy, plague, tuberculosis, syphilis, and gonorrhea to play games in politics.

The reason no one played games with deadly diseases in politics is that it is very dangerous. Playing games with disease is like playing with fire. Whether you are a democrat, a republican, a conservative, a liberal, a communist, or a capitalist you never argue about the importance of controlling the spread of a disease, finding remedy or cure for a disease, spending money in developing medicine, etc. No one has ever argued about that. All highly contagious diseases, old or new have always been a public health issue.

Since the very inception of this civilization it has been agreed upon that disease should be controlled and eradicated by all possible means. For that matter everyone's cooperation was asked for. It was, therefore, considered a crime to hide a disease allowing it to spread to some other people. A diseased person should not have any right to conceal his or her disease and there by endanger not only his or her life but also the lives of his or her family members or any other members of the society.

When we confronted a deadly disease we all used to get together setting aside our ideological, philosophical, and political differences. No one has ever objected in isolating or identifying people with a deadly

disease such as leprosy and transporting people infected with leprosy to the island of Molokai. No one has ever objected in setting a quarantine to arrest the spread of an epidemic like plague in a city. We have always drastically dealt with deadly diseases. There was no room for sympathy. If someone gets sick with small pox, we don't treat that person at home. We immediately send him or her to the hospital's intensive care. There is nothing wrong with that. If you get gangrene, the doctor has to amputate part of your body to save your life.

When it comes to deadly disease the question of discriminating or hating a person infected with that disease or the question of being unsympathetic to that diseased person does not arise at all. The question is to arrest the spread of that disease, and try to help the infected person with all possible means. This can only be accomplished if we do not keep that disease a secret, if we do not hide the fact that we have a disease. That is why this civilization has come to an agreement and understanding that if someone gets a life threatening and highly contagious disease, it should immediately become a public health issue not a private individual concern.

While it is so with all known diseases that human beings so far encountered, it is not so with an extremely deadly disease known as AIDS. Since the breakout of this disease it has been receiving a very special treatment for some unknown reasons. Some people infected with this disease don't want to go public and their wishes to keep it a secret have been granted by the government. No one has ever referred to the fourth amendment to interpret it as a right to keep a disease private and protected against unreasonable search and seizures. But it happened in the case of AIDS. Do you have the right to keep a disease to yourself and die with it? Can the society grant you that right? Some people believe it is all right to do that but, ironically, only in the case of AIDS, not in case of any other diseases.

Why AIDS should receive this special privilege? If this disease is a common human disease like all other diseases, why it should not receive equal treatment? One, therefore, cannot be blamed if he or she believes that this is not a natural disease but a very unnatural one. If it is just like another disease, why some people should feel guilty about having AIDS? Why a group of people who have chosen a different life style than the majority should believe that the reason for developing this disease is to have a different life style? They could shout to the whole world that they have nothing to do with it. They didn't bring it on themselves. There is absolutely no proof that AIDS is a disease of a special group of people. It

is just like another disease. Anyone at any time can have AIDS like cancer or Alzheimer regardless of their life styles.

Instead a group of people got organized, accepted the fact that it is their disease and demanded protection using the fourth amendment of the constitution. They are afraid that singling them out as the root cause of this disease may create hatred against their life style and they may be discriminated against. They might lose their jobs, their friends, their social status. So for the protection of an individual infected with HIV, the person must be granted the right to not go public with it unless he or she voluntarily does so.

To be politically correct, our politicians, and our elected representative surrendered to their demand to treat it as a private health issue. When the politicians did that they were thinking about not to offend a group of people which means they were thinking about getting reelected instead of thinking about the danger of allowing an individual infected with a deadly disease to consider it as his or her personal problem. Politicians are, therefore, endangering the safety and security of the public to fulfill their personal dream of getting reelected with the support of that group of people who believe that AIDS is their disease That is what I call playing games with disease in politics.

The point I am trying to make here is this the legislation, "don't ask, don't tell" can be applied to protect the homosexual community, but it cannot be applied when it comes to a disease. Unless you live in a remote pacific island by yourself, the societies around you have the rights to know whether you have a deadly disease or not. Employers should have the rights to know whether they are hiring someone with AIDS, the schools should have the rights to know whether they are admitting a student with AIDS. Wife should have the rights to know whether the husband has the AIDS, and vice versa.

It is no denying the fact that some infected people will suffer discrimination in this process. Some people might lose their jobs and have to go through life suffering humiliation, hatred, insult, indignation, and even segregation. While this is most unfortunate but this is what is expected out of some inconsiderate human beings. Not all people are sympathetic or considerate. You cannot legislate human behavior. If someone is paranoid about AIDS you cannot convince that person by the force of any law to get rid of that paranoia. Paranoia will automatically disappear when we can find a cure for this disease. As long as it remains an incurable disease, paranoia will be there and there is nothing that we can do about it.

Many write articles nowadays suggesting that we should have more education about AIDS which will dispel some myth about this disease. Since we are misinformed, we are more paranoid. But I don't think that education is going to make a difference as long as it remains incurable. The word incurable is what makes people so paranoid. Even if we could develop a vaccine to immunize people from getting AIDS, the paranoia would dissipate. We cannot force people to take this disease lightly until and unless prevention and cure come along.

When it comes to finding prevention and cure for a deadly disease, restlessness does not help. Shouting and demanding a cure and asking the government to spend billions of dollars on AIDS research won't accelerate the process of finding a cure. Besides why should government spend all its money only for AIDS research? What about other disease such as cancer, Alzheimer, and heart disease? If we want our government to give top priority to AIDS research, the entire nation must come to an agreement that we should combine all our effort and concentrate on solving this problem first. This unity cannot be achieved by force. If the AIDS activists want to deal with this problem as a political right then a debate will ensue. People affected with AIDS need sympathy and care. They don't need a debate.

If we enter into a debate those who believe that AIDS is not a natural disease but the out come of a group's unnatural life style and they brought it on themselves, will raise a question such as why should we the tax payer pay for the problem some people created for themselves? They will argue that some people wanted to play with fire. They put their hand in fire to see whether it burns. Now they are asking for an ointment to sooth their badly burnt hand. It is no different from saying that I have every right to put my hand in fire as a manifestation of my freedom of expression but if it hurts me, it is the responsibility of the entire nation to come to my rescue.

As we can see, playing political games with a disease won't help the arrest or treatment of that disease. The debate will go on and on in congress on how much money should be set aside for AIDS prevention and cure and what kind of rights should be granted to people infected with HIV virus. A furious debate will ensue and it is highly unlikely that our lawmakers will be able to unite on those issues. In such a situation even if the government succeeds in legislating some rights and privileges for Aids, society as a whole won't be sympathetic to a AIDS victims. Common people are going to say that well government is going to take care of the AIDS victims so

we don't have to take care of them anymore. There will be an apathy as a whole for AIDS victims. The people infected with AIDs will suffer more.

The best way to deal with this disease is, therefore, to treat it as all other deadly diseases that we are now concerned about. That means we have to declare this disease as a public health issue not a political right or discrimination issue. At the same time we have to ask people with HIV to go public with their condition and get registered with the public health department for assistance and direction. They should be assured of all sorts of treatment that are currently available. In the absence of such an assurance only the rich and famous will be afford to go public with AIDS. Have you ever seen an unknown and poor person declared that he or she has AIDS? Who wants to know? Why the rich and famous do not need any confidentiality when they get AIDS? Why only the ordinary people need privacy?

It is obvious that the poor and the helpless are afraid of losing their jobs, their family and friends, and their social lives. I do not know of any other disease that discriminates between the rich and the poor. I thought a disease can never discriminate. If you acquire a serious disease you are equal in the eye of that disease. That deadly disease cannot spare you only because you are rich and famous. But it appears that AIDS discriminates. If a rich and famous person gets Aids he or she becomes a hero or heroine. On the other hand, an ordinary person must hide under the protection of the constitutional rights of confidentiality. This is why I believe that AIDs has become a political disease.

Of course, this is not fair and it should not be like that. Apparently it is not such with other deadly diseases. No celebrity, rich or famous becomes a hero for declaring that he or she has tuberculosis, syphilis, gonorrhea or leprosy. People don't start shading tears, and no big condolence meetings are held with TV and Newspapers cameras present. But it happens in the case of AIDS. Why is it so? The underlying consolation in glorifying rich and famous with AIDS is to say that if a person with such and such credentials can contact AIDS, everyone can contact AIDS. So don't hate people with AIDS anymore. Unfortunately, no matter how hard one tries to change the status of a disease by associating it with rich and famous, the status will not change. No one will start respecting AIDS because rich and famous people are getting it. It is ridiculous to get comfort in thinking that celebrities are getting AIDS nowadays. It does not make the disease less deadly nor does it change the overall paranoia of people about this disease.

We have to get real and face the fact. If we have to live a fruitful and meaningful life in this world, we have to develop respect for our body. We have to stop abusing our body. It is not wise to depend on medicine. We have to believe in that old adage that prevention is better than cure. I have no control over cure but I have control over prevention. It is not wise to start abusing our body believing that if I create my own problem medicine will come along to the rescue. At the same time we have to have tolerance for the victims of the disease. It is also not nice to lecture them about morality and good conduct when they are dying. We have to take care of them and as civilized people. It should be our obligation. It can only be achieved if we practice tolerance and try to understand each otherís situation instead of trying to be politically correct when the very existence of our life is threatened.

Proud of Being Bad

I often ask myself: Is there anything in my life that I can be proud of? Before I find an answer to that question, another question comes to my mind: Is there any thing in my life that I should be ashamed of? As you can see, in criticizing your own life, sometimes you can feel proud and sometimes you can feel ashamed of yourself. People feel proud of doing good things. They feel proud of their success, their achievements, not their failures. They feel ashamed of doing bad things, and ashamed of their failures. These feelings makes us normal human beings, and I have no doubt in my mind that majority of the people's feelings are same as mine. But do you know some people who feel proud when they do something bad? Also, do you know someone who feels ashamed of him or her when he or she does something good? Yes, there are people like that too in this world and I am going to talk about that in this article.

Once I was teaching a communication course in a small business school in southern California. One of the requirements for the students was to give a presentation stating their backgrounds and career objectives. In course of her presentation one of my students, in the presence of a full class of 19 student presented this information that she worked as a stripper for five years in Las Vegas. Coming from Bangladesh, where strippers and prostitutes are synonymous, I was startled. In Bangladesh prostitutes do not come forward in public to announce that they are prostitutes, and that they are proud of being prostitutes. My student, while describing her background, appeared to be very normal as if she was telling everyone that she was working in some place as an office assistant.

But it was more puzzling and startling for me when she stated that she feels very proud of herself. She is a self-made woman and did not depend on

any one to help her out. While I mentally agreed to the fact that she should be proud of being a self made woman, I could not find any reason for her to be proud of being a stripper. The problem with me about her being a stripper was that she was talking about it just as another profession. To make sure she was not out to take revenge on the society while describing her obnoxious past life and really was proud of being a stripper, I asked her whether she feels good or bad about her past life. She confirmed that she felt good, and she is really proud of herself. She could not understand why I was so curious about and started arguing with me : Do you feel bad being a teacher? Why should I feel bad being a stripper?

I could go on arguing with her that I don't understand how someone can be proud of such a background, but I decided not to. I instantly realized that her and my senses of values are completely different. We live in two different worlds. It is not her fault either that she doesn't see why some professions should be considered bad and should be condemned. May be she was born and brought up in an environment where becoming prostitute was respectable. May be her mother was a prostitute, and may be she was never told what is good and what is bad. May be she never had seen a family life with father and mother living together. If I expect her to have the same values that I inherited from my background, I would be making a big mistake. So I let that matter go unchallenged.

But if that were an isolated incident I would be better of not to worry too much about it. I have seen many others who brag about their achievements as drug dealers, serial killers, and gang leaders, and sex offenders. They feel proud of being bad. They write books about their achievements while in jail. When they come out, they receive hero's welcome. People line up to get their autographs. Not only that some people are so proud of being bad that they want to be honored and respected by the society. They want to be recognized by the society. They want the society to approve their behavior as normal. They want every one to forget the concept of good or bad. Consequently, they want the society to approve their life style or behavior which were considered inappropriate since the very inception of this civilization.

The idea of forgetting the difference between good and bad was very intriguing for me. I pondered about it over a long period of time. How do you decide certain things are good and certain things are bad? May be some one has created this notion of good and bad with ulterior motives, and we have been following them without challenging their validity. Recently I

read an article that so called good cholesterol is actually bad for heart and the bad cholesterol is good. What do you know!

We learned as children that telling a lie is bad and telling the truth is good. If we were taught as a child that never tell the truth, always tell a lie, because it pays to tell a lie, and, therefore, it is good, we would have no doubt that telling lie is a good idea. On the other hand, telling a truth is dangerous and you might be in big trouble for telling the truth. In that case we would memorize the advice that never tell the truth. If we were taught through a religion or a tradition that there nothing wrong in killing a human being if you feel like it or when you get really angry, there would be competition in society to kill people. People would brag about how many human lives they destroyed only because they were angry. In that case murderers would become heroes.

Now that our religion, tradition, culture, and civilization have taught otherwise, we are in big trouble. We came up with certain ideas that this and that are good and this and that are bad. We punish people for doing bad thing and honor people for doing good things. From this point of view it looks all right for someone to do something as chopping someone else's head off and putting it in a grocery bag to show it to friends to brag about engaging in such a heroic act (this horrible thing really happened in Los Angeles!). To me it is horrible, terrible, and unbelievable, but for the person who did this obviously felt good and proud about it. Otherwise it would not be possible for him to do such a thing.

When I was in Bangladesh, I never got confused with the concept of good and bad. I knew what was good and what was bad. I did not ponder about that for long time. The act of virtue and the act of vice were clear and distinct to me. I knew whether I was travelling
on the path to prosperity or on the path to destruction. I was not alone in that pursuit. The family, the society, and the government are also not confused about good and bad. Even the bad people were not confused. I mean the criminals in general, killers, sex offenders, prostitutes, for example, knew that they were doing something wrong. They never claimed any celebrity status. Never bragged about their performance as wrong doers. They were never interviewed by the news media, never signed a million dollar contract for a movie or for an exclusive interview, and never appeared on daytime TV talk shows.

May be those are the reasons why I was not confused about what is good and what is bad. But things are different in the United States. The more bad things you do the more famous you become. You get invitation

from radio and television talk show hosts. Overnight you rise from the obscurity of the unknown and come to the limelight. You become rich and famous. In such a situation when you are a professional prostitute, for example, you might feel good about being a successful prostitute. There will be no sense of guilt in you. You will never thing you did something wrong in your life. Some people looking at your success might think prostitution is a noble profession. This has actually happened in the United States.

That is what made me really confused about the concept of good and bad in American context. I started thinking: Is there any such thing as good or bad? At one point I really started talking to myself: There is no such thing as good or bad. It is just a feeling of accomplishment and failure. If you become successful in whatever you do you, might think it is good. On the other hand, if you are unsuccessful in doing something, you might think it is bad. For example, if you become successful in cheating many people and accumulating a huge amount of money, you might decide that cheating people is a very good idea. Furthermore, if you start getting honor and recognition, you cannot think of cheating as something very bad after all. Why should you?

I have heard many times people say that crime does not pay. I firmly believed in that for a long time, and was happy to see many instances confirming my belief that crime really does not pay. I lived in Bangladesh for 34 years before I arrived in the United States. I was very happy and satisfied by finding examples that crime is not really paying in Bangladesh. I have never seen a criminal, rich or poor, getting away with committing a crime. Somehow or other criminals suffered the consequences of their crimes or are being punished.

But it is not so in the United States. Crime does really pay in this country. You can engage in all sorts of criminal activity in the United States. All you have to do is to make sure that you dot right. If you mess it up, that means if you fail to do a perfect crime, you will be punished. When crime starts paying in a society, it is very difficult to convince someone that it is really bad. If it pays, why should it be considered bad.

The reason a student in my class didn't feel bad about announcing that she worked as a stripper in Las Vegas is that it paid for her, and no one was ashamed of her activity. She was being praised and encouraged to do that. No one ever mentioned to her that she was doing something wrong, something very disgraceful and obnoxious. No one ever explained to her that she was destroying her self-esteem. On top of all that she got

handsomely paid. Therefore, she could not find anything to be ashamed of with that background of her life.

Eventually I realized that I was wrong in thinking that some people feel proud of doing the bad thing. It might be bad thing to me, but it is good thing to them. They of course feel proud of doing the right thing especially when they are being glorified by the society.

Shameless is the U.S

Shy people do not belong to the United States of America. This was my observation when I first arrived. Shy people belong to Bangladesh and there are lots of rooms for them in that country. They can have a good life there but not in the United States. People are shy in Bangladesh because they are supposed to be shy. To be bashful is considered a fine human virtue. If you are not bashful, you are considered an uncultured and uneducated rogue. You are looked down upon by the society. Shy people are considered gentle and sophisticated. They are considered as people with intellectual aptitude. They are adorned and respected by the entire society.

When you are born and brought up in a country where to be bashful is considered a quality, you are supposed to be a shy person. Who would like to be shameless and, therefore, termed as uncultured, uneducated or unsophisticated? So, I grew up as a shy person. I received honor, prestige, admiration, and love from the society. Obviously, I found nothing wrong with me when I lived in Bangladesh. My problem started when I brought that baggage of shyness with me to the United States. I was shy in Bangladesh even within a very friendly and familiar environment. Imagine how shy one would feel coming to an entirely unfamiliar environment. I was, therefore, doubled with shy when I encountered a foreign culture and its people. That started to take a great toll on my smooth transition to a new life. However, before I was completely doomed, I was able to become a shameless person.

The initial impact of shyness in my case was to stay hungry when I was invited to a party. In Bangladesh when you are invited to a party the host takes care of you by serving you food. Not only that the host comes back to check frequently with every single invitee whether they were properly

served often asking such question as, "Can I bring you some more rice? You are hardly eating anything today. What's wrong with you?" So, the host insists that you should eat more, unless you vehemently oppose, your host will continue serving you. You do not serve yourself frequently. If you do, people will be staring at you giving you a look that means, have not you learned any manners of eating?

That is not so in the United States. When I was invited to a party and when it was time to eat, only a simple announcement was made by somebody, the food is ready. That means this is the time you get up, grab a plate where you can find it, serve yourself and start eating. Of course this party is going on in someone's home, not in a restaurant. You go to the table as many times as you wish to get refills, walk around, talk to your friends, and eat. It is very unlikely that in a party someone is going to approach you offering to serve you food or to ask you whether you had enough. That is why I remained hungry. This is the price of bringing a baggage of bashfulness from Bangladesh and not trying to get rid of it.

I talked to some of my countryman about this problem. Those who lived in this culture for many years knew what to do. It is not Bangladesh, if you do not get your own food, you will stay hungry. You cannot be shy when it comes to hunger. Another shyness that I could not get rid of for a long time is to feel shy in eating normally in public when no one else is eating. In our culture we need privacy to eat unless we are eating with other people in a restaurant or in a party. Some people even feel shy in eating in restaurants so the restaurants had to make accommodation for them by making partitioned cubical as normally seen in offices in the United States. I have never seen such a thing in the United State's restaurants.

The consequence of not being able to eat in public, although I was hungry, was to suffer from hunger. I was appalled watching my fellow classmates bringing their lunch bags in the classroom and taking a big bite out of a hamburger or munching french fries while listening to professor's lecture on reader response criticism. I don't know whether this is a good or a bad idea. I just thought at that time if it were possible for me to do the same thing I wouldn't be hungry all the time. What's keeping me from doing the same thing what some other people are doing? My shyness! I could not get rid of it in spite of my best effort.

On one occasion one of my American friends invited me to go fishing with him, when in our casual conversation I expressed my interest in fishing. When I met him on the appointed day and time, I could easily see he was carrying a bag of most probably food with other necessary

paraphernalia to catch fish. I did not carry any food thinking that when we get hungry we would go to a fast food restaurant and gab something. But since my friend brought some food with him he was not thinking as I was. When it was lunchtime he only said, "I am hungry, let me eat something. Aren't you hungry too." Since I brought no food I felt shy and said that I was not hungry although I rally was. That was the biggest mistake I have ever made in my life. Because my friend had not ask me about eating anymore that day. He finished whatever he had to eat and I went hungry.

Why I made this mistake? Because that is what you do in Bangladesh when someone invites you to eat. You have to say I am not that hungry and your host supposed to insist, "Just eat something anyway, you will get hungry pretty soon." In Bangladesh when two people are together one never eats when the other is not eating. They are supposed to share food with each other. I thought my American friend was going to offer me some food anyway. I was too shy to admit that I was hungry. Now after living in this country for so many years and after getting used to all most all kinds ofë social customs and traditions, I feel sorry for myself thinking of those days that are gone by when I made myself a big fool being bashful. Now as soon as I hear the announcement food is ready, I stand up.

Another kind of shyness I suffered from and which did not make any sense to anyone is to feel shy in the presence of my female class friends. In Bangladesh man and woman do not mix freely, neither in schools nor in work places. In schools girls get together in a group and boys in another. If for some reason a girls need to come to boys group, she is supposed to feel shy. Same thing happens if a boy needs to go to a girls group. But that rarely happens in Bangladesh. Normally boys and girls do not need to go to a group of opposite sexes. With this background when you come to the United States and were asked to live together in a home with two other man and woman it become too much of asking.

Although we had separate rooms, it was difficult for me to live in a house with two females especially when one of them had a bad habit of going to the bathroom without any possibility of coming out soon. I did not know what to do. My friend suggested that I knock the door, "Knock it real hard. You have every right to use the bathroom." "But isn't it kind of rude to knock the door when you know a female is inside?" I wanted to know humbly. "No, not at all. You are a shy person. You cannot survive in the United States like that." So one day I exactly did the same thing. I gathered enough courage to knock the door. It worked. She opened

the door almost naked and apologized. "I enjoy reading a book in the bathroom. I can concentrate better here. Don't hesitate to knock when you need to use the bathroom." From then on whenever I needed to go to the bathroom I knew what to do but made sure my eyes are closed when the door opened.

The most serious of all the shyness I suffered from is the embarrassment of bussing tables when I was washing dishes in a restaurant. I preferred to stay with the dish washing machine, washing dishes, stacking them up and taking them to kitchen was my job. My greatest fear was at that time to go out to the dinner table and clean the table and bring the dirty dishes in. Most often I did not have to do that but when in the absence of a bus boy I was asked to do that, it was like a death sentence to me. I did not know what came upon me at that time. I wished I never had to go out to the dinning room. May be restaurant mangers were able to read something on my face. I got fired four times from four restaurants during my first encounter with dishwashing jobs.

Then I talked to my self: There is nothing to be embarrassed about bussing tables. Besides if you want to survive in this country, you have to do it anyway. So get over it. Similarly, I hated mopping the floor. In Bangladesh those who sweep, mop, and clean the rest rooms are known as "Mathors" a special group of people who are traditionally destined to this odd job. They do not come from all walks of life. They belong to the lowest rank of people in social order, always neglected, ignored, and segregated. They live with their dirty pigs in dirty places. With that picture in mind, I could not do a good job of mopping the floor when for the first time in my life I was asked to sweep and mop a floor.

That was the reason for getting fired so many times. Then some of my Bangladesh friend came to the rescue. "You have to get over this. We all have done this. This is not your Bangladesh. Besides American bathrooms are not like Bangladeshi bathrooms. There is no shame in cleaning American bathrooms. Mopping the floor! It is lot better that cleaning those toilet seats covers and toilet bowels holding a brush." Now I don't have to do those anyway other than cleaning my own bathrooms at home. However, my shyness has disappeared. Now I feel that I can do anything in this world.

I gradually learned to stand up and free myself from the self imprisoned prison of shyness. When I found myself free, I told myself: Free at last, free from the prison of shyness. I felt like breathing deeply the fresh air from my surrounding. Those who believe in shyness, those who find something

good to be bashful, the United States is going to be a hell for them. The United States of America is a country where shyness has no room. In this country shyness do not stand in your way of expressing your emotions and feelings. People do not feel shy to express their desire, sentiments, hopes, and aspirations. It happens only in Bangladesh.

Too much of shyness is killing our nation. We have to stand up and revolt against it. We cannot afford to glorify shyness any more. There is nothing to brag about being timid and bashful. Shyness should not be glorified as a human virtue. It is holding us back. I think the only reason Bangladesh is not progressing is people are too shy to do anything. We are too shy to move to this or that direction. We think too much about what others will think about us. Who cares what other think about me? If shyness makes you blind and humble, you have to get rid of it. I think it is high time Bangladesh realizes this truth and gets rid of its shyness if it really wants to move forward. It has to shake off its shyness and announce to the whole world that, we are not shy any more, we are bold, brave, and aggressive.

But when I am saying this, suddenly it dawned upon me that there is a danger in becoming shameless also. Shamelessness might make you naked when you lose all sense of decency, decorum, and respect for other's opinion. Of course, it makes sense to feel shameful sometimes. It is all right to feel shy when it comes to satisfying one's sexual desires. It is not nice to do it in public thinking that who cares. It is all right to feel shy to make obscene gesture and posture. It is all right to feel shy to expose your body in public. It is all right to feel shy to use vulgar language and it is all right to feel shy to talk in public about your sexual life.

A Social Outcast or a Hero?

A professional thief, robber, swindler, con artist, and a prostitute, have no place in the society. Society does not approve such profession, conduct, or behavior. If they get caught in their act, they go to prison and stay there for a long time. Same thing happens to a serial killer or a rapist. There is no room for them in the society, although there will always be enough room for them in the prison. When they are in prison, they are condemned to a very deplorable condition. They are doomed, gone, finished. Even if they can come out someday, their life will not be the same as it was before. Prison is a nightmare for them and they are aware of that. Once they are relegated to that place which we call a prison, they lose almost all of their rights. Once convicted and imprisoned, they are not being treated as another human being. They look different than a regular human being. People stare at them as they stare at animals when they visit a zoo.

The above-mentioned statement applies to crimes and criminal in Bangladesh. I have seen how thieves and robbers were mercilessly beaten by the public if caught red handed. No one have the patience to wait for the police to arrive. Bangladesh has zero tolerance about crimes and criminals. As if society has made up its mind forever. Society knows what is good and what is bad. What is a crime and what is not. In Bangladesh there is no looking for a reason for committing a crime. No one is interested to explore why someone has committed a particular crime. So there is no sympathy for the criminals. No psychoanalysis to decipher the mental condition of a criminal for finding the inherent reason for committing a crime. If you commit a crime, you are condemned for life. Boycotted by the society, neighbors, and even by your own family members. You are a social outcast. Don't try to give us a reason what made you a criminal. How

your society, your environment, and your upbringing gradually turned you into a criminal. No one has time to listen to that story.

Because if they listened to your story, they might get sympathetic to your situation. If they become sympathetic to your situation, you might not get harsh treatment from them. You might not receive tough punishment. They might even grant you certain rights. Make your living condition in prison more tolerable. As a result you might subsequently ask for more rights. If they continue giving you rights, if they continue showing sympathy to you, they will be sending such a message to you: You are not responsible for your misdeeds, someone and something else is. Eventually, not only criminals but also no one will feel any responsibility for any wrongdoing. In such a situation it will not be possible to put blame squarely on any body. The criminals will start putting blame on Demon or Satan when no other excuses will be available. "I did not do it, a Demon possessed me and made me do this horrible thing".

When I started to compare and contrast the nature of crime and punishment between the United States and Bangladesh, it appeared to me that the United States is very liberal about crime and punishment. Long time ago during my school years somehow I learned not to hate the criminal but to hate the crime. At that time I thought that it was a very good concept. It looked like a very sublime and honest proposition. So when I saw hatred for criminals in Bangladesh, I did not like that. I wanted to be very sympathetic to their situation. I felt like blaming the society thinking that every criminal is a product of the social injustice. If someone was not without food for three days, that individual would not try to steal food from that grocery store, I thought.

Therefore, compared to Bangladesh, I started to develop a respect for the American way of dealing with the issue of crimes and criminals. Criminals are also human beings. They were compelled to become criminals under certain unavoidable circumstances. Since as a member of this society, I also contributed to the creation of an unjust social system, I wanted to blame myself for compelling someone to become a criminal. How can I hate them? This contemplation is, of course, very civilized, sophisticated, rational, and humane. If American treatment of criminals were the result of these qualities, I would definitely feel proud of this society. But, unfortunately my research and my contemplation found completely different reasons for America's good treatment of criminals.

In this culture criminals are often respected not sympathized. Sympathy and respect cannot go side by side. To be sympathetic to someone's situation

is one thing and to be respectful for someone is another. In this culture successful criminals are respected without any consideration to what were the means of their success. If you can accumulate huge wealth by hook or by crook, you will be respected. No question will be raised about your ways and means for accumulating such wealth. When you have sympathy for unsuccessful criminals and respect for successful criminals, you are indirectly saying that I want you to be a successful criminal. That is to say that I do not care what you do, but whatever you do, do it right, don't get caught.

I do not understand how you can deter crime by sending this message to the criminals. Many people in this country are trying to be a sophisticated criminals. If you can play shrewd games in business, adopt unfair and illegal means to make huge profit and can get away with it, you will be regarded with high esteem, you will become a prominent business leader. Similarly, say for example you are a street prostitute. If an under cover police finds out you are soliciting business, you will get arrested, find or jailed. On the other hand, by tactfully avoiding getting caught you can continue your business and one day become owner of brothel and keep one hundred prostitute, you might become a leader, write a book, start a new movement to legalize prostitution, run for the state assembly, go to a TV talk show, get a chair on the middle of the stage, be admired and respected and eventually become a hero or a heroine.

The other day I watched a professional thief on a television talk show. He captured the center of the stage immaculately dressed up. He was explaining his skills to an captivated audience who showed profound respect for him. He is preparing to write a book how to steal successfully without getting caught. One day he might start a school of thievery training, start a movement to legalize thievery as a profession and demand less harassment from the law enforcement in the event that one of its members get caught. This gentle thief might become a hero for championing the cause of thievery. This society rewards those who get involved in illegal activities and come out successful. This happens not only in social or individual level, but also in government level.

There may be an inherent tendency in human being to commit a crime or to engage in unsocial activity such as to steal or to satisfy erratic thirst by watching nude dance or porno movie. One of the blessing of our civilization was to feel ashamed of engaging in those activities in public. Those desires are human, they may not be necessarily abnormal behavior. Once upon a time we used to hide them for fear of the society and family.

We used to keep those desires in our subconscious mind and were afraid of allowing those to come out in broad daylight. To give vent to those impulses and instincts, we had to look for under ground caterers of those needs. Those under ground organizations had no legal status or social recognition. People had to visit an under ground illegal organization to satisfy their animal instinct if they wanted to.

But presently in the United States, you don't have to do that any more. All under ground organizations have been given permission to come out in broad day light in the name of adult entertainment. People are hiring nude dancers in parties, and no one seems to find anything wrong with that. A new philosophy known as neo humanism has come along to support such activities. When a society starts inviting its thieves, robbers, prostitutes, and serial killers to listen to their stories and watching them perform their acts, and making hero out of them, that society is directly recognizing and approving all such kind of activities and behavior.

If this trend continuous, a serial killer one day will start writing a book describing how it feel like sticking a knife into someone's heart and pulling it out and munching it. He than will be asked to appear on a TV talk show. Eventually that person may start a movement to legalize cannibalism. It is not my intention to scare anyone by drawing such a horrible picture of the future and I know it for sure that these things are not going to happen in the near future.

The main thrust of the philosophy that I mentioned before is to allow human being to do what pleases them to do. This is what happiness is all about. You have to get rid of all sorts of traditional values, norms, ideals, religion, and ethics. This philosophy comes short of advocating the notion that if you feel the urge of killing someone , go ahead and do it. Otherwise you might suffer from depression and emotional breakdown. After all it is your life, which you are trying to protect. It does not matter if your happiness costs the life of others. Go for your own satisfaction, and don't think about satisfaction or pleasure of someone else.

This philosophy is getting momentum nowadays. Therefore, no criminal activity seems criminal anymore. If a person gets satisfaction by raping someone and if he believes in this philosophy, he cannot think of rape as a crime anymore. So, sympathy for the criminal is not emanating from the social injustice as I previously thought it was. It is a simple feeling of fellow feeling. We should not punish you for doing this. You were only trying to satisfy your needs, if I had the same courage as you have, I would

do the same thing. I salute you, adore you, and respect you more when you can do it with success.

In the face of such resurgence of philosophical beliefs, government, political, and social leaders are crying in the wilderness to stop crime. We are wasting millions of dollars to deter crimes. There is an old adage in Bangladesh that if you start chopping down the root of a tree and start watering it from the top, it won't do any good. This analogy holds good when I look at government's efforts to cut down crimes, on the one hand, and attempts to make heroes out of criminals by the society on the other.

Sounds Unfamiliar

We grow up hearing certain kinds of sounds and get used to those sounds. Those sounds come naturally to our ears. Sometimes we don't even pay attention to them. We live in a friendly and familiar atmosphere when we confine ourselves in one place, in one geographical location for a long period of time. Sounds that people make in day to day conversation, sounds of cars, buses, truck, and trains as they pass by in front of the house, sounds that comes from dogs, birds, hawkers, and beggars, all appear normal and natural to us. We become so accustomed to noises and sounds that they become part and parcel of our lives. Nothing sounds unfamiliar.

I, therefore, enjoy going to places where I can wake up with strange noises and sounds. When I was in Bangladesh, I used to visit my village home every summer. Sounds are very different there, no cars, no buses, no trucks, no hawkers, no beggars, and no airplanes. Instead I enjoyed hearing pigeons' "Bakbakum" (sounds made by pigeons) and "GhuGhu Pakhir Dak" (sounds made by a bird called GhuGhu). One day on my way to Cox's Bazaar (a tourist resort on the coast of Bay of Bengal), I decided to stay overnight at Dulahazara, a small village just few miles off the highway at a forest Beat Office. One of my relatives was stationed there as a Beat Officer. I wanted to see how he was doing in that dense forest, with tigers, and elephants.

When the bus dropped me, I instantly realized that I was in a different world. I could here a strange sound coming from the direction of dense forest across from the highway. When I enquired about that sound, my relative told me that he never heard any special sound. When I produced the sound for him and described it little bit, he said, "Oh, Yea. That sound.

I hear it every day. What's new about it?" When you live with a sound on day-to-day basis, you do not hear it. You can only hear a sound, a strange one, when you are a stranger.

So when I arrived at the Los Angeles airport for the first time, I decided to keep my ears open to listen to strange sounds, unfamiliar sounds. But the flight from Bangladesh to Los Angeles took almost 22 hours with two stop over, and I always get an earache when I stay in a plane for a long time. I become deaf temporarily. After an hour of landing everything comes back to normal. I was not willing to sacrifice that hour. When the first hour passed silently, I could here muffled voices of people having conversations. I felt like I was walking through a dream. Other sights and sounds helped create a perfect atmosphere of a dream. I talked to myself, you have to wake up and here some new sounds, you cannot dream right now.

When I got into a bus to go to my destination from the airport, I woke up with the sound of the engine of the bus. That was completely different from any bus I ever rode in Bangladesh. Not only the sounds of the engine, all other sounds that were coming out of the different parts of the bus; for example, the opening and closing of the doors and windows were also very different. I enjoyed the whole journey by concentrating on the noise that the bus was making. The journey was very comfortable.

The second unfamiliar sound I encountered when I took an elevator to go to the third floor of a building at the University of California, Riverside. Those thing we call lift in Bangladesh. However, the sound of the elevator appeared strange to me. I do not remember hearing similar sounds in a lift in Bangladesh although not too often I had the occasion to take a lift other than when I went to the government office buildings in Dhaka known as the Secretariat. There are also some miniature sky scrappers in Dhaka where you have to use lifts. Since I was not a big business man, politician, or a government officer, I had no reason to go there frequently. Whatever experience I had with elevator in Bangladesh, nothing sounded like the one I was having in Riverside.

In Bangladesh it is incomprehensible to find a calm and quite atmosphere when you are travelling through a busy thoroughfare in down town of any city. Your ears will be pierced by the honking of horn of buses, trucks, baby taxis, and rickshaws. Only in one occasion you will not hear any honking of horns when a opposition political party calls a general strike, which means no traffic on the road. When there is no traffic , there is no honking of horns. American political activists ask motorists to honk

their horns to show their support for a cause or a proposition or to protest against a proposition. Bangladesh politicians ask people not to honk their horn by staying out of the road. I have never seen a general strike in the United States as a means of political protest. That is why roads in the United States always remain busy but at the same time calm and quiet. I enjoyed that quietness of American roads when I first arrived.

United States is normally a calm and quiet place. Even if you living big cities, you have a distinct feeling that no loud noise is coming out from anywhere. Thousands of cars on the road but they are noiseless. If they make noise, they go to the muffler shops immediately. People do not honk unnecessarily; such as, to overpass or to express anger and frustration over a slow driver. People only honk here when motorists do not move even though the lights have changed from red to green. So it did not appear to me that I came to a noisy country. Considering the plight of Bangladesh, I felt the other way around, I came to a quiet country from a noisy country.

This noiselessness of the United States gave me an opportunity to concentrate on listening to strange and unfamiliar sounds. I kept my ears open to catch any strange sounds that might pass by. In doing so once I felt like I was a hunter, searching through dense forest looking for exotic animals to shoot. As a hunter steps very carefully and noiselessly, so did I. I thought, in the United States it was my job only to catch noise, not to make one.

This look out for unfamiliar sounds helped me to eliminate familiar sounds. I could concentrate better on unfamiliar sounds. Anyone who wants to concentrate on unfamiliar sounds can use my method. My advice is don't waste your precious time paying attention to familiar sounds and sights. Always look out for unfamiliar sounds and sights. You might find something very interesting there. This process will also keep you focused, concentrated, and motivated.

Another advantage of paying attention to unfamiliar sounds is that it will keep you out of trouble. You might be in big trouble if you always expect familiar sights and sounds, especially if you live in the United States. Different sounds from all over the world are penetrating here on regular basis. If you only decide to listen to familiar sounds, you will have difficulty in understanding people. Especially if you are in business and need customers, you cannot afford to stick to familiar sounds. At the same token when you are in a foreign country, it is an excellent idea to keep your

ears open for unfamiliar sounds. That way you won't be complaining about not understanding their language and culture. By keeping your ears and eyes open for unfamiliar sounds and sights, you will gradually assimilate to a new environment.

If We Have a Staring Problem

If we have a staring problem, we should stare at stars at night. We can go to a lonely place if possible and select a corner of the horizon and keep staring. We might even see a falling star, an unusual movement of a celestial body, a meteor, an asteroid, a comet, a planet, and expand our horizon of understanding of the solar system. If we are lucky, we might even encounter an Unidentified Flying Object, and get a ride in an Alien spacecraft. We will be returned to our homes safe and sound. Aliens never kill human beings. They abduct us for experiments only.

If we still have a staring problem, we might as well go to the beach, and find a lonely place away from the noise of the sunbathers, swimmers, surfers, and picnickers. We can stare as far as our eyes go and as long as we want to. We can watch the rising and falling actions of the waves. Also, we can keep staring at a passing by vessel. We can stare at sea gulls, playful dolphins, and sea lions. If we watch for any commotion in the water, we might see a large killer whale, which never wants to kill a human being anyway, as we have noticed in Sea World. If we approach them, they also become friendly. By staring at the ocean, we can expand your horizon of understanding of the creation of life and ponder about the mysteries of this universe.

Now, if nature doesn't attract us and we still suffer from a staring problem, we can go to a gorgeous shopping mall. There are plenty of them out there in this country. We can do some window-shopping. We can stare to our heart's content at all different kinds of merchandise. If we cannot afford to buy, no problem, we can continue staring. That way we can partially satisfy our craving for shopping. Shopkeepers are not going to mind. In animate objects never seem to mind.

If none of the above appeals to us, and we still have a habit of staring, let's stare at animals and inanimate objects. Even ferocious animals fall in love with human beings if we continue staring at them. Think about those lions, tigers, and wolves that human beings play with in circuses. But, we should never, never, in our slightest moment of unawareness, make the mistake of staring at human beings. Because it is dangerous. If we love ourselves, if we want to be around here in this beautiful universe, we should never think of staring at fellow human beings. Our lives will be at stake. We might end up dead! A bullet can mercilessly pierce through our arteries and stop circulation of blood to the heart. Even the presence of our wives and children won't stop that cruel bullet. So we should never stare at human beings. Human beings are the only species in the creation that do not like to be stared at.

Why is it so? Why do human beings hate staring so much that they want to kill the person who stares? Why does staring irritate human beings so much? To find answers to such questions, we don't have to be psychologists. We don't have to enter into someone's mind to decipher the mystery of human behavior. We only have to remember that we are also a human beings. We have to ask ourselves such questions, "What goes on inside me when someone stares me down? What bothers me? What makes me angry if I am angry? Why can't I be happy when someone keeps staring at me?"

If we look for answers to such questions, we will find the following answers: "I hate the way the person keeps staring at me. I can see something in his/her eyes. He hates me, doesn't he? He/she doesn't like me. He/she is criticizing me. He/she sees something wrong with me. That person doesn't like the way I look." Then we start talking to ourselves: "It is none of his or her business how tall or short my hair is. It is none of his or her business how tall or short I am. It is none of his or her business whether I am black, white, Mexican, or Asian. It is none of his or her business what I am wearing. It is none of her business what I am suppose to do and not to do in public. This is my life and this is a free country. I don't care what someone thinks about my behavior and attitude. No one can control my life. That person who is staring at me right now is trying to control my life. But before he or she can do that, I am going to do away with him or her." Here goes our hand in your pockets. We get a firm grasp on the butt of our handguns.

Unfortunately what goes on inside me might have no relation with the person who is staring at me. Maybe when I thought he or she was

criticizing or evaluating me by staring at me that person was simply unmindful, staring at me as a habit but thinking about something else. It always happens in our lives. All of a sudden I realize that I am staring at someone but my mind was wandering somewhere else. But alas, only for staring I might lose my life. This is a dangerous situation.

As we can see, we are creating our own problem and blaming someone else for it. Someone is paying dearly for the emotions we are creating in ourselves. Why do we do that? We do that because we don't have any confidence in ourselves. Our values, norms, ideals are very shaky. The life style I have chosen, the dress I have decided to wear, the attitude I am nourishing in myself are not satisfying or fulfilling for me. I do certain things without knowing why I do it. I only respect myself and don't see any reasons to have respect for any one in the whole world. When I think I respect myself, I only have respect for my wishes, my pleasures, my whims and caprices. I enjoy what pleases me without any consideration for other's concerns and feelings.

The word 'respect' has a different connotation for me. I respect my wishes means I don't control my wishes. I don't ask myself whether my wish is right or wrong. So when I wish to hurt someone, I respect my wish by hurting someone, and I get immense pleasure out of that. When I never care for someone else's feeling, I never want someone else to care for my feelings either. How can I? When that happens, I don't see any caring people around me. I only love me and since I don't care for anyone's feeling, I don't shape me up according to the expectations of others. So when they stare at me, I know for sure they are staring not with approval, praise, or admiration but with contempt. I can see hate in their eyes. That's what makes me so mad.

Fortunately, not all human beings feel that way. There are some human beings who never seem to mind when I stare at them. If I cannot move my eyes from them, they might even come closer to me and start a conversation. Why is it so? Why this big difference between human beings' behavior? Those people who don't mind when I stare at them see respect and admiration for them in my eyes. Those people who do not mind when I stare at them have confidence in themselves. They are satisfied and fulfilled with their life styles, ideals, norms, and beliefs. They are not paranoid and their values and ideals are not shaky. They have profound faith and conviction in their chosen paths. They have respect for all human beings. They want to share with everybody and care for everyone. These people are comfortable with the way they look and don't have any confusion in their

mind about their dressing and grooming. They are not in doubt about what they can do publicly and what they are supposed to do privately.

When we are completely satisfied with ourselves, when we know for sure that there is nothing wrong with us, then if someone stares at us, we don't see any sign of hate or disapproval in his or her eyes. We only see respect and admiration for us. That makes us happy. We enjoy it and feel proud of ourselves. We get a distinct feeling that we are inspiring someone to adapt our way of life. So no questions of getting angry on our part arise. That is the reason we feel like staring back at the person who is staring at us and would like to start a conversation. From such observations, it will be evident that we create most of our problems in our minds. We always have doubts in our minds about our behavior and attitude. Since we are not one hundred percent sure about our way of life, we become easily suspicious of others. Why do you think that everyone in this whole world is staring at you? You must be doing something wrong. If you are doing everything right, you won't get the feeling that everyone is staring at you.

Another problem with staring is that sometimes we provoke it. Don't instantly react by thinking that it doesn't make any sense. How can I provoke staring? Some people are in doubt about their behavior and attitude. They decide in their mind that they must grow out of the tradition, norms, and ideals of human behavior. They want to revolt, they want to change. But they are not sure that what they are doing is right or wrong. They need your approval. They challenge you. They want you to stare at them with approval. Theyë don't want you to ignore them. This is another problem. If we are not staring at them they must do certain weird acts to draw our attention. That is what I call provoking. They basically try to say they have every right to be different from us but that doesn't give me any right to be indifferent to them. So here we go. We end up staring but because we cannot stare with approval, you end up dead!

So, again it is safe not to stare at anyone. We should never, never stare at anybody at anytime. We live in a society where people cannot stare at each other with approval anymore. Rarely will we find someone that we would like to stare at with approval, with respect. So it is better to abstain from staring. Maybe in the future we can push our lawmakers to come up with a law prohibiting staring at human beings. Staring should be prohibited by law in the United States to protect innocent individuals who give their lives, in the presence of their loved ones, only because they develop a dangerous habit of staring at strangers.

Dressing Up for Learning!

We require people to wear appropriate attire when they go to work, go to a place of worship, go out to dinner, or enter into a hospital to visit a patient. We even require people to wear appropriate clothing to ride a bus, a train, or an airplane. Why should we let our children dress as they wish when they go to school? Is school a less sophisticated place than all of the above? Our society has a norm, a standard, and a conception about what constitutes appropriate attire. Decent and cultured people have no confusion about that. We, therefore, don't have to define what we mean when we say appropriate attire. But when it comes to school, this conception does not seem to work. Is it very difficult to define what is appropriate to wear in a school and what is not?

School going children are not ready yet to conform to the norms and standards of the society. Unless they see any example or are introduced to those standards, they would like to experiment with the clothes they wear just out of curiosity or to stand out of the crowd without realizing the adverse effect of such behavior. It is, therefore, necessary to show them what is appropriate and what is not in a learning environment. I believe that introducing uniforms is a right step toward achieving that goal. We have been too careless about this aspect of our culture for too long, resulting in a deterioration of the educational atmosphere in our schools. Schools are sacred seats of learning where we send our children to learn some skills to be able to do a job and to become a decent human being as well.

It is, therefore, necessary to ensure that an appropriate environment of teaching and learning prevails in our schools. If requiring young learners to wear uniforms helps promote that environment, I would, definitely, support the idea of introducing uniforms in our schools. I believe that

uniforms help the creation of a serene and sublime atmosphere of learning by promoting a sense of unity and togetherness among young learners. It also helps develop a team spirit, which is absolutely necessary for success in professional life. School is a place to concentrate on learning. It should not be turned into a dress exhibition. If we turn our schools into dress exhibitions, we will only provide a means of distraction rather than concentration. Also, a school should not be a place to experiment with weird sizes, bizarre color combinations, and brand names. If students pay too much attention to what they wear, they will not be able to pay attention to what they learn.

If students compete with one another for excellence in dressing up, there will be less competition to achieve excellence in academic areas. Uniforms, definitely, will prevent students from wearing inappropriate attire in a learning environment. Of course, what is appropriate for the beach or for a picnic is not appropriate for an office or a school. In the name of protecting our freedom of expression, or right to choose, some social and political leaders are unwittingly encouraging our children to dress as they like. As a consequence many children are polluting the atmosphere of learning by wearing sex provoking dresses in our schools. This should stop. Uniforms will certainly put an end to that practice. It will also stop those spoiled kids of the so-called rich and famous who go to school only to socialize by wearing the most extravagant clothing just out of the factory.

Another good aspect of uniforms is that it will put an end to the practice of wearing gang attire in our schools, because there will be no way of maintaining group identity in the midst of uniforms. The idea to put some clothes on is the most wonderful gift of this civilization. The necessity arose to protect us from exposure to extreme cold or hot climate conditions. Gradually we developed a sense of shyness and wanted to cover our body as the civilization progressed. Subsequently we also wanted to look beautiful. Nowadays civilized people all over the world wear clothes to reveal their personality and character, not to expose their body and become sexy. Individuals with character and dignity hate to look sexy because it diminishes their sense of decency and decorum. Our children need to learn that lesson. Uniforms in school will help them to appreciate the importance of wearing appropriate clothes on appropriate occasions and at the same time to develop respect for them.

What is Respect?

Having respect for someone is a normal part of life in Bangladesh. I grew up learning to respect people. First I learned that my father and mother should be respected. Than I learned that teachers should be respected. I also learned that anyone older than I, including my elder brothers and sisters should be respected. It never occurred to me that I can raise an objection why should I have to respect everyone? People get respect from people in Bangladesh only because someone is older than the other, if it is obvious. I thought 'respect' was some kind of natural emotion, emotion of feeling sad or happy, bored or excited. As we feel happy and sad, similarly we feel respect when we encounter someone older than I. This is what really happens in Bangladesh.

So I had respect for everyone except those who I thought did something terribly wrong. I could not have possibly respect for criminals. I also had no respect for someone who was not sincere and honest, no matter how rich and famous that person might be. In Bangladesh individuals inspire respect in people by virtue of the quality of their character, not by anything else. For example , if someone becomes a millionaire he or she never gets respect from people unless otherwise he or she is a decent human being. Similarly if someone excels in his or her profession that person does not get respect unless he or she turns out to be a nice human being.

Respect in Bangladeshi context does not depend on someone's achievement or performance in his or her career alone, respects depends on someone's performance as a human being. Therefore, to be able to inspire respect a person must be socially acceptable. A person with abnormal behavior or life style will not be able to generate respect for himself or herself in Bangladesh. I grew up in an environment where people spontaneously

respect each other. When I was a student I had profound respect for my teachers. So profound that sometimes I forgot that they are also human beings. I like to think of them as aliens, coming from another planet to educate them.

When I became a teacher, I equally enjoyed respect from my students. When I was a young 23 years old instructor of a college, I enjoyed students pushing themselves all the way to the wall in their attempt to clear the hallway for my smooth approach to a classroom. I enjoyed students standing up to show respect when I was entering the classroom. I enjoyed students touching my feet three times as a religious gestures of showing respect when they individually came to confer with me. I enjoyed students hiding or throwing away their cigarettes, if they had any, if I happened to be passing by. I enjoyed students using the word 'Sir" when addressing me.

With this background when you come to the United States and enter a classroom only to find that students are listening to their teachers putting their feet on the table, munching french fries and hamburgers, and drinking soda, and coming in and out of the classroom according to their sweet will, you will definitely get shocked. But this initial shock will quickly disappear when you will know that this is just the tip of the iceberg. This has nothing to do with showing disrespect to the classroom or to the teacher. In fact there is no deliberate attempt to show disrespect to anyone. The problem is far beyond this. There is no sense of respect left in this culture any more. Some how the sense of respect has disappeared from the life of the people of this country.

When I say that the sense of respect has disappeared from the lives of the people, I mean the real sense, the meaning of the word respect has disappeared especially from the lives of the young generation. The word respect is still there. It has not disappeared from the dictionary or from the lives of the people, but that word acquired a new connotation in American context. First of all, no one in the United States will understand why we have to have respect for someone older than we are. It will make no sense to them. They will argue that only because someone came to this world earlier than when I came, that does not give someone any right to claim respect from me. In Bangladesh people believe that by virtue of being in this world earlier than someone else that person gains more experience and wisdom. I can turn to those who are older than I am for guidance and advice. This is a realization of the fact that a person older than I am has gone through the problems of life more than I have. Therefore, in a normal situation an elderly person should inspire respect in a younger person.

Of course no one is supporting having respect for elderly people indiscriminately. If a person older than I, is found to be a criminal that person cannot inspire respect in me. The other factors remaining the same a person gets respect from me only because he or she is older than I am. This kind of contemplation is impossible in the Unite States. I have never seen anyone, parents or teachers giving this advice to anyone. No one is saying in this culture that, one should have respect for the elderly people. I have seen many textbooks on communication, psychology of success, and professional development where the importance of to be nice, polite, and sensitive to everybody has been discussed in depth but the word respect has never been used.

Americans likes to use the word respect for special people and on special occasion. Generally they do not use the word. In the United States successful people are being respected. Americans measure success in terms of money only. If someone can accumulate huge amount of money in a relatively short period of time that person gets red carpet treatment. People talk with him and about him with respect. That person gets lots of admiration and eventually becomes a role model, a hero. If sometimes that hero falls from his glory being accused of adopting illegal or unfair means, people don't condemn or hate that person instead they become apathetic.

Similarly if someone makes an outstanding achievement in sports that individual can generate enough respect for him or her. Successful athletes are another category of people who can easily inspire respect for them in the United States. Americans do not mind to stand in line for hours together to get an autograph of a famous basketball, baseball, or football player. Which is unthinkable in Bangladesh. No one even thinks of collecting autographs from players. There is no such thing as baseball cards or any cards of that nature. People enjoy games, admire the players for their skills and performance but don't develop a respect for them. They don't create an image of an athlete in their minds, they don't think of an athlete as a role model. they know that an athlete has nothing to offer them except a temporary sense of enjoyment and excitement.

Bangladeshi people believe that life is not all about excitement and enjoyment. They believe that they need to relax sometimes watching games, but they don't think about sports but they don't think about sports beyond a source of temporary means of relaxation. No one is obsessed with sports. They forget all about sports when they come out of the stadium and enter into the real world. In that world players has no room. Their

faces become faint, their names obscure, there is no such thing as sports fan in Bangladesh.

Players no that very well too. They realize that they only provide temporary relief to people. They don't expect people to respect them and make a hero out of them. So the athletes do not like to identify them as players. Being only player is an absurd and ridiculous thing in Bangladesh. All players make their living by doing something else. Besides playing they have career of their own. Same thing is true about people in movie making industry. Producers, directors, actors, actresses of hit movies become rich and famous in the United States. They are considered as special people. Although they may not have accomplished much as a decent human being and have no definite contribution towards the progress of society, people tend to believe that they deserve respect. In contrast Bangladeshi producers, directors, actors, or actresses have no social recognition and acceptance. No one wants to invite them as a chief guest in any kind of special celebration or occasion. They live a segregated life respected only by the people of the same trade. They are not considered intellectuals. They have the status of an entertainer. People enjoy their performance but don't pay any regard to them.

That is why I said that special people and special occasion get respect in the United States. These special people are rich people, winners in games and sports, and prominent actors and actresses and singers. People know their names. Like to talk about them during lunch break, show respect for them, and like to get their autographs staying in line for hours together. Special occasions are considered as winning a game, hitting a box office, winning a jackpot, suddenly getting rich, engaging in pernicious and covert activities and getting caught, becoming a serial killer, doing something very unusual such as killing more then one person at the same time, killing own father, mother, sons, or daughter. This people somehow earn the celebrity status in the United States. They get instant recognition, name and fame , become nationally known. Business people make some moneymaking T-shirts, hats with their names and pictures on. Some people talk about them with respect. People involved, no matter what they did, start feeling good about them. So good that they feel like writing books about themselves although they never attempt to put together two sentences in their lives. Suddenly they discover themselves as great litterateurs, philosophers, and thinkers.

On the other hand, real litterateurs and philosophers remain unknown. No one cares to know who is the founder of new philosophical movement,

who created a new theory of literary criticism. Very few people know who won a Nobel Prize in Economics or Physics this year. Those are not considered interesting events in the United States. A Nobel laureate, a famous philosopher, a great social reformer, a prominent political scientist never get any recognition from the contemporary world. They die unwept, un honored, and unsung although generation after generation might enjoy the fruits of their hard work, their dedication, and their sacrifices.

But thing are very different in Bangladesh. Those who make outstanding achievements for the advancement of science and technology, literature, art, and philosophy are remembered and honored. They receive all kinds of social recognitions and respect. No one remembers the name of a soccer player in Bangladesh for more than three days, but they clearly remember names of poets, novelists, historians, and famous professors. They have profound respect for those people.

So, it is not true that Americans do not know the meaning of respect. They have respect for the wrong people, and when you have respect for the wrong people, the word respect loses its charm and significance. That is what exactly happened to the word 'respect' in the Unite States of America.

Who Are Racists?

I thought I knew who racists are. They are, of course, human beings who hate other human beings. They possess a notion of the superiority of their own race over the races of people from other cultures. I am not trying to oversimplify the concept of racism. I fully realize that racism can manifest itself in various forms and shapes, but the underlying factors behind all of them is definitely the fundamental belief that people of some races are genetically inferior than other races. I was happy and satisfied with my own way of understanding racism. I, therefore, believed that Hitler was a racist, and his hatred for the Jews culminated in mass killing of millions of human beings. I, therefore, was afraid of racist people and always tried to avoid any confrontation or contact with a racist if it so happened that I came upon one.

Presently I am not so sure about what racism really is. Recently I read some articles in national newspapers in the wake of the protest against affirmative action. Some writers are coming up with new definition of racism to prove that they can talk against affirmative action without being termed as racist. Their greatest fear is that if they advocate against affirmative action they might be termed as racists. Certainly no would like to be termed as racist. So they decided to come up with a new definition of racism.

To give us a new definition the advocates for the abolition of affirmative action contend that most of us have a very superficial knowledge of racism and they have they real knowledge of racism. According to their definition if you believe that race brings changes in human behavior you are a racist. You cannot believe or think that people of different races may act or think differently. You have to believe that human beings are human beings and

all human beings are equal and they, by virtue of being human beings, are suppose to act, behave, and think exactly alike. Race do not change pattern of human behavior or thinking. To believe that race has profound impact on humans way of reacting to the external events is to become a racists.

From such an observation opponents of affirmative action accuse the supporters of affirmative action as racists. They argue that if you believe in giving preferential treatment to people of minority races, you are actually saying that those people really need preferential treatment meaning they cannot make it on their own. That is some races are inferior to other races. This is an irony. So long I thought that if I believe in affirmative action and preferential treatment I am not a racist. I am very sensitive to people of other races and culture. I am willing to give everyone a chance. How can I be a racist? Now according to this new interpretation of racism I become a racist with my all-good intention to get along with the people of other cultures, with all my intention to help everyone by giving them an opportunity, by opening door for them. Because I believe that I can reach that goal through affirmative action and preferential treatment, I become a racist! How can that be?

I, therefore, decided to think it over and examine this new definition of racism very carefully. It appears to me that it is impossible to ignore the difference that really exists between people from different cultures. First of all people are physically different. Some people belonging to a race are short and others belonging to different race are predominantly tall. People of some races are black and some are white. Some has black hair and some has brown hair. People do not come in same size, shape, and color. So human beings are different physically. No matter how hard one tries to prove that all people are created equally, outwardly you cannot see that.

Now, are all people genetically same? No, if we were all genetically same, we all would have same kind of physical features. Scientists believe that genetics not only determines physical features it also shapes up behavioral pattern of human beings. If we were all genetically same we would have same kind of physical and behavioral pattern. It is true that race has nothing to do with genes. People of a certain race may not possess the same genetical characteristics, but genetically human beings can again be regrouped. For example, it is possible to determine that people with certain genetical characteristics are supposed to be fat while others with different genetical characteristics are supposed to be skinny whether that person is a black, a white, an Asian or an European.

At this point the supporters of "All people are created equal" may

raise an objection that they are not talking about physical or genetical differences between human beings, they are talking about the intelligence and ability to perform a particular job. In that respect all human beings are equal. But it is also possible to present evidence that all people are not equally able to perform certain tasks and all people do not have the same kind of intelligence. That is why we have such words in our vocabulary as late bloomers or even more derogatory terms as stupid. From my many years of teaching experience in traditional classrooms, I have noticed that some students understand some concepts better than others or faster than others. This is why if you believe that all people are not created equal you do not become a racist. You become a racist only when you generalize by saying that all black people are genetically and intellectually inferior to white people.

But to believe that people of a particular race has some general characteristics which distinguishes them from other races does not make one racist. For example, if I say that Japanese people are short and American people are tall, it does not make sense to call me racist. Because in the first place by mentioning this physical difference between Japanese and American, I am not in any way expressing any general hatred against a group of people.

When I was in Bangladesh, I always believed that Americans are mostly honest, sincere, and hard worker compared to Bangladeshi people. I know this is a generalization. There are many Bangladeshi honest, sincere, and hard worker. On the other hand it is always possible to find some Americans who are far from being honest, sincere, and hard worker. But this generalization does not make me a racist. Of course I do not hate my own race. This is just a realization, a self-criticism. It is also an attempt to compare oneself with others to find fault with some nations national characteristics.

Therefore, it is not a good idea to term someone as a racist only because that person can see the difference among people of different races. What makes you a racist is your sense of superiority over other races and your hatred for people of other culture. But the new definition does not recognize that. The new definition suggests that if you believe that people of different races may have different national characteristics you are a racist. The purpose of defining racism as such is to keep some people of same ethnic background who share some common characteristics and behavior from getting organized and demanding fair treatment if they believe that they are not receiving proper treatment. It is to say that don't ask for

proper treatment, you are acting like racists. This is a very convenient way of depriving a group of people from their legitimate share and then blame them for voicing their concern. This is what the foes of affirmative actions are doing right now.

If all people of this world had exactly the same behavior pattern, same ability to understand an instruction, same intelligence and same amount of tolerance and patience, yet they are found superficially categorizing and identifying themselves with certain common characteristics only to take advantage of certain governmental program such as affirmative action, I would vehemently object to that. Let me imagine a country where all employable people are equally qualified for a particular job. All of them received equal treatment traditionally. They were never termed as minority or disadvantaged. They all received equal education and training, and then a group of people out of that population started talking about getting preferential treatment just because they belong to a different ethnic group than the majority. The question would naturally arise than do we have to give them preferential treatment because of their ethnicity? Does not make any sense to me.

As we can see to become color blind and get away with affirmative action and preferential treatment, we need a country where people have never been discriminated against. where people have never been given the status of a second-class citizen. where human beings have been respected as human being irrespective of their physical features. In that case there is no reason for someone to ask for affirmative action or preferential treatment. The question of affirmative action and preferential treatment arise when we do not live in a perfect world as I imagined. Where people hate people so much that they divide themselves as majority and minority. When people hate one another so much that they don't want to see someone with a different skin color in their neighborhood, then it becomes the obligation of an organization known as government to design programs to teach people the value of tolerance and justice.

Let us look forward to a future when human beings will stop hating each other only because they look different, speak a different language, behave in a different manner, or believe in a different religion. If we can envision a future like that only at that future land you will not need any affirmative action or preferential treatment. Until then if we try to play innocent by claiming that we do not see any difference in human being, we are colorblind and therefore we are not racists, unwittingly you also become a racist by being insensitive to need of people who have never

received equal treatment in their lives. So, coming up with a new definition of racism only to depict the defender of affirmative action as racist does not make any sense. Those who support affirmative action at least don't hate people. They are very sensitive, and sensitive people cannot be termed as racists.

Women's Right to Choose

Back in 1960s when I was a college student in Bangladesh once I came upon an article in a medical journal entitled, "Don't Have an Abortion". I forgot the name of the journal and name of the writer. I remember that it was written by a professional. The writer was trying to point out the adverse affect of having an abortion on women's body. The writer was explaining the health related hazards of terminating a pregnancy. The article had absolutely no comment on religious, moral, and ethical dilemma regarding abortion. It was a factual step-by-step scientific explanation of the problem of having an abortion. The article was really scary, but at the same time it was so academic that it did not appear to me as just another scare tactics by a pro-life activist in the disguise of scientific research.

Surprisingly since then I don't remember reading any thesis or dissertation asserting the fact that having an abortion has its dangerous side affects. I, therefore , assumed that medical science has made tremendous progress since 1960s and eliminated all possibility of having side affects from an abortions. In other words scientists have perfected the procedure, so there is no risk or danger involved in having an abortion. Still I was not very happy and satisfied with that assumption because from time to time scary news of complications after an abortion came to my attention from friends and acquaintances. I don't remember the precise nature of hazards involved as was pointed out by the physician long time ago, but somehow I believed that if you go against the nature, you have to pay dearly for it in some form or other.

Getting pregnant is a natural phenomenon, and terminating pregnancy requires some drastic steps to stop a process that naturally started in a woman's body. So to proceed with the decision to have an abortion anyway

being aware of the adverse affect it might have on your health, you must come up with a very good reason. It must be considered an absolute necessity, an emergency for that matter. You have to come up with this conclusion that in your case to carry the baby for nine months and giving birth is more dangerous than the health hazard you might have in the process of having an abortion.

If you look at this issue from this point of view, it will be evident that this is not a matter to choose between two equal options whether to have a baby or not to have a baby. Options are not equal. You have to be forced or compelled to have an abortion. It is not your choice. Because if you do not have an abortion, for example, you might die or your baby will be born with serious birth defects or something very serious of that nature, which will justify risking the possibility of side affect by having an abortion. So women's right to choose is a wrong slogan. When you are forced to do something, you are not choosing.

Besides considering the risk involved in the procedure (stopping abruptly something in progress), abortion should be performed under emergent situation and under serious consideration. It should not be taken lightly; such as, to decide not to watch TV tonight and to go to bad early. Since you have to pay a price for terminating your pregnancy (not the doctor's bill!), you have to think it over very seriously. Therefore, it is not a choice, it is a circumstance, and it should be an unavoidable circumstance when you don't have a choice.

When pro-abortion activists raise the slogan, "Women must have the right to choose", they are sending a wrong message to the society as if the women have the right to give birth to a baby or terminate a pregnancy according to their sweet will. By uttering this slogan the pro-choice activists only pick a fight instead of serving the cause of women who really need an abortion. This slogan makes many people very angry and frustrated. This slogan that you have right to choose whether to have or not to have a baby after getting pregnant is wrong from many different points of view other than one I just mentioned.

First of all, the very attitude behind this slogan is bad. Let's pretend that there is no danger involved in having a pregnancy terminated. The modern science has made this procedure one hundred percent foolproof. Do you jump in joy thinking, "Good! now I can terminate my pregnancy whenever I wish." You may feel secure and safe knowing that there is no health hazard to you if you terminate your pregnancy. You might feel good that you can have an abortion just in case the situation arises. But if you

start jumping in joy, you will be sending this message to the society that from now on you can have worry free sex with any body and at any time and enjoy your sex-life. There is no way to stop you. But would you really like to announce this to the whole world and be proud of yourself?

Asking for a right to choose, therefore, comes closer to asking for right to have indiscriminate sex without having to worry about getting pregnant because safe methods of abortion are available. No cultured and decent woman should be happy about getting a risk free abortion so she can enjoy sex. No matter how safely done stopping a growth is a destruction. You should not be happy about safely destroying the progression of a life. No matter whose life it is. So this should be considered as a last resort, not as an option or a choice or as a means to enjoy sex. Question of having an abortion comes after you get pregnant. Do you worry about abortion before you get pregnant? Certainly not! If you do, you have a problem. Everyone dreams about getting pregnant, having a baby, and enjoying a baby once in a while. If you are afraid of getting pregnant and worry about the right to have an abortion just in case you get pregnant then, definitely, you have a mental problem. You need to see a psychiatrist, not a pro-choice activist.

As I can see it clearly, two different kinds of emotions might generate in a woman's mind when a woman gets pregnant. First, it can be the most expected thing that happened to you. You wanted to get pregnant and have a baby. So you will be very happy and jumping in joy. Second, you might be very sacred, disappointed, and depressed when your pregnancy is the most unexpected and undesirable. Now when pregnancy makes you happy, abortion does not come into picture. If all the women in this country get happy when they get pregnant, no one will think about abortion. When they will not think about abortion, they won't worry whether abortion is legal or illegal. If pregnancy creates a sense of achievement, a fulfillment, an accomplishment, a positive feeling, a pride, who would bother about whether she has the right to have an abortion? Pregnancy would be considered a blessing of nature.

If you want to get pregnant and have a baby, you will be more than happy when you get pregnant. You would like to protect your pregnancy with all the resources available to you. This is so because getting pregnant does not depend on your sweet will. You might want to get pregnant but there is no guarantee that you will get pregnant, no matter how desperately you want it. It is not up to you to decide to get pregnant. You can only

wish. That is why once you get pregnant, you will be jumping in joy. Therefore, abortion does not come to the picture.

Now, let's look at the other side of this scenario. If you do not want to get pregnant but get pregnant accidentally, you will be extremely disappointed, frustrated, nervous, panicked, depressed, and sad. Depending on your background, support, and your social and economic status, the intensity of those negative feelings will increase or decrease. You will be left with an overall negative feeling. You will feel as if this pregnancy will ruin your life, your career, will hold you back from making any progress, so on and so forth. So you would like to have your pregnancy terminated. When that happens to you, you are not choosing from two options. When compulsion forces, options disappears. The word choosing has a positive connotation, which indicates that you are not under compulsion or pressure. When you are compelled, how do you choose? Choosing means to choose from two acceptable, one is more other may be less. When you are looking for abortion you are obviously not accepting anything less. Your emotion is totally negative. So, you are not choosing at all. You are under tremendous emotional pressure to terminate your pregnancy. Don't tell us that you have chosen to have an abortion. Because you really did not. You have in fact decided to have an abortion. I would accept the slogan, "Women's right to decide" but not "Women's right to choose." Choice is a very inappropriate term when it comes to life and death. It is inhuman to say, I have chosen to stop the development of a life. It is better to say, I had no choice rather than to decide to terminate the progression of a life.

At this point, you might think. "Oh, well. Big deal! I have not chosen but decided to end my pregnancy. Whatever it is, I need my right to terminate my pregnancy. After all it is my body, and no one should have any right over my body. This contemplation is all negative and inappropriate. First of all, if the father of your baby gets involved, you cannot decide unilaterally whether to keep or abort. Since you cannot get pregnant by yourself, your baby is not going to be your baby only, legally you cannot terminate a pregnancy without the consent of the father, unless you can prove that it was a rape. Father might also ask for his right to protect a pregnancy, in the event that he comes to know that mother is thinking about terminating the pregnancy. Getting pregnant should be considered as a joint venture, and one party cannot dispose it off without the approval of the other.

If, on the other hand, the father of your child is not in the picture, or if you are not sure who the father is, you might think, "Now I am

absolutely free to make my own decision. If the society does not like the word "choose", I will announce that I have decided to have an abortion". Not so fast. Wait a minute until you announce that decision. Do you need any help to have an abortion? Can you do it by yourself? Of course you need some professional help if you want to do it safely. When you need help, can you ask for a right? Is not there a contradiction in demanding a right when you need help? Help should come spontaneously. You cannot force someone with the authority of law to help you. For example, if for an unknown reason all the doctors of the United States decide not to perform abortion, can you force them to do so? Can you create a new law or amend the constitution to compel them to perform abortions? What about their freedom to choose whether to perform abortion or not? Did you know that they had to take an oath known as ìHippocratic Oathî at their graduation ceremony that they are never going to destroy a life?

Before you ask for a right to do certain things, you must realize that human rights refer to normal and natural condition of life. To impose any limitations or restriction on those normal and natural status of life is an infringement on someone's right. For example, you have the natural ability to walk. If I restrict your movement by my power, and leash you like a dog, you should fight for your right to walk away. Now, if you break your leg in an accident and become unable to walk and then start shouting all day long for your right to walk, no one will be able to give you that right, they can only give you a cold shoulder. Similarly unwanted pregnancy should be considered as an accident in women's life. Therefore, when you get pregnant and get depressed you don't shout for your right, you shout for help. Everybody will be sympathetic to your situation and will come forward to help you out, to stand by your side and assist you to cope with a very difficult situation. If instead you ask for your right, no one will be sure what to give you.

I, therefore, believe that the main debate on abortion is revolving around the issue of granting rights to have an abortion, not against having an abortion that much. I have talked to many anti abortionist who are very much willing to help someone to have an abortion who has no other visible option than to have one. There concern is you cannot claim it as your right. They are always willing to go to the extent of providing an alternate solution of your problem other than having an abortion. But if you have to have an abortion for psychological or physical reasons, such as the pregnancy is the outcome of a rape, or the pregnancy is life threatening, no one is standing on your way of putting your life together by having an

abortion. The slogan "Women's right to choose" does not promote any of the above consideration. It brings out an adamant attitude, a challenge to the society that I shall be irresponsible, I will do what pleases me to do, and then the society must grant me the right to destroy the growth of a life within me. It is nothing short of asking society's approval for one's erratic and irresponsible behavior. Society can allow abortion as a privilege not as a right.

Society must be able to weigh a women's decision to abort a fetus very seriously. Therefore, every pregnant women who have to have an abortion must come up with valid reasons to have one. They should be required to fill out an application form to be submitted to an appropriate authority formed by the government and entrusted by the society asking for permission. Those application must be supported by fathers' endorsement and doctors' recommendations, and in case of teenage pregnancy, parents' approval. The merit of each application should be studied individually and permission granted or denied accordingly. This is the question of terminating a life, a death sentence to an innocent prospect of life. We even hesitate to give a death sentence to a serial killer. In this case the seed of life will be up rooted just because the women's have a choice! I don't get it.

The Other Side
Part 2
Letters to the Editor
Published in The Ventura County Star

OPINION

LETTERS

■ Editor, Star-Free Press:

I would like everyone to understand that looting is a natural and integral part of lawlessness. During wars and riots, looting takes place. Looting takes place in the absence of law. Crime takes place in the presence of law.

Looting has an age-old tradition. As we have seen in history, when someone invades a country and conquers it, looting takes place. When the invader establishes law and order, looting stops. When citizens want to take law in their own hands, for whatever reasons, riots begin.

This tendency is inherent in human nature. The activity that takes place in the absence of law cannot be called criminal activity, so all looters cannot indiscriminately be called criminals. Their action has nothing to do with crime, which usually takes place in normal situations — in the presence of law.

I understand that thousands of law-abiding citizens of Los Angeles were arrested during the three-day riot on charges of looting only. They should immediately be released if they have no previous criminal records.

QAZI N. UDDIN,
Ventura

Letters on the riots

The Star-Free Press has received 153 letters on the verdict in the Rodney King beating trial, the riots in Los Angeles and related issues.

174

What kind of kids?

Editor, Star-Free Press:

RE: your Sept. 13 Associated Press article, "Study: Infants don't need nuclear families":

One researcher, in a conference of the World Association for Mental Health, has found that infants can develop emotionally without a traditional family. The researcher, Charles Zeanah, claimed it took him 10 years of research to establish this fact. He further added that only one adult must show interest in the baby.

I wonder why it took him 10 years of research to find that out. I came to the United States from a Third World country with a little knowledge of western literature, and it took me only six years to do research and earn a Ph.D. from a prestigious university in the United States. What I am trying to say is that it does not take 10 years of research to find out that infants do not need a traditionally family to develop emotionally. They just need someone to take care of them during their growing period so they can survive.

Of course they will develop emotionally. But what kind of emotion will they develop? A fulfillment, a satisfaction of being loved by both parents, or an emptiness, a dissatisfaction of being rejected by one parent? And what about the emotion of not knowing who the father is?

It is very unfortunate that people who want to follow a particular lifestyle are trying to convince everyone in the name of research that they are doing the right thing. If you want to discard the traditional values, just do that. You have every right to do that in this country. But don't try to convince everyone that there is no harm in doing so.

Also, don't try to justify your stand in the name of some ridiculous research. The researcher further said that, "Babies don't know what a nuclear family is." Of course they don't know. They won't know it anymore in the future when we will produce babies in laboratories, and nurses will take care of them until they are ready to go to schools. Schools will teach them safe sex, math, language, science, medicine and engineering. I am sure we will get some kind of human beings in the near future, but not human beings with love, affection and concerns for others.

QAZI N. UDDIN,
Ventura

Maybe what we need is a president who has no hair

John Quincy Adams

Editor, Star-Free Press:

Can the people of the United States of America afford to be delayed at the airport so their president can get a luxurious hair style, blocking the runway for one hour? In a democracy, we elect our representatives to work for us, not to pay too much attention to their hair.

If they continue doing so, we might decide to elect bald-headed presidents next time. Three of our first 10 presidents — John Adams, John Quincy Adams and Martin Van Buren — were bald-headed. During their presidencies, this great nation made wonderful progress.

Unfortunately, since 1841 we haven't had a single bald-headed president. It's about time to get one in the White House.

QAZI N. UDDIN,
Ventura

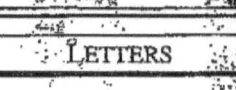

LETTERS

5-8838; Opinion Page Editor: Timm Herdt, 655-7957

For a noble cause

Editor, Star-Free Press:

I am extremely surprised and shocked by Reese Lamar's comment (Letters, July 30) that acquiring land from someone, by the concept of eminent domain to establish an educational institution, is morally wrong. I think it is morally wrong for a person not to sacrifice his or her land, if he or she can afford to, for the establishment of an educational institution, which definitely should be considered a moral, noble and serene cause.

It has been a standard practice, since the very inception of our civilization, to acquire land from persons who are unwilling to participate in noble causes. Of course they have been fairly compensated (shame on them). Civilized people donate land and money for the establishment of schools, hospitals and libraries.

In this case we are paying the owner the current market value of the property. I don't see anything wrong with the concept of eminent domain.

QAZI N. UDDIN,
Ventura

Letters

No right to privacy

Editor, Star-Free Press:

The Fourth Amendment should not be used to protect a person accused of committing a crime. It is very dangerous for a society to let someone use the constitutional right of privacy when he or she is accused of a crime. I think the law enforcement authority must be given enough power to violate someone's privacy if it results in producing evidence supporting the accusation. We should allow the police to decide whether they would like to intrude on someone's privacy or not. We have to amend the Constitution to allow police to do so.

Also, all law-abiding citizens must be mentally prepared to sacrifice their privacy, if the situation warrants, to ensure that real criminals cannot abuse this concept of privacy.

For example; if you find a police officer knocking at your door in the middle of the night to tell you that he or she has reason to believe that a criminal is hiding in your house, you can only ask for the officer's identification, and then should allow him or her to search your house. It should be an obligation of all citizens to co-operate with law enforcement if they want to get rid of criminals.

I do not see any reason to have such a law that does not allow the law enforcement authority to use an evidence, simply because the evidence was gathered without a search warrant. Do we create laws in this society only to protect people accused of committing a crime?

Did it ever occur to anyone that by allowing a person accused of committing a crime to use the Fourth Amendment, we are actually allowing that person to destroy evidence? Would you in your right mind let go a murderer because the police made a mistake in collecting evidence although they have solid evidence connecting an individual to a crime? This is ridiculous.

QAZI N. UDDIN
Ventura

SOS initiative stirs passions on both sides

Those who are in favor of Proposition 187 are basically saying that people who are illegally staying in this country shouldn't receive any kind of social services, including health and education.

By providing services to them, the state is spending billions of dollars, which it should not. Opponents of the proposition argue that those who support it are racists. They argue that illegals do contribute by paying taxes through Social Security, unemployment and disability insurance deductions from their paychecks, although they never receive any benefit from those.

They work very hard in our agricultural fields. They are the backbone of the state's economy. So it is not fair to deprive them of certain benefits from local or federal programs.

I think both supporters and opponents of this proposition are missing one very important point. The proposition is aimed at illegal immigrants, while the issue is illegal immigration. We certainly do not want to send home all the people who are living in this state illegally for generations. It is an absurd and impossible task.

The issue is to stop the influx of further illegal immigration. Proposition 187 cannot achieve that goal. Besides, immigration is a federal issue and only Congress and the federal government can make laws or adopt measures to stop illegal immigration. The state government has no authority over immigration laws.

The purpose of this proposition is not to control immigration, but to deny responsibility for those who are here illegally. The truth is: California needs illegal people to keep its agricultural industry alive. Everyone knows that without the hard work of mostly Mexican illegal workers, California's economy will be doomed. This is an open secret. Besides, illegal workers are taking care of all sorts of odd jobs (with below minimum wages and substandard living conditions) that legal people hate to do.

So it is not that California doesn't want illegal workers. What this proposition wants is basically this: since you are here illegally, just work hard for us and die for us. If we need some more workers, we will let them in, and let them work hard for us and die for us, but we are not going to take any responsibility for them. I think this attitude is very detrimental toward the progress of any civilization and culture.

If they do not want Mexicans to work here, go start working in strawberry fields. Don't let them have any jobs. It's not fair then to deny taking care of them, depriving them of their basic human rights such as education and health.

—Qazi K. Uddin,
Ventura

iore

DON'T BE SCAR MISTER QUA AS JUST N DRESSED A VAMPIRE!

YOU WERE MY EX-WIFE'S ATTORNEY.

OPINION

YOUR L

What is a 'criminal'?

I have noticed a tendency among the supporters of Proposition 187 to use the word "criminals" when they refer to illegal aliens, as if "illegal" and "criminal" are synonymous. Radio-TV talk-show hosts, newspaper columnists, politicians and those who have something to say supporting this proposition find it very convenient to label all undocumented aliens as criminals, on the grounds that those who break laws must be termed "criminals."

Indiscriminate use of the term "criminal" to mean illegal aliens gained momentum when Section 1 of the proposition's text stated that the people of California "have suffered and are suffering personal injury and damage caused by the criminal conduct of illegal aliens in this state."

How can illegal aliens legally be termed as criminals? As far as I know, all laws are classified as civil and criminal laws. Those who break civil laws are never considered criminals. For example, it's against the law to drive more than 55 mph. Many of us break this law once in a while and get pulled over. Do we consider ourselves criminals, or are we termed as criminals? Of course not! It is a civil offense, not a criminal one.

What kind of law do the illegal aliens break when they enter the United States? They break federal immigration laws, which cannot be classified as criminal laws and should, therefore, come under the jurisdiction of civil laws. How can people be termed criminals for breaking civil laws? I do not know of a single country in which a person is termed a criminal for illegally entering.

It is not my intention to encourage or justify illegal immigration. For the time being, it would be nice to stop using the word "criminals" when we refer to illegal aliens. We should not express any hatred toward fellow human beings by calling them criminals when they are really not.

— Qazi N. Uddin,
Ventura

Monday, Jan. 23, 1995   The Star FC

Pray for concentration

Most of us have a wrong conception about the true significance of the term "prayer." I believe that if we can separate prayer from the concept of God and religion, no one would object to introducing prayer in school. We associate prayer with praying to God as a manifestation of certain kinds of religious beliefs. Of course, many people do pray out of their convictions, but that does not necessarily mean that one cannot pray to oneself for one's own improvement. This kind of praying to oneself, as an eagerness to do a good job, may be termed as contemplation and concentration.

No one can deny that when we pray to God or to ourselves, we try to concentrate. The importance of concentration to do a good job or to learn something well cannot be overemphasized. Since praying helps to concentrate, and concentration helps learning, I do not see any harm done in praying, whether to God or to oneself, for just a minute, in a place which we call an institution of learning.

Since this will be done in silence, no one will know whether I am praying to God or to myself and what my religion is. This should be considered as a unique opportunity to help students learn or practice concentration through prayer, irrespective of whether the student is praying to God or to himself.

If you do not believe in God, pray to yourself. Address your mind with such words as, "Oh, my mind, I know you have a mind of your own. You have a tendency to wander around somewhere else when I need you the most. Please stay with me for a while so I can accomplish this difficult task." On the other hand, if you do believe in God, just change the word "mind" with "God," but pray. Praying is good and healthy. It keeps you concentrated, motivated, and focused. We cannot achieve anything without concentration. Praying generates concentration.

So, please don't confuse prayer with God and religion and abandon prayer altogether. Do not bring here the Constitution and the issue of freedom of religion or church-state separation. Also, please don't bring the issue of conservatism or liberalism. All of us need to pray or to concentrate. When I ask for just a minute of silence to be able to concentrate, I do not bring religion to my school or to my workplace, I bring a highly motivated mind.

— Qazi M. Uddin,
Ventura

Get rid of discrimination before trashing affirmative action

By Qazi N. Uddin

A big debate is looming large in the horizon, which will determine the fate of affirmative action. The well-intentioned California Civil Rights Initiative is now under attack, and Californians are preparing to lead the nation in the right or wrong direction.

I believe that we have to do some serious thinking before we make up our mind on this issue. One wrong move will not only push the state, but also the entire nation, 100 years back.

Opponents of affirmative action believe that this concept has been abused to the extent that the once oppressor has become oppressed, and quality has been sacrificed in the name of achieving diversity. They, therefore, want the government and society as a whole to become color-blind. This approach seems innocent and appropriate.

There is nothing wrong with this, except that it proposes to do away with preferential treatment as a means of wiping out discrimination. It is to believe that if we become color-blind, discrimination will magically disappear.

An ostrich buries its head under the sand when it senses an approaching storm, thinking that the storm will disappear. Becoming color-blind is a good idea when you deal with people who have been receiving equal treatment traditionally. It is a decent approach if you believe in human beings as human beings, not as black, white, or Asian. To apply color-blindness, we need a country where people were never classified as majorities or minorities.

After keeping a group of people as slaves for 100 years and discriminating against them for another 100 years, if we suddenly declare that we are going to be color-blind starting tomorrow, do you see the implication of this intention? It is no different from challenging someone to fight after starving him for 10 days. Is a sensible human being, can you allow that to happen?

Affirmative action was intended to narrow the gap and to create a balance. It gives a chance to a starving person to get some food and gain strength so he can accept the challenges. Affirmative action was intended to make competition fair.

I do not believe that by giving preferential treatment, we are sacrificing quality or merit; we are just opening doors. We are only becoming sensitive to people of different cultures, giving them hope and courage.

> To apply color-blindness, we need a country where people were never classified as majorities or minorities.

I can declare that I have five openings in my office, I prefer to hire three whites and two blacks, according to their proportionate representations in my community. But they must possess certain qualifications to get these jobs. Of course, they have to be able to do their jobs! Setting a quota serves the purpose of giving incentive to historically ignored people. It motivates them to get ready, to prepare themselves to qualify for those jobs.

Similarly, schools can declare: We have 500 seats and these seats will be distributed proportionately to blacks, whites, and Asians, according to their representations. But this is our admission requirement. If you do not meet this requirement, you do not get admission. Your quota will be filled with other deserving candidates.

No one should ask for lowering standards either to get a job or to get admission in school. It is very disgraceful for any group of people to demand any lowering of standards of tests or to change curriculum only to accommodate them. In that case, they will have no self-respect, no sense of achievement. Lowering of standards is another manifestation of racism in disguise of liberalism, which presupposes that people of certain races are intellectually inferior to others.

I would, therefore, vehemently oppose lowering standards but like preferential treatment to stay until such time as human beings are not termed as black or white, majority or minority. Preference should be given to correct the mistakes of the past, and it can be given without sacrificing any quality.

— Qazi N. Uddin lives in Ventura.

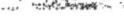
Democracy has built-in safeguards

☐ The United States is known all over the world as the father of modern democracy. People of the rest of the world have profound respect for the democratic system that prevails in this country. In the history of the United States, no government has ever been thrown out of power violently by the opposition party or by the Army. That image has recently been shattered at home and abroad, not because of the Oklahoma bombing, but due to the fear of their own government as expressed by some politicians, radio-TV talk show hosts, columnists and by support for a militia movement.

Whether the bombing has anything to do with the militia movement is completely a different issue. But worrying that militias might have something to do with this bombing, some journalists jumped to find an excuse for such an act on the part of militias. They believe that the federal government is encroaching on individuals' freedom. So there are valid reasons for Americans to be afraid of the federal government and start supporting the militia movement as a means of keeping the government under check. This kind of interpretation serves the purpose of promoting violence against the government, which is undemocratic.

The United States has never supported terrorism, no matter what the reasons. Why then, this sudden shift in some people's thinking? It is nothing but a paranoia about losing their individual freedom. It is very disturbing to note that when a tragedy of that magnitude struck the nation, instead of condemning the act of violence and empathizing with the victims' families, some people are paranoid about losing personal freedom and making a hero out of the militia by asking them to come forward in the media as champions of the cause of protecting individuals' freedom against the federal government.

The Constitution of the United States provided for a well-regulated militia for the security of a free state. Militias must be formed by the state and must be regulated by the state to ensure freedom of the state, not to secure the freedom of individuals. U.S. armed forces have nothing to do with guaranteeing individuals' freedom. Similarly, a state's militia has nothing to do with securing freedom of people by resorting to terrorism. It may secure the political freedom of the state from federal intervention, if it ever happens.

In a democracy, people's freedoms do not come from the barrels of guns. People organize against their government and change the government peacefully by their power to vote. Democracy does not allow individuals to take the law into their own hands. If we do not like some federal regulations that restrict our personal freedom, we should fight through our elected representatives to change those regulations. We should not get afraid of the government and start organizing a militia movement to overthrow the government, should we?

— Qazi M. Uddin,
Verchere

Blame the molesters

Now that Susan Smith is behind bars, should we breathe a sigh of relief believing that a demonic mother, who has killed her sons, has been punished and the society has been saved from the horror of the recurrence of such a horrible crime? Wrong!

We can't relax. This society is capable of creating more Susan Smiths as long as we have animals among us like Beverly Russell, the stepfather of Susan, who sexually molested her when she was 15.

This society is capable of creating more Susan Smiths as long as fathers or mothers of this society have to commit suicide over divorces. (Susan's natural father committed suicide over a messy divorce.) This society is capable of creating more Susan Smiths as long as teen-agers have to attempt suicide to escape sexual assault from stepfathers. (Susan attempted suicide as a teen-ager.)

If we do not want to see any more Susan Smiths, we have to get rid of child molesters like Russell. Is Russell responsible for Susan's act? Of course he is. He has already confessed about his contribution in creating an offspring-killer in Susan, not out of a guilty feeling but to save her from the death penalty.

Were Susan's father and mother responsible for her act? Yes, they were. Who contributed in shaping up Susan's attitude toward life? Obviously, her parents and stepfather.

I wonder how a society can remain silent about the crime committed by Russell. If we do not eliminate child molesters like Russell from the society, if fathers and mothers do not learn to sacrifice their own pleasure for the sake of their children, instead of sacrificing their children to satisfy their desires, we will see more mothers starving their children to death (as happened in Ojai), or dropping them in the river from a bridge (as happened in Los Angeles).

— Qazi N. Uddin,
Ventura

Speak out against unjust verdict

■ Are we really civilized?

When a violent crime takes place in a civilized society, it is normal for all decent, sensible, peace-loving and law-abiding citizens to be concerned, sad and depressed until the culprit is apprehended and punished. When O.J. Simpson was accused of committing a horrible crime, we had some consolation that at least someone was accused and that the individual might be found guilty. A crime of that proportion cannot go unpunished.

Now that O.J. Simpson is found not guilty, we should, naturally, be more concerned, sad and frustrated thinking that the real killer is still out there somewhere. This notion is very depressing that the real killer is getting away unpunished. As sensible human beings, how can we jump for joy and celebrate the acquittal of an accused at this point? Instead of sympathizing with the victims' family and friends and sharing their anguish and frustration, how can we celebrate? Are we really civilized?

Of course, I can understand, the accused and his family and friends have enough reasons to jump for joy and celebrate, but can the rest of us participate in joyful celebration of an acquittal? Is it all right for the news media to follow O.J. Simpson to his house to find out how happy he and his family are when the victims' families are crying in utter frustration?

What is more appropriate for civilized people? To share the sufferings, anguish, and despair of victims, or to jump and dance only because someone is not found guilty?

If we start jumping and singing, it shows that we are very inconsiderate people. We don't care for the victims, we don't care whether a criminal gets punished or not. We are fanatics and care for only those whom we support. This is not only undemocratic, but also inhuman.

I, therefore, understand those who expressed their frustration and stuck with

the verdict, but don't understand those who are jumping for joy. This is not an occasion to celebrate, but an occasion to shed tears.

— Qazi N. Uddin,
Ventura

BILINGUAL EDUCATION

Teaching English saves in the long run

Good intentions . . .

By Qazi N. Uddin

I will prove there is no such thing as bilingual education.

The term means giving bilingual education to monolingual people. Doesn't it sound contradictory to start with? Why do we need bilingual teachers to teach monolingual students? For example, if a student speaks only Spanish, why do we need a teacher who speaks only Spanish and a textbook written in Spanish? In this case, we are using one language. So what is bilingual education?

There is no denying the fact that many students come to this country from various linguistic and cultural backgrounds, and they need to educate themselves.

It is also true that it is very difficult to learn a subject using a foreign language. But the solution to this problem does not lie in getting a bilingual teacher and books translated into one's native language. It is not practical because a bilingual classroom may turn into a multilingual classroom with 20 students from 20 different countries. Is it economically feasible to hire one bilingual teacher for one student? Besides, specific textbooks in translation may not be readily available. On the other hand, it will be extremely difficult to find one teacher with multilingual ability in eight languages. (I am an exception.)

However, it is not altogether impossible to form a class with a group of students speaking the same language, such as Spanish. Since they do not understand English, we are teaching them geography, for example, in Spanish. In that case, why should we need a bilingual education? We need a teacher who can teach geography using the Spanish language only.

But in doing so, what are we really trying to achieve? Are the students learning geography in Spanish able to use their knowledge in the United States? Besides, it is going to be very difficult to form one-language bilingual classes in localities with diverse ethnic populations such as Los Angeles.

Under the banner of bilingual education, some educators are doing something completely different. They are grouping together some students with limited proficiency in English and some with no proficiency at all, and relegating them to a special class with a bilingual teacher to help them out.

Their cause is noble. They want to help those students who have problems with English, but want to continue their studies and finish the course to graduate. It is wrong and dangerous, because this approach, in reality, is keeping some students from achieving their goal of learning English and assimilating into this culture.

This segregation of students diminishes their self-esteem and makes them timid and nervous. Furthermore, instead of fostering racial harmony and tolerance on the campus, it creates different groups of students with superiority and inferiority complexes, and hatred and apathy for one another.

If the purpose of bilingual education is to help non-English-speaking immigrants, then we have to divide that population into various categories. We have to design curriculum according to their levels of proficiency in English. But the focus must be on teaching English, not any other subject matter.

I believe that to accommodate all groups of non-English-speaking immigrants, we have to design minimum four and maximum six levels of courses. A placement test will determine who is suited for what level. After successful completion of that course level, students will be eligible to get regular courses. Placing a student in a particular English class and letting the student finish that course will definitely prepare that student mentally and academically to enter into a regular program where the medium of instruction is English.

The fact is, if we want to help non-native speakers of English, improve their conversational, reading and writing ability, we have to put them in a class where only English is used. They may suffer initially, but eventually, they will start enjoying it.

While I am advocating against the bilingual method of learning and teaching, it is not my intention to downplay the importance of being bilingual or multilingual. I can handle eight languages. I don't see how the so-called bilingual education can help either to learn a foreign language or to become successful in a foreign country.

— *Qazi N. Uddin lives in Ventura.*

ENTURA COUNTY
PULSE

WEAPONS:
people carry them?

■ Average Americans have a profound love and respect for guns. When guns give us power and power gives us a country, the existence of a country depends on guns. If, on the one hand, we justify or glorify the role of guns to protect our freedom, we cannot downplay the importance of feeling powerful in our individual lives by having a gun.

The point is, we do not hate physical or brutal power, we love it. That love is manifested in our attempt to create more sophisticated weapons and more destructive power. This trend is not peculiar to the United States, which is why the arms race is still going on.

Asking people to get rid of guns should be supported by asking all nations of the world to get rid of their weapons and armed forces. It is a double standard to keep guns in government, but to disallow them for individuals.

The main thrust of democracy is to recognize and respect the power of the people, not the power of the gun. Those who believe that democracy can be secured or restored through the power of guns are wrong.

Democracy thrives in an atmosphere where there is no threat of application of power. Democracy gains momentum in a society that believes the pen is mightier than the sword.

Human beings' progression from the love of brute physical force to the power of knowledge is the history of civilization. Asking to possess a gun at this juncture of our civilization is to deny this progression.

— Qazi H. Umar,
Ventura

YOUR LETTERS

Schools not factories

To understand why the Ventura County Board of Education has rejected a federal grant of $2.5 million, we have to understand the difference between education and training.

Education gives a person profound knowledge of a subject matter and creates a cultured human being. Training only creates workers. These workers may be good at performing specific jobs, but they lack in general knowledge. Workers are not able to make independent decisions. They are afraid of doing anything else other than what they are trained to do. Surely, we don't want to create only workers in this society. We need to create sensible and intelligent human beings.

School-to-Work is a concept that wants to sidestep this process, because it is time-consuming and expensive. Instead, it wants to create workers only because it is convenient and a shortcut to supply workers to workplaces. Obviously, this should not be the purpose of education. We cannot turn our schools into huge job-training centers or robot-making machines. Uneducated but trained workers are nothing but robots.

The job of regular schools is to educate students in general, irrespective of what kind of jobs they are going to do in the future. Educators are dedicated people who not only teach but also touch a life and change it. Trainers do not get any chance to build character. They are in a big hurry to show someone how to do the job. All of our social problems are the result of not having enough educated people, although we have many trained workers. We, therefore, cannot let our industries dictate our curriculum.

It may be a federal government's headache to create more robots, but it is not fair to ask all regular schools to adapt programs or design special programs to create more workers instead of educating our children. It is an insult to their intelligence.

It is the job of industries to train their workers to meet specific needs. Besides, we have trade schools for that purpose. Let the trade schools get the federal money to create workers.

Ironically, even the trade schools cannot remain satisfied by training someone to do only a particular job, because if they teach a particular skill without teaching some human relation skills, such as communication and professional development, and human psychology, students do not get prepared to become productive members of the society. It is easy to train an educated person, but it is very difficult to educate a trained person.

— Qazi N. Uddin,
Ventura

True prediction

Re: your Feb. 8 article, "Libraries must yank best sellers":

In 1953, Ray Bradbury wrote a book, "Fahrenheit 451." He had foreseen a future when there are no books. Libraries are forced to burn their books because of the complaint that books are offending many people and are making people think. I believe that Bradbury's prediction is coming true now, 43 years later.

It is very unfortunate that we fail to pay attention to philosophers' predictions. Sometimes we even make fun of such predictions. While reading your headline, it came to my mind that paying attention to great thinkers' forecasts is a good way to avoid future catastrophe.

The problem with our libraries is not that we don't have money to run them; in fact, we don't have any thinkers in this society. People believe that all the thinking has been done for them and they are here only to enjoy their lives. We don't have thinkers because we don't have readers. Reading inspires thinking and thinking generates writing, which creates books. No money can keep a library open unless society develops respect for reading. Bradbury envisioned it 43 years ago.

— Qazi N. Uddin,
Ventura

THE STAR

OPINION

• OPINION PAGE EDITOR: TIMM HERDT • 655-5837 • THURSDAY • APRIL 25, 1996

till

› do

ree years, the
nen-owned
reased 43 percent
employing 15.5
s. The number of
essions and in
o dramatically
will continue to;
enter for Education
nates that in 2003
illion women will be
npared to 4.5 million

enetrated male-
tplaces, they initially
to the male work
nsumer base with
ing power.
sses may aspire to
uitable management
sense of fairness,
iscover that it's

will have done their
eir presence is a
nat.

YOUR LETTERS

Run from the border: How to respond?

Those who provoke law enforcement bring rough treatment onto themselves. It is absurd not to suffer the consequences when one picks a fight. Strangely, we do not want to understand this true nature of human behavior. Police officers are just like any other human beings with flesh and blood. Isn't it too much to expect police officers to act timidly when you provoke them?

It is very unfortunate that human rights' advocates and politicians do not see the consequences of playing with fire. They are trying to make the police beating of two illegal Mexican immigrants an illegal immigrant-bashing issue, which clearly it is not. If the police officers went to a factory and started beating illegal workers, we could say that this is illegal immigration-bashing.

I hate to see police offices whipping their batons on any human beings. I expect them to act professionally. But again, they are human beings and can get easily carried away in extreme situations. The point is, politicians and human rights' advocates should not take advantage of this situation and distort facts.

In fact, police did not beat them for illegally entering the United States. Police beat them for ignoring and provoking. The other day a truck crammed with illegal immigrants overturned, killing seven men and critically injuring 19 others. It is better to beat two to save seven lives.

— Qazi N. Uddin,
Ventura

YOUR LETTERS

Get emotional

The recent vandalism in Oxnard's newly built and state-of-the art high school is the outcome of this society's tendency to distance itself from the cause and effect of crimes, and a strong desire to go on with its day-to-day business. We have a tendency to feel that no matter how serious the nature of the crime is, it should not have any impact on our normal way of life. Nothing should stop.

That is why some people believed the graduation ceremony should go on at Oxnard High. All students should not be punished for the unscrupulous behavior of the few. Further, there is an assumption that we have nothing to do about it. The law enforcement will take care of the problem. If we cherish and nourish such an attitude toward crime, the number of crimes will increase manifold.

There are other societies that believe everyone should suffer for one's crime. I lived in such a society for 34 years before coming to the United States. Once I announced that if a single student was found cheating on an examination, I would cancel the entire examination and, as a consequence, the students' graduation would be delayed. No one criticized me by such words as, "This is ridiculous." Instead, I was able to inspire a real respect for me in that community.

It is only possible in other countries, not in the United States. Wrong! I kept that habit of giving vent to my emotions against all evils even when I moved to the United States. It happened in the most crime-infested area of Oxnard, which is Colonia. I was teaching at the now defunct Jade American School. One day I found graffiti on some buildings. I announced immediately that I was not going to teach in a school that has graffiti. Who cares? Next morning all the graffiti was gone! Yes, even criminals care when you get emotional to uphold truth, beauty, serenity and sublimity.

If I were the principal of Oxnard High, I would not only cancel the entire graduation, but also would resign or probably go on a hunger strike until the culprits were apprehended. Our leaders should set examples of how emotional they can be when it comes to serving a noble cause.

— Qazi N. Uddin,
Ventura

)PINION

OXNARD COLLEGE

■ I am extremely shocked and surprised by James A. Merrill's Aug. 2 letter. "College needs leader," wherein he provided a telephone number asking public pressure on the college district's governing board to submit to the wish of the hiring committee.

I served as president of a college in my country for seven years before coming to the United States in 1979. One of the many reasons I left my country was that my people have a tendency to take the law into their own hands. They have little respect for the system or for the authority. For example: one of the members of the college's hiring committee created a big hullabaloo and mobilized the public to put pressure on my governing body to oust me only because I refused to hire one of his favorite candidates for a teaching position.

I have now lived in this country for a considerable period of time and can assess fairly the culture of the United States. I believe that this is a country where people in general have respect for the system and for the authority. But that belief has recently been shattered by Merrill's letter and the politics going on at Oxnard College over the selection of a president.

I believe that it is ridiculous to question the authority of the governing board to cancel a search process. We should assume that the college's best interest is always in the governing body's mind. Also, the hiring committee is not an independent body. It is a creation of the governing board. The governing board has the absolute authority to dismantle a hiring committee if it so desires. Therefore, it can also call off a search process at any time and at any stage of the progression of the search. It is meaningless to question the governing board's authority when there is a system in place and one has respect for this system.

To do otherwise, one has to come up with a new system declaring that henceforth the hiring committee will have the supreme power to conduct a search and to select a candidate for a job and the committee's decision will be final. Until then, we have to have respect for the governing board's decision. The attitude expressed by Merrill and his supporters at Oxnard College is anti-American and more like the people of the country that I left behind.

— Qazi N. Uddin,
Ventura

STAR

OPINION

◆ OPINION PAGE EDITOR: TIMM HERDT ◆ 655-5837 ◆   FRIDAY ◆ NOV. 29, 1996

s

ig

er

. It's as
nd the

ory of
d left in
re
l't on
ve to
igine
ick
s of a
uld
a such
is that

and
k isn't

is story,

Quest is worthwhile

Re: your Nov. 16 article, "Does Academic Decathlon stress winning over learning?":

I find it very hard to believe that there are some veteran teachers who feel like criticizing the Academic Decathlon. The purpose of Academic Decathlon is not to supplement the high school curriculum, nor is it a remedial course. It goes well beyond that.

The students with extraordinary intellectual aptitude are chosen for this extracurricular activity. I don't understand what's wrong with putting emphasis on "recalling facts." Do the critics realize that recalling facts is objective, and critical thinking is subjective?

In a competition, it is only fair to assess someone's performance objectively, not subjectively. However, it is not true that the Academic Decathlon emphasizes only recalling facts. One of my daughters is in the Academic Decathlon and she has to deliver a speech. Don't we need critical thinking in preparing a persuasive speech?

Besides, what's wrong with preparing students for this competitive event throughout the year, when a school can afford to do that without sacrificing anything? The only sacrifice of students is their time, which is beneficial in the long run.

Fortunately, we have dedicated teachers who do not hesitate to use their own time for such a noble cause. Who can find something wrong in arming students with knowledge? Have we forgotten that knowledge is power? Can someone put a limit on how much knowledge one should acquire to win in a knowledge contest? Is overlearning bad?

Critics said that Academic Decathlon stresses winning over learning. In a knowledge contest, can someone win without knowledge?

It is absurd to believe that participation in Academic Decathlon can take a toll on a student's academic performance, as might be the case in sports where the emphasis is not on the intellect but on physical stamina.

In this society when academic institutions chase headlines in their achievements in sports and devote time and money, probably sacrificing academic performance of the participants, no one seems very concerned.

It is very unfortunate that there can be critics, even among veteran teachers, against devotion to Academic Decathlon, which only promotes a quest for intellectual achievement that is essential for the sustenance of a civilized society.

— Qazi N. Uddin,
Ventura

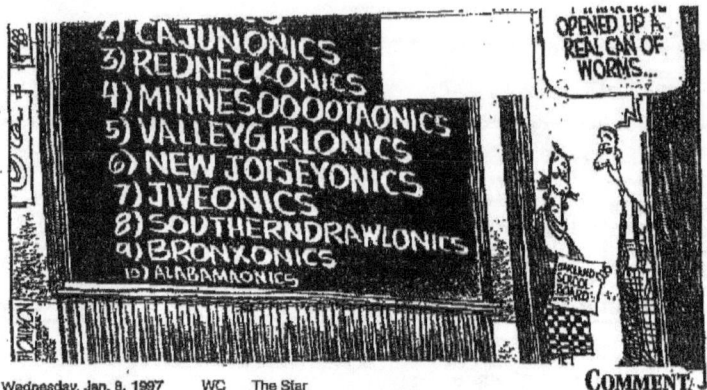

2) CAJUNONICS
3) REDNECKONICS
4) MINNESOOOOTAONICS
5) VALLEYGIRLONICS
6) NEW JOISEYONICS
7) JIVEONICS
8) SOUTHERNDRAWLONICS
9) BRONXONICS
10) ALABAMAONICS

OPENED UP A REAL CAN OF WORMS...

OAKLAND SCHOOL BOARD

Wednesday, Jan. 8, 1997   WC   The Star

COMMENT

Common ground

Re: recognizing black English:

I am totally appalled by the decision of the Oakland school board to recognize black English as a means of imparting formal education. I have been teaching business English, communication, and English as a Second Language in the United States since 1985. One of my biggest challenges was to teach my students that there is a difference between home language (dialect and slang) and business and academic language (standard). There is nothing wrong in using one's home language for day-to-day communicative purposes within one's own community, family and social environment. After all, the purpose of language is to communicate.

But the purpose of business and academic language is to seek a universal and common ground of understanding, agreement and acceptance. For example, if you write a business letter to another business using your own English, and that business fails to decipher the meaning of your message, the purpose of business or communication will not be served. Therefore, when I taught my students how to write a business letter, I told them it was not OK to write "he don't" and "I been." According to the Oakland school board's decision, I won't be allowed to do that anymore. I have to recognize those expressions as black English.

I have no problem with recognizing and respecting all languages of the world. I can claim that I am a devout learner of languages, literatures and cultures since I can handle eight languages. But I believe that we have to draw a line when it comes to business, academics, universal acceptance and understanding of a particular language.

If we continue allowing every group of people in a country to use its own way of communicating, there will be no communication at all. There will be chaos and confusion. The Oakland school board may have good intentions, but it is totally wrong in believing that this approach will help black students.

— Qazi N. Uddin,
Ventura

194

THE STAR

PINION

WEDNESDAY ◆ MARCH 26, 1997

PAGE EDITOR: DAVID M. SMITH ◆ 655-5837 ◆

Asking too much?

Re: your Feb. 23 article, "Unions ask for benefits to partners":

It is very annoying and disturbing to know that Ventura County Community College District's teachers are asking coverage for same-sex, unmarried companions. To ask for such coverage is to ask society and the government to recognize a relationship between two individuals that defies the traditional family relationship. We have been blaming the deterioration of our family values and collapse of our traditional family structures for most of our social problems. Now, imagine our teachers, who are supposed to stand in front of our young generation as role models, demanding to recognize their controversial lifestyles and give them benefits!

I have no problem with people adopting any lifestyle that pleases them. But they should do so without asking for approval and

governmental support. Especially when one chooses to be a teacher, one should be able to sacrifice his or her own desires for the greater benefit of the society. Whether one likes it or not, students have a tendency to look up to a teacher and follow his or her lifestyle. Teachers don't only teach, they touch a life and change it forever. Therefore, a teacher has a great responsibility. Teachers are supposed to be dedicated individuals. They are not supposed to pay attention to their own desires and fight for the recognition of their own lifestyles and get benefit out of it. They are supposed to sacrifice.

It is not to say that teachers should not have any personal philosophy, preferences, religion, or beliefs. But they should not use their positions as teachers to express their philosophy or give vent to their personal frustrations, if any. They should remain above their own emotions and feelings, especially when they confront any controversial issues. Otherwise, they don't belong to this noble profession. When they stand in front of our young generation, who are going to shape up this society in the near future, all teachers should leave behind their domestic life, their sexual orientation, and their personal demands. We like them to become universal human beings, not to represent any particular groups upholding any personal agenda. I don't think it is asking too much of a teacher.

— Qazi N. Uddin,
Ventura

WHERE TO WRITE

■ We welcome your letters on current events. Keep them brief, please. All letters are subject to editing. Sign full name and address and give telephone number for verification; only name and hometown will be published. Send e-mail to VCStar@aol.com. Postal address: Editor's Letters, The Ventura County Star, P.O. Box 6711, Ventura 93006. Fax: 650-2950.

Teacher's Day

On May 15, I got the biggest surprise of my life when, in the middle of teaching a class, all my students suddenly stood up and started clapping and chanting a song that ends with "Rah... Rah... Rah."

Before I could find out what it was all about, to my further astonishment, they pulled out a gift packet and presented it to me with a beautiful card. I immediately opened the card and there it was, "Teacher's Day."

Teacher's Day!

Tears rolled down. I have never heard of such a thing in my 32 years of teaching life. Students have observed my birthday occasionally if they somehow came to know about it. But a "Teacher's Day"? A day for an ordinary teacher who has never received any award for excellence in teaching. It had never happened before. When I was able to gather myself, it was explained to me that it was a Mexican tradition of honoring teachers on that particular day each year.

The purpose of this letter is not to give vent to my emotions and sentiments. I don't believe we have a day set aside as "Teacher's Day" to be observed nationally on a particular day. If not, I would like to suggest that we accept this wonderful Mexican tradition of honoring teachers by observing a "Teacher's Day" here in the United States. This day could be the last day of school during the month of June each year before the summer vacation. I would like to see readers' response to this proposal.

— **Qazi N. Uddin,**
Ventura

"I've been fired, Honey. The boss caught me reading 'Dilbert.'"

OLD GLORY

Do we need an amendment to protect the flag?

By Qazi N. Uddin

■ The Supreme Court decided that freedom of speech extends to freedom of expression, but expression of what?

When our Founding Fathers decided to use the word "speech," they were very careful. Why did they use the word "speech" if they had "expression" in mind? Because they wanted to make it clear that we have freedom to express ourselves, but we have to use language or speech. We cannot use any other means. When our cave-dweller ancestors were speechless, it was quite appropriate for them to set a fire in a house or to a piece of cloth to express anger. The gift of civilization is that we don't have to do that anymore.

Burning involves physical destruction. By speech, we cannot physically destroy anything. If my anger can take the form of expressing itself in a small fire, that small fire can get out of control and turn into a big one.

Some people believe that we have to understand freedom of speech in its wider context of freedom to protest against government. We not only protest by giving speeches or by writing in newspapers, we can also, among other things, call a strike, hold rallies and processions, and picket.

As long as the protests are nonviolent and victimless, there is nothing wrong in adopting those methods. Flag burning is one such method. Making this act illegal may result in making similar protests also illegal, and the government may turn to dictatorship. So say supporters of flag burning, who are paranoid that by outlawing flag burning, the government can take away their rights to protest. The main flaw with that argument is that while flag burning may be a nonviolent protest, it is opening the door to violence. A fire is a fire, no matter how small, and it has the potential to start a big one. Let's everyone carry a match box so we can instantly start a fire when we want to make a political statement. Why not? This is easier than sitting down with pen and paper and organizing our arguments.

I do not agree with the Supreme Court's interpretation of freedom of speech as freedom of expression, which would allow a flag to be burned. Unfortunately, whether you like it or not, some people will still go to the Constitution to support desecration of our flag. It is, therefore, necessary to amend our Constitution to outlaw flag desecration.

What is consent?

Re: Joseph Perkins' June 9 essay, "A new definition of rape," and Betsy Logan's June 20 letter, "Whose rules?":

Logan completely misunderstood Perkins' essay. Perkins is one of those intellectuals and philosophers who just does not write to "blame the victim." He was also not lamenting the loss of "golden girls" in this society. His essays demand more serious reading and interpretation than done by Logan.

What he is telling us is that it has become extremely difficult nowadays to conclude what is consent and what is not. Nowadays, women have every right to become aggressive in courtship and to become extremely provocative.

Women do not have to bear any responsibility or worry about the consequences of their actions. The burden is on the man. He must be extremely careful. Any advances by him, even under extreme provocation, may turn into a sexual or physical assault.

Logan believes, "Buying a woman a drink, paying for a woman's dinner, or room; making out with a woman..." do not constitute consent."

I understand "drink" and "dinner," but I do not understand how a "room" (hotel?) doesn't constitute consent. It is very foolish to put your hand in fire to check how hot it is and then ask the fire

to behave nicely. This is what Logan is asking for in her criticism of Perkins.

Logan claims, "Until a woman says 'yes' to... she is saying 'no,' loud and clear"

I believe that until a woman says "no", loud and clear, she is saying "yes."

There is a proverb in Sanskrit, "Mownong sammati lakshanam," which means, "Silence is the sign of consent."

I believe that giving indulgence to a man in the manner of accepting gifts, dinner and drink (not to speak of a hotel room) constitutes consent. If you go out with a man for a long time silently, the man reaches a decisive moment. Any "no" at that moment (no matter how loud it is) becomes meaningless.

So until you say "no" loud and clear to any advances by a man at the very early stages of your relationship, you are constantly sending a message that translates to "yes."

If you have any self-respect, you should not accept any favor or gifts from a man in the first place. When you lose self-respect, you cannot expect others to respect you. Respect is something one cannot command or demand; it can only be inspired.

— **Qazi N. Uddin,**
Ventura

198

YOUR LETTERS

Forgiveness in order

Suppose your teen-age daughter went abroad to study for a semester under a government-sponsored, foreign-student exchange program and you found out she would have to spend the rest of her life in a foreign prison. How would you feel?

Also, if you found out that a teen-age foreign student living with you as a family member unintentionally inflicted fatal injury to your 8-month-old son, how would you feel? A cultured society must answer all such questions before bragging about its criminal justice system and imposing harsh punishment on anyone.

The pain and suffering of parents at the loss of their loved offspring cannot be overemphasized. I have no intention of diminishing the torment and anguish that the parents of the 8-month-old boy are experiencing. Also, I have no intention of blaming the victims and sympathizing with the criminal. But in such an unusual case, how can the pain and suffering of both the parents be redeemed? Where can we put the blame squarely? Whom do we punish?

Louise Woodward has no criminal record. She is not a serial killer, a rapist, a child abuser or a molester. She is not a monster, as the mother of the 8-month-old boy said. It happened on the spur of the moment. No one knows what came upon her in that perilous moment. Such a bizarre case well deserves psychiatric research and evaluation. It does not come under a typical crime-and-punishment case.

Punishing Woodward for her involvement in this tragic mishap is not going to make anyone breathe a sigh of relief. Instead, it will add more misery to the feelings of all cultured and sensible human beings. This is why many people along the both shores of the Atlantic Ocean are crying for a retrial and acquittal of Woodward.

I think the best solution to this problem is for Woodward to admit her guilt and apply for mercy, and the best comfort for the victim parents is to forgive Woodward.

— Qazi N. Uddin,
Ventura

would

ow,
aring
a
iy
hook,

ess,

thing,
. Let's

— just
or,

f

ted of
w

is

d the
r and

who

PINION

EDITOR: DAVID M. SMITH ◆ 655-5837 ◆   SUNDAY ◆ DEC. 28, 1997

LETTERS

Respect for workers

Re: your Dec. 19 article, "4 die as gun battle rages at Caltrans' yard":

It appears that killing co-workers, supervisors or employers by a disgruntled employee has become commonplace. Nowadays going to work has become just like going to a war. No one knows whether he or she will be able to return home safe and sound. Everyone seems to be very worried about it, but nothing has been done other than talking about strengthening security in workplaces.

No one realizes that strengthening security is not the solution to this problem. If we really want to stop or reduce such tragic incidents, we have to go to the root of the problem. The root of the problem lies in the culture of American workplaces, which needs to be changed. The atmosphere that prevails in our workplaces is highly charged with productivity, which diminishes the existence of human beings. In the eyes of employers, workers do not exist if they are not productive.

I am not advocating making concessions for unproductive workers. But I believe most employers do not consider their employees as human beings; they consider them as tools for making profit. Using the plea of staying in business, American business owners justify putting tremendous pressure on their workers to produce more and more. They also enjoy having enough freedom in treating their employees in any form or manner they wish.

The days of slavery have gone but a new kind of slavery has emerged, which has tarnished the sense of decency and decorum, and shattered a feeling of security and stability. Sometimes those feelings push a human being to the edge. Unless our employers make an effort to honor and respect human beings as human beings, not tools of making profit, they will create many disgruntled workers and workplace massacres will increase.

I would urge everyone who manages, supervises or owns businesses to develop respect for their workers. This is the time of the year when we should learn lessons from the past mistakes and look forward to developing a harmonious relationship between the employees and the employers.

— Qazi N. Uddin,
Ventura

please. All letters are subject to editing. Sign full name and address and give telephone number for verification; only name and hometown will be published. Send e-mail to letters@staronline. com. Postal address: Editor's Letters, The Ventura County Star, P.O. Box 6711, Ventura 93006.

YOUR LETTERS

PRESIDENT CLINTON

Since antiquity, meanings of certain words have been changing and acquiring new connotations. Some words have been able to retain their original meanings. "Character" is one of them. I thought I knew what the meaning of the word was. Its meaning has become so universal and fixed that even time has not been able to desecrate it, until recently when British Prime Minister Tony Blair came up with a new definition of character.

In his attempt to protect Bill Clinton against the accusations of allegedly lying and cheating to satisfy his libido, Blair has come up with this definition of character: Character is about public performance, not about private behavior.

If we accept this new definition, we have to get rid of our age-old conception of character. When I was in school in the early 1950s, my teachers told me, "When wealth is lost, nothing is lost; when health is lost, something is lost; but when character is lost, everything is lost." I grew up with the belief that the whole self of an individual manifests itself in his or her character. That is why we call a person an individual, an entity that cannot be divided. The character of a person molds his or her personality and shapes up his or her philosophy of life.

Blair wants us to believe that an individual may develop two entirely hostile entities simultaneously. A person can lie, cheat, steal and engage in adultery privately, and yet can perform well his or her job-related responsibility publicly, even though those responsibilities may require honesty and integrity.

I am totally confused. It is to claim that privately a person can be a liar, a thief and a cheater, but publicly the same person can be honest and sincere. Say, for example, psychologists believe that it is quite possible. But what happens when one's private life becomes public? Besides, to say that private behavior has no bearing on public performance is to endorse stealing, lying and cheating, without the knowledge of the public. Politicians may need this new definition of character, but we, the people, do not.

— Qazi N. Uddin,
Ventura

THE PURPOSE OF HIGHER EDUC[

Learners go to school these days to buy a skill

By Qazi N. Uddin

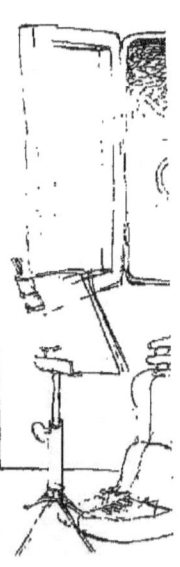

In the late 1950s, after graduating from high school, when I was getting ready for college, my father told me to go to college, not to find a job, but to be educated. Therefore, I was in college with the sole intention of getting some knowledge. I was there to know myself, know the world, know the history of civilizations and develop my mind, not to build a career. It was not very surprising for me, therefore, to realize one day that I had really learned something that had changed my thinking process forever. I learned that "education" is one thing and "training" is another.

I believe that the word "education" had a different connotation 50 years ago in the United States and around the world. The connotation of that term has drastically changed in this country over half a century. Half a century ago, "education" meant receiving knowledge to become a cultured and sophisticated human being. Educators were considered dedicated individuals who not only taught a skill but also shaped minds and brought refinement to the crude state of a human mind. An educated person was considered a refined individual.

Nowadays, learners go to schools to buy a skill and to do a job, not to develop any qualities that make one a decent human being. Educational institutions have turned into shopping centers. Teachers have become salespeople and students customers. Customers do not have to develop any respect for salespeople. Education has become a buying and selling business. Everyone forgot that "education" cannot be bought or sold. Money cannot buy "education." Money can only provide some "training." Therefore, the words "education" and "training" have become synonymous. If we can change our attitude toward education, we can educate our next generation in the true sense of the term.

— *Qazi N. Uddin is the director of Golden State College in Oxnard.*

YOUR LETTERS

Both sides must bridge cultural gap

When I arrived in the United States in 1979, I called the telephone company to get a phone. The lady who took my call gave the impression it was impossible to communicate with me. "I don't understand what you are talking about," she said. "Speak English." So I uttered every single word: "I am speaking English with an accent that you are not familiar with," I said. "You are also speaking English with an accent that I am not familiar with. The reason I understand you is I need to. The reason you don't understand me is you don't have to. The burden is on me to make you understand, but not on you to try to understand me."

I expected her to hang up on me, but she apologized and I was able to get my telephone.

Guest column

Qazi N. **Uddin**

Many Americans consider America's advancement as an indication of superiority of this nation's culture. So, when someone from another culture comes here, Americans often assume that person must be coming from an inferior culture. This belief manifests itself in a superiority complex.

Communicating across cultures becomes very difficult when we develop such a complex. Many suffer from such a complex when they encounter the culture of an underdeveloped country and find themselves unable to communicate.

Some wonder why we have to be culturally sensitive? People will come here anyway. Let them assimilate to this culture if they really want to improve their lives. The burden is on them.

Those who think this way have preconceived notions. They believe people of other cultures have bad habits. Becoming sensitive is making some accommodation for those habits.

Certain habits are universally considered bad. No one would argue about the importance of being punctual, for instance. If I brought to the United States the bad habit of arriving late for work, it wouldn't be fair to call my employer insensitive to my culture if he reprimanded me.

We are not asking for the endorsement of bad habits. We would like to suggest that, when someone from one culture moves into another, he or she should ask "Am I bringing bad habits of my culture to this one?"

It should be the newcomer's responsibility to develop respect for the host culture.

The host culture cannot expect only imitations of itself from the guest culture. Those of the host culture who demand assimilation from the guest believe the host is superior to the guest. Cultural sensitivity reveals itself when one asks such questions to oneself: "Is there anything in my culture by which I can hurt the feelings of someone from another culture?"

Communication across cultures will be possible if both sides start asking such questions.

Qazi N. Uddin, Ph.D., is director of education at Golden State College in Oxnard. The views expressed are those of the author and not necessarily those of any church or organization. This weekly guest opinion column is open to contributors of all faiths. For guidelines, write to Star Hunter, the Star, P.O. Box 6711, Ventura, CA 93006.

YOUTH VIOLENCE

$$.22 \div 33 \times 30.06 = \frac{(AK-47, M-16 \div 45)}{006 \times 44 - Caliber}$$

$$(38 \div 44 \ MAGNUM) = \frac{}{.22}$$

Parents hold the key

Did Jonesboro, Ark., produce such a bizarre incident that it should be attributed to demonic possession of those 11- and 13-year-old boys? If we could believe that and perform exorcism on those kids, we could breathe a sigh of relief. Unfortunately, we cannot conveniently do that anymore. We have had so many incidents of violent behavior in kids that if we wanted to attribute such violence to demonic possession, we would have to perform exorcisms on lots of our kids.

I, therefore, would urge everyone to refrain from using the word "bizarre" when referring to violence by kids. Instead, we should accept this as a very rude reminder of our total failure as parents to raise our kids. Isn't it absurd to believe that we parents are not responsible for the behavior of our children? If we don't blame the parents, we have to blame Satan or another kid on the block or in school (peer pressure?). The other kid's parents are going to blame whom? Satan again?

Can we take some comfort believing that this is not unique to the United States, that these things happen all over the world? Not really. I was born and raised in a Third-World country and lived there for 34 years. Now I have lived here for 20 years. During all those years, not a single incident of students killing students or teachers has occurred in educational institutions in my native country. I can also guarantee that this is not going to happen in a million years in that country.

How can I be so sure? Because I know the culture of that country. In a country where parents can happily sacrifice their lives for the sake of their children, children do not get a chance to get angry and consequently violent. When we have examples, it is a good idea to look at those to solve our problems.

— Qazi N. Uddin,
Ventura

⊞ ᵀᴴᴱSTAR

PINION

PAGE EDITOR: DAVID M. SMITH ◆ 655-5837 ◆   MONDAY ◆ JUNE 1, 1998

YOUR LETTERS

Set an example

Re: John Sherffius' May 13 Opinion page cartoon:

It is too naive to expect India to remain fixed in time and space, nurturing Gandhi's philosophy of nonviolence forever. It is also naive to believe that the British just wanted to hand over independence to Gandhi as a gesture of deep respect and regard for Gandhi's philosophy of nonviolence. If Gandhi's contemporary detractors had not started freedom fighting (no matter how hard the movie "Gandhi" tries to depict him as the solo achiever of Indian independence through nonviolence), I doubt very much whether the British rule of India would have come to an end precisely at that moment.

Those who have studied Indian history know very well that India fought many wars against many aggressors, including the British. Amazingly, most westerners think of India as Gandhi's India, as if the people of India have no philosophical difference with Gandhi. Why were the Indian people rejoicing on their achievement in emerging as a nuclear power? Why did not the Indian people demonstrate against their government for devising such a violent weapon of mass destruction, if they were so totally immersed in Gandhi's philosophy of nonviolence?

The fact is India took time but is now coming along to follow the trend. It is a very sad reality, and it is an unavoidable outcome of the dangerous trend that the nuclear arms race by the superpowers has created. By upholding and promoting an agenda that violent force is necessary to maintain supremacy over other nations, by believing that violent force is necessary to maintain peace around the world, we cannot expect other nations to remain nonviolent.

Therefore, to expect India to just stay with Gandhi's philosophy is very unrealistic. When you draw a picture of Gandhi with tears rolling down his eyes, and of mushrooms in his eyeglasses to signify atomic blasts, do not expect Indians to feel guilty. Instead, it is the superpowers possessing nuclear weapons that should feel guilty for seeing India, Pakistan and other nations craving nuclear weapons.

If the United Nations Security Council members want other nations to stop producing nuclear weapons, they should start by scrapping all of their nuclear weapons first.

— Qazi M. Uddin,
Ventura

Nation humiliated

It is better to humiliate one person than to humiliate the entire nation.

When the president of a country confesses to wrongdoing and sin, it is absolutely meaningless to question the legality and intent of the investigation and detailed report of his inappropriate behavior. I expected President Clinton and his staff to remain quiet and submissive, and let the House of Representatives decide the president's fate. Instead, Vice President Al Gore came to the president's rescue by addressing the nation that the purpose of the Starr report was to humiliate the president.

I expected the entire nation to mourn, the national flag to be lowered to half-staff, prayers to be said in churches, synagogues, temples and mosques that we would have the courage to endure this insult on our prestige as a civilized nation. I also expected the observance of one minute of silence in educational institutions and workplaces to cope with our anguish and frustration.

On the contrary, some people, including our president, want the whole thing to disappear like magic and let the nation unite behind the president so he can remain in his office and do a so-called good job! I expected all to distance themselves from the president's behavior, every one to scream that this president does not represent America's character. Alas! His supporters do not realize that by keeping him as president they will humiliate the entire nation. I believe that it is better to humiliate one person than to humiliate the entire nation.

— Qazi N. Uddin,
Ventura

Religion letter

The significance of a confession

If anyone ponders a minute over the significance of the word "confession," it will be evident that this word suggests a total submission of one's self.

Therefore, confession cannot stand side by side with defense. One either defends himself or herself or totally submits. There is nothing that can come between those two elements. We either try to defend our action, try to justify it, find an excuse for engaging in an inappropriate behavior, or confess that we are wrong. There is absolutely no defense, no justification, no argument over the definition of inappropriate behavior.

That is why all religions made provisions for human beings to make confessions. There is no denying the fact that human beings are vulnerable to all kinds of temptations. It is very easy to succumb to one of those, but then religions come to the rescue by giving us an opportunity to face ourselves, to repent. Some religions even suggest elaborate rituals to purify one's self, so one can get rid of his or her past and seek a new meaning of life.

Therefore, confession must come out of extreme repentance, extreme desire to suffer the consequences and to be re-born. Instead, if we find that some one is trying to defend his or her action, that individual's confession becomes meaningless.

According to Christian theology, confession signifies acknowledgement of sin to God in order to obtain absolution. This can be done privately in the presence of a priest or in public before the congregation. But the purpose remains the same, which is absolution.

The legal implication of confession is not exactly the same as it is implied in religion. In law, any acknowledgement of guilt made in court becomes judicial if such acknowledgement is not procured by force. Such legal confession does not necessarily imply that an individual is going to reform. Instead, it might imply that an individual accused of a crime is entering in to a plea bargain to qualify for immunity from harsh punishment. So there is a big difference.

Therefore, when an individual publicly confesses of wrongdoing or sin, it is a good idea to find out whether such confession is religious or legal. If a confession is religious, obviously the individual will not try to defend himself or herself. In such a case the individual may be forgiven, and given a chance for a new beginning. On the other hand, if the intent of confession is legal or event political, the question of forgiveness does not arise because the individual is not promising to change or begin a new life. The individual is only using the word confession to run away from his or her crime and get immunity from punishment.

— Qazi N. Uddin
Ventura

— We welcome your letters on religion issues. Please keep them brief. All letters are subject to editing. Sign full name and address and include telephone number so we can verify your letter; only name and hometown will be published. Send letters to Marty Bonvechio at The Star, P.O. Box 6711, Ventura, 93006; Fax 650-2950.

PINION

Not a typical character

Re: your Oct. 15 article, "Strohmeyer gets life, gives reasons":

Now that we have put Jeremy Strohmeyer, molester and murderer of 7-year-old Sherrice Iverson, behind bars without the possibility of parole, should we rest in peace believing that a monster has been eliminated from society? Not quite so. The question still torments many minds whether David Cash, a friend of Strohmeyer, could have saved the precious life of an innocent girl. If we don't find an answer to this question, our pain and suffering won't fade away soon.

The question that looms large on the horizon is whether we have reached a threshold of our civilization when we don't have to care for lives of others and can passively be the spectator of heinous crimes being committed in front of our eyes. Has this civilization brought us to this point when an individual's right to remain passive becomes more valuable than another human being's right to live?

Why then do some people jump into the ocean to save a life? Why do some people enter burning homes or cars, risking their own lives to save others? Fortunately, Cash is not a typical character of this society. His attitude and his philosophy of life, as revealed through his recent interviews, are very bizarre and scary. This type of character needs psychiatric evaluation and treatment. He is a threat to the values and morals this civilization has been able to achieve through trials and errors of many centuries.

— Qazi N. Uddin,
Ventura

PRESIDENT CLINTON

Loyalty sacrificed

The acquittal of President Clinton once again proved beyond the shadow of a doubt that it is impossible for politicians to sacrifice their political future to uphold morality, honesty, decency, decorum and strength of character.

No matter how hard the Senate members who voted for acquittal try to convince us that politics did not play a role in their decision making, it becomes absolutely absurd for us to believe such claims on the face of not having a single Democrat voting for conviction, and even some Republicans' defections (John Chafee, Susan Collins, Jim Jeffords, Olympia Snowe and Arlen Specter, who acquitted Clinton on both counts).

But it is one thing to strictly adhere to one's party interest, sacrificing personal conscience, and another to break ranks. I thought one can only sacrifice a party's interest for a noble cause, not for personal political interest. I understand those Democrats who sacrificed the cause of morality for the cause of party politics, but I have only condemnation and hatred for those Republicans mentioned above who decided to sacrifice their loyalty to the party for fear of being unpopular by convicting a popular president.

They sacrificed both loyalty to the party and adherence to moral values. They measurably failed to show strength of character and utterly succumbed to their call for very personal political interest.

— **Qazi N. Uddin,**
Ventura

Negative attitude is key to education's problems

By Qazi N. Uddin

Since Gray Davis took office as governor, the issue of education reform has once again been moved to the front page of the newspapers. Apparently this move is very encouraging. However, one can not but notice the enthusiasm on the part of the politicians to point fingers at the teachers for all of our educational problems. Along with Davis, who wants to make teachers accountable for student test scores, Assemblyman Tom McClintock, R-Simi Valley, has recently joined the bandwagon of teacher bashing by urging parents to look for good teachers and reward them.

Now, what is a good teacher? I was a student for a long 22 years in two different countries and never felt like blaming a teacher for my poor performance! A student may not like a teacher's style, manner, attitude and methods of presentation, but that does not necessarily mean that the teacher does not have the academic qualifications and knowledge of the subject matter. I do not believe that anyone can face a group of at least 20 to 30 or more students every day without the knowledge of the topic and without imparting any information whatsoever. The learners will not accept such a teacher for an indefinite period.

So, what we do have here are teachers with different styles, personalities, and methods of presentation. It is absurd to expect all teachers (human beings, not robots!) to come up with an identical method and style of presentation. Some teachers might have more ability to organize their thoughts and to present information than others.

I do not believe that anyone can face a group of at least 20 to 30 or more students every day without the knowledge of the topic and without imparting any information whatsoever.

I believe that to ask teachers to improve their performances is to relieve the students of their responsibility for learning. This move is very detrimental to the success of any educational systems in any social conditions. Once we start blaming teachers for students' poor performance, students will not try to change their attitudes toward learning. Some students will find an excuse to attribute their failures to the inability of the teachers to teach them. This is definitely a negative attitude.

I strongly believe that any honest and sincere attempt to reform education must start with teaching students to take their job of learning very seriously. The society and the parents must combine their efforts to teach students to develop respect for their educational institutions and teachers. If they do not really like a particular teacher it is their job to challenge that teacher. This means challenging a teacher to come up with strategies to teach a very demanding and aggressive learner. When the learners are active, the teacher can not remain passive. When a student demonstrates a positive attitude, the student sees everything positively. A serious student with a positive attitude can learn from anyone.

Unfortunately our political leaders are doing a great disservice to the process of teaching and learning by not emphasizing the fact that the negative attitude of the learners, lack of respect for education, and the indifference on the part of the society and parents are the main causes of deterioration of our educational standards.

— Qazi N. Uddin is a resident of Ventura.

VIOLENCE AT SCHOOL

Teachers' hands tied

On April 13, 1998, I wrote a letter to the editor to express my feelings over the tragedy of Jonesboro's school shootings. Is it a coincidence that after a year I have to write again to express my anguish over the shootings at Columbine High School?

I could not but write, being an educator and being active in changing lives of many students who have been shortchanged by our society and educational institutions.

In my previous letter, I held the parents responsible for their inability to positively influence the lives of their children. Although I strictly adhere to my conviction that it is the parents who can diffuse any frustration or anger that a young mind can build up due to the lack of childhood parental care and affection, I strongly believe that teachers can have a very positive and enduring effect on their students.

While we, the teachers, could alleviate some of the torments of a disturbed mind that resulted from the absence of parental guidance, we are being deprived by the society of our sacred duty of shaping a life to achieve positive results.

We have been advised by the school administration (under pressure from the society) not to bring any ethics, morality, religion and prayer to school.

Instead, we have been told to encourage deviance among our young learners, allowing them to do whatever pleases them to protect their freedom of expression. Nowadays, a school may be sued by parents or students if it tries to teach some values other than the subject matter.

Therefore, in the absence of both parents' and teachers' guidance, if some tormented, abused and neglected teens find themselves in a vacuum, deviate from the norm, see the meaninglessness of their existence and finally become destructive, how can we not understand it?

— Qazi N. Uddin,
Ventura

211

OPINION

THE EDITOR: DAVID M. SMITH ✦ 655-5837 ✦ SUNDAY ✦ JULY 18, 1999

Your Letters

Motives questioned

Re: your July 14 article, "Gallegly terms INS effort 'patriotic';

It is very annoying that Elton Gallegly should take advantage of the surrender of the railroad killer, Rafael Resendez-Ramirez, to give vent to his anti-illegal immigration sentiments. He did not waste a moment to find a correlation between illegal Mexican immigrants and criminals. He wishfully decided to deny a killer is a killer and that it has nothing to do with immigration status.

Gallegly became very angry with the Immigration and Naturalization Service for having let Rafael Resendez-Ramirez slip through its

fingers on June 2, 1999, when he was picked up by Border Patrol agents. Gallegly wants the INS to make sure everyone picked up for illegal entry is not a criminal. At the same time, he wants the INS to crack down on illegal immigrants with criminal backgrounds.

While it looks like a very noble effort, one cannot help but notice the emphasis on illegal immigrants. Why not crack down on all people with criminal backgrounds? It is dangerous to play political games when killers are at large, whether legal or illegal. What Border Patrol agents did was routine, picking up someone at the border and sending him back. The INS has a very well-defined and specific job to do. The

INS does background checking on people who apply for legal status. It can try to stop people from entering illegally and catch and deport people who are staying illegally.

Please do not take advantage of such isolated incidents and blame the INS, as if they do it on regular basis, and ask everyone including schools, colleges and employers to crack down on illegal immigrants, believing they are all killers like Rafael. Gallegly should stop this practice, which is clearly aimed at gaining political advantage, not at solving the real issues involving illegal immigration or crime.

— **Qazi N. Uddin,**
Ventura

212

COMMENTARY

Prenatal execution

Re: your Aug. 8 article, "Abortions get credit for lower crime rate":

This is too much! I have seen various kinds of research by university professors that cater to the needs of all sorts of philosophies, but never have I encountered such a bizarre study in my life. Your article mentions that well respected researchers at prestigious universities found out that legalizing abortion eliminated many "would-be" criminals, which explains the decline of crime in the United States in 1990s compared to 1970s.

The point is some people never got a chance to be born to become criminals. They received capital punishment before they could commit a crime! What happened to the notion in our criminal justice system that one is innocent until proven guilty? The assumption is that children born to poverty-stricken people with drug and criminal backgrounds are most likely to become criminals. According to this logic, it is good that they are allowed to abort their babies. If we take this study seriously, we have to ask all poor people to abort their babies to help eliminate potential criminals. At the same time, we have to ask all rich people not to abort their babies because their babies will receive all the love and affection they need, and will grow up as decent human beings.

To find a correlation between legalization of abortion and decline in crime, we have to believe in two things. First, that the majority of the poor people necessarily abort their babies. Second, that the majority of the babies born to poor parents engage in criminal activity. If we believe this to be true, why don't we eliminate poverty or try to narrow the gap between the rich and the poor? Why don't we make sure that babies born to poor parents get proper care and affection to grow up as decent human beings? One could just as easily conducted a study proving a relationship between an increase in the amount of Diet Coke consumed and the reduction of crime. Merely because two events occur concurrently, it does not necessarily follow that there is a cause-effect relationship.

Do we believe that killing the criminals before they get a chance to be born is a civilized approach to our problem? Besides, how can you be so sure that babies of poor and criminals are going to be criminals? This assumes that some people are just born evil, and further assumes that there is a correlation between poverty and ill will. Is a Third World country, riddled with poverty, one in which no one should reproduce? Have we not seen many people coming out of negative environments becoming successful? And likewise, have we not seen the children of rich and famous parents turn out to be killers?

If we get very excited about this study, while we may abort many aspiring criminals, we might end up aborting many human beings who might turn out to be productive members of the society, such as doctors, teachers, philosophers and writers.

— Qazi N. Uddin,
Ventura

We have freedom of religion, not freedom from religion

By Qazi N. Uddin

It is said that the first wave of immigrants arrived in the United States to escape religious persecution in their native land. That is why the Founding Fathers provided religious freedom in the Constitution as such: "Congress shall make no law respecting an establishment of religion, or prohibiting the free exercise thereof," which, of course, means freedom to observe someone's religious practices without any constraint, obstacle or intimidation.

Keeping that purpose in mind, the separation of church and state was heralded by our Congress. The idea was to prevent any domination of a particular religion in our public life.

No one would say that the concept of freedom of religion can be interpreted as freedom from religion. However, it appears that those who do not like religion want to take advantage of this constitutional provision of freedom of religion as freedom from religion.

In their effort to eliminate the observance of religious rites and rituals from society, such as observance of a moment of silence to say a prayer, they argue that religion should be a private matter and should not be brought to any public event.

Is this the free exercise of religion the authors of our Constitution envisioned when they wanted to guarantee the freedom of all religions in the United States? Are there not some elements of intimidation inherent in forcing all people to keep their religious beliefs at their homes?

What is the total picture of a life if it is only private? What is our life if we are afraid of making our private devotional feelings and beliefs public?

Human existence in this universe cannot be only private. We must have a social life. Our social existence depends on our interaction with other members of the society. Civilized and modern governments all over the world provide means of such interaction through government-sponsored and subsidized infrastructures known as public educational institutions and community centers.

To see that such infrastructures are not dominated by a single group of people with one religious belief is the responsibility of the government. But to say that one cannot use those infrastructures for religious purposes is to prohibit people from the free exercise of their religion.

Therefore, those who believe that organized prayer before any public events is unconstitutional are wrong. Those who want to protect religious freedom by denying people the ability to express their religious feelings before school athletic events, for example, are unwittingly supporting the cause of those who want freedom from religion.

A government cannot be the government of a section of people who want to eliminate religion from people's lives.

I strongly believe that freedom of religion becomes meaningful when we let people perform all religious rites and rituals, including prayer, not only privately but also publicly.

Of course, freedom should come with a price tag, which is tolerance. We have to get ready to tolerate one another's religion in public places. Everyone should be invited to pray in accordance with his or her faith in a public ceremony, such as a ground-breaking of a public building, an athletic event or a graduation ceremony.

In a free society, no one should be asked to keep his or her religion at his or her home. All religions of this universe have provided some wonderful concepts for the upliftment of the body and the mind. Prayer is one of them.

Every citizen of the country must have the right to devote and concentrate (say prayer) when he or she deems it appropriate, whether publicly or privately.

Ironically we allow many objectionable, controversial and even widely recognized deviant human behaviors to organize and to exhibit themselves publicly (in the name of freedom of expression), and when it comes to religion, we need privacy. Why?

What is wrong with expressing publicly some sacred and sublime feelings of human cultures that are manifested through all religions over the span of the history and helped build our civilization?

— *Qazi N. Uddin lives in Ventura.*

PRAYER IN PUBLIC SCHOOLS

Is Halloween more than fun and games?

Festivities hide dark side of celebration

By Qazi N. Uddin

Prehistoric cave-dwellers used to cut holes with painted stones in the skulls of tribe members who showed abnormal behavior, believing this would allow their demons to escape. They also hung scary faces and objects at the entrance to their cave to scare away demons and wild animals.

Our civilization has progressed tremendously since then, yet it appears that some societies are unable to shake those primitive traditions and beliefs.

While one could expect such primitive traditions to continue in some undeveloped cultures, amazingly, in a highly developed culture like the United States, it has survived in the observance of Halloween.

If it is only for fun, it is easier to accept this prehistoric tradition as harmless. The big problem in desiring to be something other than what we really are is its effect on our personality. If we wear funny-looking attire, we have to act funny. If we dress like a demon, we have to act like a demon. This desire to act out can be dangerous.

However, people like Halloween. Schools, businesses and offices are decorated with spooky, ghoulish objects and figures. Students and workers are urged to put on costumes befitting the occasion. Horror movies are televised. Movie theaters run scary movies, and most houses are decorated with skeletons and other ghostly apparitions along with a huge pumpkin.

My first reaction to Halloween was critical. I thought that it was a very shallow way to have fun. I then wondered if there are similar festivities in my culture. The comparison not only confirmed my belief that this is a very shallow way to have fun, but it also gave me more reason to despise Halloween.

Indian society is based on the caste system, which segregates people into four different classes, the lowest being the untouchable. Untouchables are destined to do odd jobs such as cleaning lavatories. They live on the outskirts of a city in dilapidated huts generation after generation and raise swine. They have their own holders and their own culture. One of their holidays exactly resembles Halloween. They dress up peculiarly, drink, dance, kill swine and have fun. People belonging to higher classes are not supposed to engage in those kinds of activities.

While I do not support stratification of human beings on the basis of religious beliefs and would like to fight for the emancipation of these wretched untouchables, I cannot convince myself to adopt their lifestyle and culture. To help them does not mean to become one of them.

Enlightened and cultured people do not find enjoyment and entertainment in such things as wearing funny-looking dresses. Cultured people cannot even think of expressing such behavior. I do not know of any other country where such a thing as Halloween is observed with such enthusiasm and excitement.

I have talked to many Americans who believe that Halloween is obnoxious. In fact, I have not seen too many intellectuals dressing up for Halloween. The problem with the United States is that the intellectuals do not control the culture of the country. Intellectuals do not always like the popular culture, but cannot control it.

It is difficult to accept a culture when we decide that this is a culture of the uncultured. Wearing strange outfits may be fun for children, but not for adults. The problem that can go with being childish is developing destructive behavior.

The destructive child always tries to find an outlet to exhibit his or her abnormal behavior. In a normal situation, it is difficult to give vent to one's harmful childish behavior. So, the child has to wait until Halloween when he or she can go to burn a house in the neighborhood, rob an individual, vandalize a neighbor's car.

Considering all the negative aspects that are associated with Halloween, I never felt motivated to participate. I can see the importance of having fun in life, but adults and children should not see the same source to have fun. People need to grow up and become mature and decide what kind of fun is appropriate and what is not.

— *Qazi N. Uddin lives in Waukau.*

OUNTY GOVERNMENT CRISIS

Staff photo by Chuck Kirman

HAPPIER TIMES: David Baker, right, was smiling as he left the Board of Supervisors meeting Oct. 12, with Mike Saliba, president of the Taxpayers Association. Three days after starting his job, though, Baker resigned.

CEO needed

This is not only unfortunate, but also a very embarrassing, humiliating and insulting situation for Ventura County that its newly appointed chief administrative officer, David L. Baker, resigned within three days of assuming the responsibility of his office, alleging that the Board of Supervisors did not disclose the challenges that he will have to confront, not in the unforeseeable future, but immediately!

If the allegations are true, the Ventura County taxpayers should be very concerned about them, and ask the Board of Supervisors to show cause as to why disciplinary actions should not be taken against them for doing such a sloppy job.

It is absurd for us to believe that our supervisors are so foolish and selfish to contemplate that they would be able to save the county from imminent danger by hiring a new CAO, not a chief executive officer.

Normally, an efficient and talented CEO can save an organization from its financial turmoil because of his or her executive power. It is impossible to bypass the authority of an executive office.

On the contrary, it is very easy to bypass an administrative officer who merely administers decisions made by the board. Department heads often ignore the CAO and get direct approval from the board members to fulfill their self-interest, instead of the interest of their organization. This is perhaps what was happening in Ventura County.

It would only be wise and prudent for the board to look for a CEO and place the real problem in front of the candidates selected for interviews and find out who would be willing to accept the challenges. Instead, the supervisors daydreamed that their problems would magically disappear, if they could hide them and dump them on the shoulders of an unsuspecting CAO and make him a scapegoat. However, it did not work.

Baker was smart enough to smell a rat and escape before contracting the plague.

— **Qazi N. Uddin,**
Ventura

216

COMMENTARY

Heroes deserve more

Re: your Jan. 14 article, "Heroes just can't stand by":

I felt a deep sense of satisfaction and pride as a human being after reading about the heroic act of Brian Wiggins, who rescued two children and their mother from the frigid water of Channel Islands Harbor in the dead of night.

Some human beings feel a strong urge to endanger or sacrifice their lives for the sake of saving others. We have seen firefighters entering burning homes, motorists approaching cars in flames and bystanders jumping into oceans, rivers or lakes to save others.

Because of the presence of such people among us, life becomes meaningful and we feel proud of ourselves.

However, we also have such human beings as David Cash, who decided to wait outside a restroom calmly so his friend Jeremy Strohmeyer could molest and murder 7-year-old Sherrice Iverson.

While we feel proud of our heroes and express our anguish over people like Cash, the real issue here should be how we as a society react to such incidents both of heroism and heinous crime.

Apart from a picture and story about him in the newspaper and some phone calls mentioning his act as "awesome" and "wonderful," it is likely that nothing more will be done to honor, recognize or show respect to Wiggins. Soon this act of heroism will fade into oblivion.

On the other hand, Cash got national publicity for his stubborn and remorseless attitude and behavior, on the plea of proving loyalty to a friend and protecting the right to remain silent. Strangely enough, many people came forward offering sympathy toward Cash's situation.

I believe that all acts of heroism deserve recognition by society, not only locally, but also nationally. Local administration ought to arrange a civic reception in honor of Wiggins. For national recognition, he should be interviewed by national TV and radio talk-show hosts and national newspapers. If we do not glorify our heroes, but instead become overly concerned with protecting the rights of criminals, we will not feel any more pride for being a member of the human species in the near future.

— Qazi N. Uddin,
Ventura

Tuesday, May 9, 2000   WC   The Star

Important objective

It appears from letters to the editor that some people are not happy about too many so-called nosy questions that the Census Bureau is asking. They believe that the Constitution allows the bureau to count only the number of people living in each home.

If we take the Constitution literally, how are we going to count our homeless people? As you can see, no government can remain satisfied by knowing how many people live in a country. What purpose is it going to serve by knowing only the number? The government must know the category of people to devise plans and programs to fairly and effectively distribute its resources and services.

Our society is not classless, nor is it colorblind, free from poverty, illiteracy, prejudice and discrimination. Therefore, it will not be fair to allocate resources and design programs only on the basis of the number of people.

Resources must be allocated according to needs, not numbers. The government must identify the different categories of people, such as how many are poor, rich, illiterate, jobless and homeless, etc.

It is the job of the Census Bureau to gather such information at the time of counting heads. It is only by asking some unpleasant questions that the bureau can achieve its objectives.

— Qazi N. Uddin,
Ventura

Thursday, June 22, 2000   WC   The Star

Disturbing situation

Re: your June 5 article, "U.S. Russia nod to missile threats":

It is very disturbing that President Clinton, who once opposed President Reagan's proposal for a spacebased missile defense program, is now trying to persuade Russian President Putin to support his own version of missile defense system. Does Clinton want us to believe that there is a difference between Reagan's space based system and his "limited missile shield"?

I believe that any attempt of protecting a country's air space from an oncoming missile is utterly futile. It can only create a false sense of security. First of all, mistakes can be made and the system might receive false alarm, misfire, or simply falter. Secondly, it is absurd to believe that only a few rich countries will be able to come up with the technology of missile shield and keep it a secret, without the possibility of the invention of a counter devise to frustrate the shield.

In this age of global information revolution if a country or a group of countries want to preserve their absolute supremacy over the rest of the world, they are living in a fool's paradise. Poor countries sooner or later will come up with the same technology. For example, India and Pakistan now possess the capability of launching nuclear missiles.

If we believe that we can protect ourselves by erecting an umbrella over our heads, we are wrong. This will only escalate the arms race. The only way to protect us and the human race from the perils of nuclear threats is to work together by agreeing to reduce plutonium stockpiles, not to build a shield against missiles coming from North Korea, Iran, India, or Pakistan.

— Qazi N. Uddin,
Venisera

Testing our democracy

Vision of true democracy has been shattered

By Qazi N. Uddin

I was born and raised in Bangladesh, a Third World country mostly known to the western world for its poverty, illiteracy, epidemics, natural calamities and political disasters. I lived there for 34 years before I thought "enough is enough" and decided to move to the United States in 1979. I lived through many communal riots, epidemics, famines, furious cyclones and finally a civil war that wiped out one fifth of its population, including one of my own brothers.

I presided over two polling places during two national elections in my country. According to the system of Bangladesh, presiding officers of polling places are selected with the approval of contesting parties, to ensure that officials involved in supervising polling places are not biased or prejudiced against any candidates. Even though I was chosen twice (earning approval of the parties concerned) because of my reputation as an educator not as

When I became an American citizen . . . the political system of this country was able to inspire a real respect in me for its democratic process of changing government.

a politician (I was president of a community college), on one occasion I had to call law enforcement to control a rioting mob who demanded my removal from the polling place because I refused to allow some voters to cast votes without proper identification (as if I knew who they were voting for!)

This is only one out of many incidents that prompted me to leave my native country behind, to seek a new meaning of life in the United States (father of modern democracy). When I became an American citizen, I developed a sense of security and stability in myself, and the political system of this country was able to inspire a real respect in me for its democratic process of changing government.

However, that sense of security and stability has been shattered recently by the incidents in Florida. It is unimaginable for me that 19,000 votes had to be discarded because people did not know how to vote or the authority did not know how to print ballots! Over and above, people are now talking of conspiracy, fraud and of bringing lawsuits. I thought these things can happen only in Bangladesh where political leaders always try to litigate and bully themselves to leadership instead of accepting the verdict of the people.

It therefore appears that the only difference between Bangladesh and Florida is that Bangladesh is a country and Florida is only one of the 50 states in the United States. Let us hope that other states do not follow suit.

— Mr. Uddin is a Weston resident.

The skinny on public nudity

If law is required to make people wear clothes, so be it

By Qazi N. Uddin

According to California Penal Code Section 314, in order to prosecute someone for public nudity, we have to provide proof that the intention of that person was sexual gratification.

Under the protection of this law, one can pose naked in a public place and, when confronted, claim that he or she had no intention to get, or excite, sexual gratification. Simi Valley and Thousand Oaks city councils have, therefore, good reasons to outlaw nudity in public, regardless of the naked person's intention.

Taking it for granted that the individual had indeed no such intention, the fact remains that the individual is naked! His or her intention cannot cover the naked truth! The point is, the intention is not observable, the behavior is.

Therefore, it will be difficult to provide proof that someone is having sexual gratification just because that individual is exposing his or her body in public. However, regardless of the intention of the person who decides to pose naked in public, the onlookers may feel sexually excited or harassed.

For example, one can claim that he or she does not care what the intention of a naked person is, but his or her sense of decency, decorum and civility has been severely damaged by the public nudity of an individual.

While it is difficult to prove someone's intention, it is easy to understand someone's shock and feeling of harassment at being exposed to a naked human body in public.

Why? Because the idea to put some clothes on is the most wonderful gift of human civilization. The necessity arose to protect human beings from extreme cold or hot climatic conditions.

Gradually, we developed a sense of shyness and wanted to cover our bodies. Subsequently, we also wanted to look beautiful. Generally, civilized people all over the world wear clothes, not only out of necessity, but also to reveal personality. This is why it would be extremely difficult for human beings born and raised in a traditional culture to ignore the naked body and look for the intention underneath.

If the law of the land allows an individual to roam around naked in broad daylight because that person is not getting sexual gratification out of it, then the law of the land should also protect the rights of those individuals who feel harassed and shocked by the action of that naked individual, regardless of his or her intention.

It will, therefore, be evident that such a law that protects the right of an individual to stand naked in public, depending on his or her intention, is utterly meaningless. I wonder how such a law came into existence in the first place. According to my understanding, such a law can only exist in a nudist settlement where nudity is the norm and ideal of the people who call themselves naturists.

In a nudist colony, someone can bring a lawsuit that a particular individual is getting sexual gratification or provoking sexual excitement, and the accused can defend himself or herself by claiming that he or she had no such intention.

But it does not work for the rest of us who live in a traditional society and have developed certain norms, ideals and values over a long period of time. There is no denying the fact that we feel shocked and harassed by the presence of an innocent-looking living and moving nude human body in public places.

It brings to mind the incident of 1992 when Andrew Martinez, a student of the University of California at Berkeley, decided to attend classes naked. The university could not prove that "the naked guy" had any bad intention.

Finally, the university officials were able to ban him from campus, charging that his behavior constituted sexual harassment.

When we live in a society where everyone is wearing clothes in public, it is absurd to feel innocent and claim not to have any bad intentions in exposing one's body. If the time comes when the majority of Californians start going to the grocery store naked in the summer, a naked person can claim not to have any bad intentions.

Until that happens, I think it is a good idea to put some clothes on before going out. If someone fails to understand this very simple fact of life (unless the person is mentally ill), the force of a law is necessary to regulate such a person's behavior.

— *Qazi N. Uddin lives in Ventura.*

Focus on caste system unfortunate

By Qazi N. Uddin

Re: your Feb. 8 article, "Houses gone, but caste system remains":

The article states, "But there's one structure that can't be shaken in India, even by a killer earthquake — the caste system." The article states that the caste system is hindering the distribution of aid to victims, since relief workers were presented with six lists of residents, divided according to social status.

It is not only insensitive but also very rude to focus on the caste system of India and to blame it for the inconvenience in the relief effort. I find it very hard to believe that people who are struggling to survive are concerned about who are Brahmins and who are Sudras, or who are Muslims and who are Hindus.

While it is unfortunate that in some remote, rural areas of India people are still adhering to the caste system, based on their religious beliefs, it is not fair to generalize that the entire Indian society has remained frozen in time and space upholding the meaningless, primitive caste system.

The Indian societies have been able to move steadily since the dawn of the 19th century through the tireless efforts of many intellectuals and social reformers. Nowadays, although the vestiges of the age-old traditions can occasionally be traced here and there, the impact of the caste system can hardly be felt in the majority of Indian societies.

On the contrary, one can find ample examples of people extending their helping hands to people, regardless of their religious beliefs, ethnicity and caste. Amazingly, instead of focusing on the harmonious relationship that exists among people of various social categories, the Western world often prominently depicts the negative aspect of Indian societies.

For example, newspapers in the United States failed to publish an article headlined, "Hindu quake victims run Muslim blood in their veins," reported by Amrit Kumar of the Press Trust of India, which appeared in many Indian newspapers. The article stated, "The Muslim youths, hailing from Behrampur, Jamalpur and Bagdiwal localities of the walled city, have saved the lives of nearly 100 Hindu quake victims by donating their blood."

It is sad that the West has seldom been presented with such positive news about India. To say that even a natural disaster cannot bring people together is a glaring example of that typical Western attitude. Why not prominently publish Pakistan's help to Indian earthquake victims or the news of Muslims' blood saving Hindu lives?

Being born in British-India, I have witnessed how the ruthless British empire instigated riots to thwart the independence movement by using its divide-and-rule policy, while blaming Indians for racial intolerance.

Ironically, the British society is still strictly maintaining its caste system of nobility, clergy and commoner, which also shaped its political infrastructure in the form of the House of Lords and the House of Commons.

On the other hand, I witnessed how a Muslim saved the life of a Hindu from a lynching mob, and how a Brahmin jumped into the river to rescue an Untouchable. Such stories of pro-social behavior of human beings will prove, beyond the shadow of a doubt, that common people do not hate one another because of their differences in race, religion, color or caste.

It is the tyrants and bigots all over the world with power and position, such as political leaders, who are responsible for dehumanizing and demeaning human beings in order to exploit, extort or even exterminate them if necessary, be it India, Bosnia, Somalia or America.

Therefore, it is not a good idea to pick on India's caste system, especially in the aftermath of such a natural disaster.

— *Qazi N. Uddin is a Ventura resident.*

Reflections

But one Lord is the Object of all devotion; but is the Subject of all wisdom; but one Lord is the all activity. One Lord and therefore one humanity Lord, and therefore Oneness through the whole of the Lord; one Lord, one Life, one Brotherhood wise will help with their wisdom, the busy with their activity, the devotees with their love, and they will together and make one perfect body.

— Anrit

"Hints on the Study of the Bhagav

growth standards

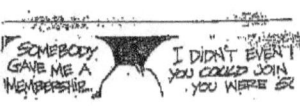

Should sex education program bare all?

It's up to parents to set a positive example

By Qazi H. Uddin

There is a negative element inherent in the approach to impart so-called sex education in our schools. The negative element is the assumption that our young generation is engaged in unsafe, indiscriminate and premature sex, resulting in the possibility of unwanted pregnancy and contracting AIDS. Therefore, proponents believe sex education is a must. I believe such an assumption is negative.

Worst of all, it denies the very essence of our civilisation. The progress of our civilisation from cave-dwellers up to the present time bears testimony to the fact that we, as human beings, are able to modify, control and regulate our natural instincts. Our prehistoric ancestors were indiscriminate and regulated by primary urges when they felt the urge to satisfy their libido. Gradually, they laid the necessity of developing loving relationship, privacy and a sense of discretion when it came to sex.

The creation of our family and social life was this outcome of our ability to regulate our sexual activity. If we failed to control our sexual behaviour, we would not have been able to sustain our society and our civilisation.

Anthropologists, biologists, psychologists and sociologists all agree that part of our becoming human is natural or instinctive, and part is social experience. Our nature and nurture create our culture, and are transmit our culture from one generation to the next. Our children do not acquire something from thin air; they acquire their experience by observing social behavior.

The very moment a child is born, we start educating him or her without even realising that we are doing so. So, to assume that we, the adults, are fine and we just need to educate our children about sex is a very wrong, negative and unrealistic assumption.

The way I see it, if anyone needs to receive sex education, it is the parents, not the children. If we believe that our children are gradually becoming models to control and regulate their sexual activity we have to admit that they are learning it from our behavior. We are providing role models.

In a society where children see their parents are not living together to take care of them, fathers or mothers have girlfriends or boyfriends, and parents are unable to discipline and control their libido, it is merely futile to try to educate them about appropriate sex.

Our good old days were not that bad. Our parents never heard of AIDS and teenage pregnancy. Were our parents better educated about sex than are our children? I can't remember ever receiving any sex education. The behavior of my parents and the society as a whole gave me sex education.

Therefore, I have no doubt in my mind that the concept of sex education that also promotes distribution of condoms originated from the negative attitude of such parents who miserably failed to provide any positive example of disciplined sexual behavior for their children, combined with the attitude of a society that glorifies inappropriate sexual behavior, but does not want to take any responsibility for the consequences.

— Qazi H. Uddin Noor is Nedunat.

Our failure, too

While I was watching the news in the aftermath of the shooting at Granite Hills High in El Cajon, I heard one official state that the shooter could be sentenced to life in prison plus 47 years if convicted. The purpose of making such a statement was, of course, to threaten disgruntled teen-age students with the consequences of their actions, believing that such harsh punishment will serve as deterrent to further school shootings.

If we believe that those who go to their own schools with a gun to kill other students and teachers are concerned about the consequences of their action, are scared of punishment, or have respect for their own lives, we have got it all wrong.

Teen-age school shooters are not criminals and do not engage in indiscriminate killing like career criminals, while committing crimes. So we cannot punish them in the traditional way we punish criminals. The threat of harsh punishment may be appropriate for regular criminals, but threat of punishment cannot and will not keep an angry, frustrated and depressed student from going to school with a gun.

Why not? Because such students have already been punished for being born in this world! They have been punished (abused, molested, tortured and neglected) to the extent that they have lost all respect for their own lives and, consequently, for the lives of others.

They could only feel the meaninglessness of their existence in this hostile universe. Being deprived of love, affection and guidance that they so desperately needed, they started living in a vacuum, felt pushed to the edge and, ultimately, decided to strike back in a destructive manner.

Therefore, considering them as criminals and threatening them with the consequence of harsh punishment will not help the situation. When their families and friends failed them, they expected their schools to provide comfort and guidance. Unfortunately, their schools also failed them miserably, leaving them unprotected, at the mercy of the bullies and gang members and putting the blame on their family's shoulders.

If we really want to do something about it, we have to accept their failure to cope with their anger as our failure to diffuse their anger as parents, teachers, administrators and friends. If the shooters receive punishment for their failures, we have to receive punishment for our failures, too.

From this perspective, I would suggest a drastic solution to the problem of school shooting. Next time a shooting occurs, the parents of the shooter should be charged with the accusation of failure to diffuse the anger of their child. The principal of the school should be asked to resign immediately. What about their constitutional rights?

But the point is, we want to stop school shootings; we do not want to go to the Constitution to avoid responsibility and punishment.

— Qazi N. Uddin,
Ventura

224

Tuesday, July 31, 2001   WC   The Star

Sad situation

In any civilized country, the accomplishments of exceptional children are measured by the recognition they receive from such an organization we call the government.

I had a notion that the highest honor and recognition our promising children could be accorded was the award of internships by our federal government, enabling them to work with our presidents in the White House or with congressional members in the Capitol.

However, such a notion that I harbored and nurtured for a long time has been shattered by the repeated incidents of inappropriate behavior of some of our leaders in Washington, D.C. I don't know about other parents, but I lost all my desire as a father to see my extraordinarily talented children going anywhere near the White House or the Capitol for any purpose whatsoever.

Concerns for our brilliant children's safety, dignity and well being have wiped out all my desire to see them receiving any internships from my own government.

I would like to see them honored or recognized by any other local societies or even international organizations, but not by our own Congress or the president anymore. How sad!

How dare some people in our government claim to be our leaders when they are miserably failing to lead their own family lives. How absurd it is that they get support, sympathy, and protection from their colleagues in the government. We hear about removing one bad apple to save many. Are we lately having too many bad apples that like to stick together so they cannot be separated?

It is about time to stand up and demand that our government clean up its house before another tragic incident of disappearance and inappropriate treatment of interns occurs.

—Qazi N. Uddin,
Ventura

Tuesday, July 31, 2001   WC   The Star

Sad situation

In any civilized country, the accomplishments of exceptional children are measured by the recognition they receive from such an organization we call the government.

I had a notion that the highest honor and recognition our promising children could be accorded was the award of internships by our federal government, enabling them to work with our presidents in the White House or with congressional members in the Capitol.

However, such a notion that I harbored and nurtured for a long time has been shattered by the repeated incidents of inappropriate behavior of some of our leaders in Washington, D.C. I don't know about other parents, but I lost all my desire as a father to see my extraordinarily talented children going anywhere near the White House or the Capitol for any purpose whatsoever.

Concerns for our brilliant children's safety, dignity and well being have wiped out all my desire to see them receiving any internships from my own government.

I would like to see them honored or recognized by any other local societies or even international organizations, but not by our own Congress or the president anymore. How sad!

How dare some people in our government claim to be our leaders when they are miserably failing to lead their own family lives. How absurd it is that they get support, sympathy, and protection from their colleagues in the government. We hear about removing one bad apple to save many. Are we lately having too many bad apples that like to stick together so they cannot be separated?

It is about time to stand up and demand that our government clean up its house before another tragic incident of disappearance and inappropriate treatment of interns occurs.

—Qazi N. Uddin,
Yonkers

Divorce

Don't have kids if splitting is an option

By Qazi N. Uddin

I came here from a country where people get married to stay together for the rest of their lives. In Bangladesh, the prime consideration for getting married is to start a family life. No one ever thinks of getting separated or divorced in the near or distant future.

Once married, husband and wife become one entity. One's destiny becomes the other's destiny. They might both work, but they do not keep track of their income separately. They do not maintain separate bank accounts.

In other words, two lives become one. There is no "you" and "me," there is always "we." They make decisions together and look forward to a beautiful future when children will illuminate their house. When children come, husband and wife become father and mother.

Their names change to "Babla's father" or "Runu's mother." They become known by their children. I have seen how my father's and mother's lives revolved around me and my brothers and sisters, how many sleepless nights they passed taking care of us.

They did not want anything for themselves. Our pleasure was their pleasure. After all this, did they have to tell us that they loved us?

Now, let me talk about the United States. People get married in this culture to get separated and divorced. Why do they get married in the first place? It is beyond me. I heard a radio talk show host the other day providing statistics that the average marriage in the United States lasts for seven years.

If you want to get separated or divorced, you can find hundreds of reasons. For example, the talk show host mentioned one caller complained that her husband does not know the proper way to squeeze toothpaste. That irritates her so much that she is thinking of a divorce. On the other hand, if you want to stay together, you do not have to find any reason whatsoever.

In this culture, people get married for all conceivable reasons other than to start a family. I have no doubt in my mind that married couples' lives do not revolve around their children in this culture. They have other priorities.

They can heartlessly dump their children on a baby sitter to go to a party and dance. They justify this dumping when they go to work. But there are other things they have to do, without any justification whatsoever. For example, they go on vacation by themselves, leaving their children behind.

Fathers and mothers in the United States never realize that their children love to see them living together. They love both father and mother jointly, not separately.

Since parents do not make any sacrifices for their children, their love and affection for their children are not so obvious as in Bangladesh. They are well aware that their children may be in doubt about their feelings for them.

I cannot remember any social event in my life where I went by myself leaving my wife and children behind, unless it was strictly work or business-related. They are part and parcel of my life, and I cannot imagine my existence without their presence. The same with my wife.

If someone invited us and we knew children were not welcome, we politely refused to accept that invitation. Now, my daughters go to universities. Sometimes, they do not enjoy going with us whenever we go somewhere.

Sometimes they say, "Why don't you go by yourself, Mom and Dad, and leave us alone? Don't you think we are grown up and can take care of ourselves?" When they say this, we really feel like going. We tried, but that trip turned out dull and monotonous. We enjoy ourselves best when we are all together surrounded by our children.

Fathers and mothers in the United States never realize that their children love to see them living together. They love both father and mother jointly, not separately. They naturally believe that it is normal for their father and mother to live in the same house, sleep in the same bed, eat at the same dining table and relax on the same couch.

They feel good when they see that Mommy loves and takes care of Daddy, and that Daddy loves Mommy and takes care of her. They feel proud of themselves. They believe it is for them this is happening. They get a sense of fulfillment, safety and security.

In such a situation, it is useless to explain: "Although your mommy and I do not live together any more, it has nothing to do with you. I love you very much. So does your mommy."

They listen to this explanation intently, they try to understand its meaning, but do not understand. "But it does not make any

sense to me. I do not like to be loved separately by my mother and father. What about my feelings? I want both of you to love each other. Because you are my daddy and my mommy. That makes me happy.

"When I see you do not live together, it breaks my heart. I feel frustrated and defeated. I feel I could not bridge the gap between you. No matter how hard you try to convince me both of you love me separately, it does not lessen my pain."

I do not think that I am making up these responses. If you have any doubt about what goes on in children's minds when they learn their parents are planning to divorce, you can go back to your past and put yourself in their shoes.

If you are one of those lucky kids whose parents never got divorced, find out how it feels by asking your friends' kids or a school counselor. They will be able to give you a clear picture about what goes on in children's minds when their parents file for a divorce.

I think divorcing is the worst form of child abuse this civilization has ever encountered.

The message parents send to their children by separating or divorcing is, "You are not the most important thing in my life. I have a life to live, and I want to live it to the fullest of my satisfaction."

The true meaning of that satisfaction becomes apparent when Father brings home a girlfriend and Mother brings home a boyfriend. The children get the message that sex is more powerful and more important than love, affection and concern for one's own children.

A child's emotions, safety and sense of security have no room in a world where sexual desires proclaim their supremacy above anything else. Under such a situation, how can parents demand respect from their children? And how can they ask their children not to place too much importance on sex; not to become frustrated; and to say no to drugs?

Children lose all respect for their parents and any norms and ideals or the values of society. They feel defeated and cheated. No matter how hard you shout, "I love you," it will never make sense to them.

So, think twice before you decide to get married. If you have any such doubt in your mind as, "If we don't get along ..." then please don't get married.

Also, once you get married, please don't plan on having children if you have any concern that you won't be able to stay together.

— Qazi N. Uddin lives in Ventura.

RECALL

Tabloid journalism on relationship

Re: your Sept. 10 article, "Moorpark College instructor writes of love with Arnold":

I am surprised and shocked to see this as a news article and on the front page of The Star.

This is a glaring example of how American people, culture and society have lost all sense of decency, decorum and dignity of living a sophisticated and honorable life. My first reaction was, who cares? Who wants to know? Then, I thought, yes, people care and people want to know because it is Arnold Schwarzenegger.

Then I wondered, would Barbara Baker even venture to publish her so-called "memoir" if Schwarzenegger was not running to become governor of California? Did she see an opportunity to attract a publisher and sign a contract for a million dollars? This is so disgusting.

In a democracy anyone can run to become a governor. That does not make a person a role model. We have to wait and see a person in office to know whether that person can inspire some respect. Even then, people should not dig into their past to connect themselves with that person either to bring that person down or to glorify him or her. What happened to self-respect?

This article just provided me with an example of tabloid journalism and tarnished the love and respect I have developed for the Ventura County Star over the years.

— Qazi N. Uddin,
Ventura

Your letters

Judge lacks education

Re: your Oct. 18 article, "Judge limits bilingual dad's language":

A district judge of Sarpy County in Nebraska ordered the father of a 5-year-old daughter not to use his native language, Spanish, during visitation. The mother, who is Polish, does not like her daughter to be exposed to Spanish. It is disturbing to find that the judge would go along with such a racist attitude.

The judge believes, "And if you put her in a situation where people are not communicating in a language that she understands, that is not fair to the child." Thus, the judge threatened the father with the consequence of speaking Spanish with his daughter: further limitation on visitation.

Some people believe they have knowledge of all issues because of the position they hold. However, most of the time they do not know what they are talking about. Therefore, I suggest those who receive specialized education to become professionals, such as physicians, engineers and judges, should receive some general education involving language and society.

If they receive education on language acquisition, they will know age 5 is the best time to acquire languages. I was able to use words from four different languages when I was only 4, being exposed to Bengali, Hindi, Urdu and Arabic. Such exposure enabled me to acquire English, French, German and Spanish. Both of my daughters are also multilingual.

It is disappointing that a judge believes a 5-year-old should not be exposed to many languages. He said, in effect: You can visit your daughter, but you have to leave behind your language.

Luckily, the poor father was bilingual, as the judge could order him not to use Spanish. I wonder what the judge would do if he were monolingual. Tell him to keep his mouth shut when he visits his daughter?

— Qazi N. Uddin,
Ventura

No dumpin

(This letter pastor of Santa Oxnard to his ¡
— Editor)

On Oct. 26, nearing the end looking forwar parish and gett you, the parishi Santa Clara Ch

Unfortunatel be relaxed and another newspa yet another law scandalous acti inactive priests new — same st some persons

SHOULD SAME-SEX COUPLES BE ALLOWED TO MARRY?

Find another name for union besides marriage

By Qazi N. Uddin

A close observation will reveal that the so-called gay marriage controversy is not related to conservatism, liberalism, or individual rights.

Without even referring to religion, ethics and morality, conservatives can make a strong case against gay marriage.

Conversely, if liberals believe that by referring to individual rights and pursuit of life, liberty, and happiness they can defend gay marriages, they are wrong also.

The fact is, both conservatives and liberals have the wrong attitude when they confront the issue of gay marriage.

First of all, those of us who have studied etymology know that certain words have been able to acquire specific connotations over a long period of time by virtue of their association with long-standing social and cultural tradition. The word "marriage" is one of them. As soon as we use this word, it creates a picture, an image, an emotional attachment. No matter how hard one tries, it will not be possible to isolate it from that picture.

Married couples go home to opposite-sex husbands and wives. The words husband and wife also signify male and female, respectively. It is impossible to demand that, beginning tomorrow, we will change the meaning of wife to signify male, and husband to signify female. This is exactly what the same-sex people are doing when they want to name their relationship "marriage."

Long before the advent of religion, the primitive human species started thinking about how to regulate their sexual activity, take care of children, and be supportive of one another for the sake of their own survival and existence. Religions definitely have a contribution in reforming our culture and civilization. However, religion did not create the concept of getting married, it only endorsed it.

Through marriage, we create a primary group that performs some essential functions, including regulating sexual activity, taking care of children and providing emotional support and protection to the members of that group. Subsequently, this group has acquired another connotation we call "family." Social scientists call families "building blocks" of a society.

It is not whether someone is a conservative or a liberal. No one will be willing to do away with the society and civilization, either to protect religion, morality and ethics, or to protect individual rights.

We have to accept the evolution of society and the history of our civilization on a scientific basis. This basis clearly indicates that "marriage" and "family" are built-in components of society and civilization. So, their connotations cannot be destroyed without destroying the very structure of the society and civilization.

Etymologically speaking, these built-in concepts that refer to male and female union and that are designed to perform essential functions for the sustenance of the civilization can never be used by same-sex partners to signify the same concept. We are not trying to regulate any relationships here. We are not suggesting that people should not have different sexual orientations.

Speaking of individual rights, gay people should have the right to claim they have a relationship that is similar to heterosexual marriage, but they should find another name that will make the distinction between homosexual and heterosexual relationships.

Why is it so important that we should recognize homosexual relationship as "marriage"? It is not necessary to bring up religion to speak against using the word "marriage" by gay people. Also, it is not necessary to claim that gay people are exercising their individual rights by calling their relationship marriage. It is impossible to destroy the etymological significance of a word, and no one should try to do so.

— *Qazi N. Uddin lives in Ventura.*

Your letters

Flynn best for supervisor

Re: David Katz's Jan. 30 letter, "Flynn deserves re-election":

I fully endorse the view expressed by Katz. I have lived in the city of Ventura for 17 years. Although I have written regularly on social, cultural, educational and social issues, I have never felt like endorsing any candidate running for any political office.

One of my reasons for staying out of local politics was that I always considered myself a foreigner, who should not poke his nose into a most sensitive area that is "local needs." But suddenly I realized that I have never lived for 17 years continuously in one city, even in my native country. So why not join the local politics, which has a tremendous effect on my day-to-day existence in this county.

As an educator helping disadvantaged students of this county, I have seen the faces and actions of many mayors, council members and supervisors. I have had occasional interactions with them when I needed help for my own educational institution. I had to reach out to the elected officials for help and support. No one ever volunteered to find out what problem I was encountering.

John Flynn is an exception. In 1996, when the Indo-American School in Oxnard was in financial trouble, he came to find out what was wrong. I was teaching English as a second language the night Flynn showed up. No one asked him to do so.

I strongly believe Flynn is independent, honest and, above all, free from bias and prejudices. We need more politicians like him in this country. I would, therefore, be very happy to see him re-elected.

— Qazi N. Uddin,
Ventura

PULSE

HOW SHOULD WRITING BE TAUGHT?

Look at the big picture

By Qazi N. Uddin

A s an educator, who has been teaching writing in Bangladesh since 1964 and in the United States since 1985, I feel a strong desire to air my experience on this issue. My West and the East experience and the United States brought me on this.

I started teaching composition at Sussex County College in New Jersey and then at Monmouth College. Subsequently, I taught composition and English as a second language in various American secondary educational institutions in Western County.

Going over the composition papers of my students, who had already graduated from high school, I was astonished. What were the teachers doing in high school? I knew I learned how to write in high school. I thought, meaningful content and well-formatted essays when I was in high school. They were not just grammar; I remembered that my high school teachers also did not correct my essays and write comments. They simply returned my essays, asking them to write them over.

That is why I don't believe that students' low performance in writing in the United States is related to their teachers' inability to correct essays. The problem is deeply rooted in American culture. Over the last 50 years, the culture has developed an educational system in which students are required to gain understanding of concepts by filling in the blanks, choosing the different answer from a multiple-choice list, and matching statements with corresponding expanations.

These methods of evaluation require only recalling of information and, obviously, no critical thinking. Students don't have to organize their thoughts and write essays to demonstrate their understanding. Essay-type questions have disappeared from our classes.

Composition cannot be taught in isolation of reading, critical thinking and discussion. It is impossible for a person to become an effective writer who does not read, think and engage in debates.

We have no time to talk from a multiple knowledge of a democratic society. I am a physics, biology, geography, or philosophy.

When I see a lot of essay-type questions included a generation of poor writing, our education, on the demand of employers, horrid

discussions. Our students do not read newspapers and books. Instead, they watch TV, play video games and listen to music. Our curriculums have been designed to quickly prepare students for the job. When we realize that they cannot write, we blame teachers for not correcting essays.

If we really understood the importance of writing, we have to change this attitude. There is no shortcut in learning. We have to answer multiple-choice questions and introduce behind essay-type questions only literary studies.

Also, we have to emphasize the fact that writing skills are essential for all disciplines, not only literary studies.

Since I learned how to read and write in Bangladesh, I was never asked to fill in the blanks to identify the correct answer from a multiple-choice list.

to correct the problem by recruiting so-called "composition" experts for college students. Those of us who studied rhetoric and theory of composition know that composition is not something that can be taught like math or PowerPoint. No one realized that waiting starts with the question "What to write about?" Students learn to have something in mind that they want to express for that reason, they need to think about issues, and to think about issues, they need to read and participate in discussions.

If we don't take care of this problem immediately, we have to face a whole means of communication that helped transmission of knowledge, culture and history from one generation to the other.

— Qazi N. Uddin lives in Western

Hopelessness is the real problem

By Qazi N. Uddin

Homelessness is not a unique problem to Ventura. If the city believes it is going to deal with this problem from its own perspective, it is all wrong. We have to understand the real problem.

When I was first introduced to the word "homeless" in the United States, I thought it must refer to a lifestyle chosen by some mentally ill or eccentric individuals. It has nothing to do with poverty. Some people do not like to live in homes. This interpretation made sense to me. The United States being one of the richest countries in the world, it was impossible for me to think of some people so poor they could not afford to provide a roof over their heads!

The word "homeless" has never been used to mean poor in my native country, Bangladesh. A majority of the people in Bangladesh are poor, but they are simply known as poor, not homeless. The poor are not homeless either because they live in a makeshift home, a dilapidated home, but a home, after all. Most live in some kind of homes. People love their homes, and poor people do not like to be called homeless.

In big cities of Bangladesh, some people like to live in parks, under the bridges, or in abandoned buildings. They are known as vagabonds and worthless people, not as homeless.

Then, I learned "homeless" is synonymous with "poor" in America. Every country has some poor people, no matter how rich the country is. So, the United States has poor people and they don't have homes. Politicians and social reformers talk about doing something to alleviate the sufferings of homeless. They blame the government for not taking care of these poor people.

I wondered how a rich country could produce such poor people. What is wrong with this system? Then I compared my own situation regarding being poor and homeless in the United States.

In 1979, when I landed in the United States with only $10 in my pocket, I was homeless. I had to spend the night at the Los Angeles International Airport sitting in a chair waiting for the sun to rise. When I faced a new world, not only did I manage to earn my own food and shelter, but was able to learn the English language and educate myself with a master's degree and a doctoral degree from two prestigious universities. I was homeless only for one night!

Therefore, I do not understand what money has to do with becoming homeless in the United States. If homeless people needed only money to buy homes, it would be easy for the government to provide

> The problem of homelessness is in no way connected to poverty. Money cannot solve this problem.

homes for them. But the homeless people do not need a home, meaning a place to sleep. They need real homes — homes that can provide love, affection and a sense of security and belonging.

The problem of homelessness is in no way connected to poverty. Money cannot solve this problem. This problem can only be handled if we do not call these people "homeless," but identify them as "hopeless." I believe people become homeless when they become hopeless.

When an individual finds no reason for his or her existence in a society, he or she loses all respect for traditional norms, decency and decorum.

When some people cannot lean on their past to relax, cannot enjoy their present life, and don't see anything happening in the future, they abandon all hope. First they become hopeless and then homeless. Those of us who live in homes have a notion of the past and present and we look forward to the future. Time appears terribly static for some who suffer from an acute sense of nothingness of their existence, who live in a large vacuum of emptiness and cannot come out of it.

If they could come out of it, they would feel like making good use of their time and would feel like looking forward to a bright future.

The complexity of human life creates a sense of meaninglessness for some people. They find no way to shake it off to proceed toward a new beginning or to search for a new meaning of life. They want to pass their lives with this feeling of nothingness, which makes them utterly hopeless.

As it will be apparent, homeless people are mentally unstable. They are not out of their homes; they are out of their minds. To categorize them as homeless is a big mistake. Because in doing so, they get mixed up with poor people. This is a wrong diagnosis, and a wrong diagnosis will not cure a disease.

Homeless people of Bangladesh are not mentally ill. Some of them are homeless because poverty has driven them out of their homes. Once upon a time, they had a small home in a village. They had a piece of land to grow food, a pond to grow fish and some

cattle to raise. They suffered through the exploitations of the greedy landowners, natural calamities, flood, drought and epidemics. During the turn of the century, the Industrial Revolution shattered the peace of their homes. They were forced to leave and flocked together around big cities to survive. Some of them found a new life. Some slipped through the cracks to become homeless.

The root cause of such homelessness is poverty, not a mental condition. While Bangladesh can solve its homeless problem with money, the United States cannot. The factors that drive people toward homelessness vary from society to society. In the United States, some people discarded their homes due to the disintegration of traditional family life, values, norms and ideals, not because of poverty. Some people lost all interest of living in a home or in a family environment. They developed a new philosophy of life. They started to revolt against the establishment. Home is an establishment.

There was an attempt to alienate oneself from society and find a new meaning of life in mysticism or in gang membership. The hippies of the 1960s bear testimony to such observation. This eagerness of some angry young generation to break tradition and to evolve out of economic crises. Rather, its origin may be traced to disintegration of family values.

It is so tragic, but a truth that most children in this country cannot call a place their home although their parents may have a million-dollar home. A place where father and mother do not live together does not feel like a home to children. It is an open secret. Nobody wants to talk about it. Some decide to leave their homes as a manifestation of their anguish and hatred they accumulated over a long period of time because of the abuse they received from their families. They lose all attraction for their homes.

If proper research is conducted, it will be apparent that poverty did not generate the problem of homelessness in the United States. A group of people wanted to revolt against the system. Obviously, they did not see any hope for themselves in a home devoid of a traditional nuclear family. They developed an alternative philosophy of satisfying the purpose of life by using drugs or alienating themselves from society. These people can be categorized as hopeless; they are not really homeless, meaning poor.

If we call them homeless, it looks like they want to live in homes, but because of economic disparity, they have been deprived of living in a home. But the truth is far from this. Hopelessness is a mental condition. Hopeless people like to live in a vacuum, and openly provide that vacuum.

If Ventura wants to fill that vacuum, the city has to provide a real home for them that can bring meaning and hope to life, not a temporary shelter.

— Qazi N. Uddin lives in Ventura

HURRICANES

Chittagong and New Orleans: What's the difference?

By Qazi N. Uddin

I was born and raised in Bangladesh, a Third World country. I lived there for 34 years and I survived famines, epidemics, civil wars, communal and political riots and cyclones.

Cyclones frequented a city where I lived most of my life educating myself and subsequently working as an educator. Cyclones pummeled the coastal city of Chittagong twice during my stay there. Cyclones killed 25,000 people in Chittagong and its coastal areas in 1895 and 40,000 in 1970, according to official estimates.

During the second cyclone, corrugated iron sheets from the roof of my house were twisted away just like cardboard, leaving me exposed under open sky. I survived because tidal waves could not reach me. My house was on high ground, where a handful of professionals — rich and affluent segments of the population — could afford to live.

Bangladesh is one of the poorest countries in the world. Chittagong is situated by the Bay of Bengal. There are 2,500 big and small islands offshore where people live in dilapidated houses. Most of them make a living by fishing and working in agricultural fields. When a cyclone hits, it brings with it huge tidal waves. The houses collapse like sand castles, and all living beings are washed away into the Bay of Bengal People living in the low-lying coastal areas of the mainland suffer the same consequence.

So, when in Bangladesh, I learned that the difference between being rich and poor was the difference between life and death. It was not a difference between quality of life.

Also, I was told by our government and intellectuals of the country not to worry about it. Nothing could be done to save the lives of poor people in a poor country where the majority was living from hand to mouth. Making plans for evacuation and building shelters on offshore islands and coastal areas sounded like a daydream. People were just advised not to live in those dangerous areas.

So I decided to escape and go to a country where nature does not discriminate between rich and poor. Where natural disaster affects everyone's life equally. Where people do not die just because they are poor, a country that is well-prepared to accept challenges of nature's fury, a country where the difference between standard of living, not a difference between life and death. The United States appeared to be such a country to me.

Since moving to the United States in 1973, I have been happily living here with the perception that this is the ideal place to live. This is the place where nature does not get a chance to kill thousands and millions of poor people. Then, one day in 1991, when I was driving to work, came the devastating news. A cyclone hit Chittagong again. According to an official estimate, 125,790 were dead. That was enough to confirm my belief that we leave the poor people to die under the open sky in Bangladesh. A poor country cannot undertake any rescue effort prior to a natural catastrophe or in its aftermath.

W hy could the United States not protect its poor people from the devastation of a hurricane?

However, that perception has recently been shattered by Hurricane Katrina. This is a very rude awakening for me — to realize that the most powerful and the richest country in the world has to sacrifice its poor people to nature's fury. Why? Why could the United States not protect its poor people from the devastation of a hurricane? It's beyond me!

The United States is not Bangladesh. The government and the people of Bangladesh may feel hopeless to tidal waves, but why should the United States feel hopeless to combat Katrina? A country that can fix democracy and freedom of people around the world cannot raise the standard of living of its own people so they can survive a natural calamity? They could not escape because they had no transportation. People died in nursing homes because they were abandoned! Some people starved for three days because no one could supply food to them!

This is the United States of America? How ironic and how sad! Is this because poor people are destined to die regardless where they live in this world. Chittagong or New Orleans?

— Qazi N. Uddin lives in Weston.

Tuesday, May 2, 2006   FC   The Star

Spanish anthem a sign of love

Re: your April 29 article, "Bush rejects national anthem in Spanish, plans for boycott":

It is very unfortunate that the president of the United States, along with others, is offended by the idea of a Spanish-language version of the U.S. national anthem. In a recent statement, President Bush bitterly criticized this idea of expressing patriotism for the United States in Spanish!

I understand the reasons behind anguish and disappointment of some uneducated, uncultured and unintelligent low-class people on this issue. I have no doubt in my mind that the negative attitude they express is emanating from blatant racism, anti-illegal immigration sentiments, bias and prejudice. Such people are so blinded by their ignorance, intolerance of diversity, and lack of cultural sensitivity that they fail to see the good-heartedness and patriotism of a group of immigrants who want to make the national anthem of their new country their own and keep it close to their heart. They just want to express their love for their new country wholeheartedly, using their own language.

Nothing is more valuable for human beings than to be able to express their love, emotion and feeling in their mother tongue. It is definitely a clear and sincere sign of love and respect for the United States that people of different languages and cultures want to create their own version of their American identity.

When I saw The Star's article, I thought those who are offended are unfortunate illiterates, bigots and narrow-minded citizens who utterly fail to see the good intentions behind such a move. However, I was immensely shocked and surprised to find out that our president is also one of those who failed to see the goodness of heart behind this wonderful idea.

— Qazi N. Uddin,
Ventura

YOUR LETTERS

SANTA BARBARA NEWS-PRESS

Be fair to readers

Re: your July 23 article," Turmoil at paper fractures a city":

In all fairness, we, the readers, should know when we are reading news and when we are reading advertisement. When newspaper owners accepts money or are motivated by their own agenda, bias or prejudice and ask their employees (editors, columnist and reporters), to run an advertisement in their newspaper claiming that this is news, there starts the real trouble.

The true significance of a newspaper is undermined then and there. This is what the owner of the Santa Barbara News-Press needs to realize. Of course, we, the readers, are not so naïve as not to be able to detect bias and prejudice in reporting a news event, but journalists are entitled to their opinion, too. No matter how objective they try to be in reporting, they sometimes cannot avoid being opinionated. That is when we complain and criticize news reporting and, also, that is when the owners should intervene to protect the decency, decorum and ethics of journalism.

However, the owner at Santa Barbara News-Press is doing just the opposite. This is one thing to have an opinion, but completely different to force the journalists to accept an advertisement as a news item.

People who want to do business using such commodities as news, education, cultural and social service need to realize that they cannot change the connotation of news, education, culture and society just because they own the business. It is about time for the Santa Barbara Business Press owner to realize that.

— Qazi N. Uddin,
Ventura

236

Missions are history; restore them

Re: your Aug. 16 article, "State rejects plan
for tax money to repair missions":

If I propose that, from tomorrow, let's
forget about history, do not teach it, it's
meaningless and a waste of time, everyone
will oppose me vehemently. We believe the
study of history is necessary. It provides us
with valuable information we can use to shape
the present and future.

The importance of history reveals itself
in such adages as "history repeats itself"
and "we have not learned anything from the
lessons of history."

However, many of us failed to realize
history cannot be selective. We have to get
the entire picture of our past through our
history. We have to understand that, whether
we practice our respective religions or
not, we cannot ignore them. Religions are
integral and essential parts of our history.
Most historical architectures and edifices are
manifestations of religious beliefs, emotions,
and sentiments.

Having respect for history and, at the
same time, ignoring historical symbols,
relics and edifices because of their religious
affiliations do not make any sense to me. Not
to protect historical religious edifices on the
concern of church-state conflict is akin to
throwing out the baby with the bathwater.
We have to wake up and cultivate common
sense. Nobody is asking the state to endorse,
protect or promote any particular religion.
We are just interested in protecting our
history, by preserving and repairing historical
monuments.

I strongly believe the U.S. Constitution
should be amended to make it clear history
cannot exclude religion.

Therefore, preserving historical
monuments and places of worships (missions,
churches, synagogues, mosques and temples)
is not the same as endorsing or promoting
any particular religion.

— Qazi N. Uddin,
Ventura

YOUR LETTERS

The Dutch goofed

Re: your Nov. 18 article, "Netherlands to ban 'burqa for security'":

I don't understand what security problem burqa-clad Muslim women pose in The Netherlands.

I have visited Amsterdam twice in my life and never spotted any burqa-clad women. It is estimated that about 30 women wear burqas in that country.

The issue here is intolerance and hatred for other religions and cultures. It is so inherent in some people that they do not hesitate to shoot at hijab-wearing women walking with their children in the broad daylight.

It is so ironic for any government that claims to be on a high moral ground and civilized compared to other religious and ethnic groups to try to legislate human culture. How would you feel if the U.S. government tried to define safe and secure dresses for its citizens by banning the wearing of shorts in public?

Muslims never wear shorts, even in their living rooms. A country may be paranoid because of 9/11, but to express that paranoia by legislating drastic measures against another religion or culture is dangerous.

Think about how the rest of the world hates American culture. I have traveled extensively in many Third World countries and in many European countries. People all over the world believe Americans dress very inappropriately, even when they are in foreign countries.

In 1978, when I was in Chittagong, Bangladesh, I, along with many others, was dumbfounded watching a half-naked American woman shamelessly walking in public. But nobody wanted to kill her, nor did Bangladesh pass any law prohibiting foreigners from wearing inappropriate dress.

The action of the Dutch government is not only silly, but also dangerous. It will set a precedent of intolerance around the world and may promote violence against foreigners in many countries.

— Qazi N. Uddin,
Ventura

"Do you sky dive? Ever been a critic of Putin?"

in his third month of kindergarten   ... ... lawyer and in the

238

Sunday, April 29, 2007   WJC   1B

PULSE

VIRGINIA TECH MASSACRE

Extend a hand

By Qazi N. Uddin

I am searching for an answer. I as everyone else is. I searched for an answer, too, when the Jonesboro tragedy, in a letter to the editor on April 13, 1998. At that time, I had responded because 11- and 13-year-old boys were involved. I searched for an answer and wrote again May 27, 1999. After the Columbine tragedy. That time, I took myself as a teacher and my colleagues as teachers and our being able to provide proper guidance and seeking for answers.

I am still seeking for answers. This time, it is a precarious situation where mature and responsible journeys can enter for pursuit of knowledge and wisdom. Now, I am really exasperated. I don't know whom to hold responsible. It appears that the disease is spreading at a very fast pace, and challenge the very fabric of our existence as a sustainable society.

Since Cho Seung-Hui sent a package to NBC between shootings, we know what was going on in his mind. I can see how this student from South Korea felt isolated, stressed and emerged in Virginia Tech. Was it America's culture of violence, America's apparently complex that prompted him to write: "Did you decided to spill my blood. You forced me into a corner and gave me only one option. The decision was yours. Now you have blood on your hands that will never wash off?"

I am not trying to justify I am trying to understand the root cause of human demeanor and behavior. If we want to deliver anger and frustration and abnormality, we have to look at our own attitude toward people of other cultures. Living in a rich and powerful country, I will not probed us anymore. The world think whether we are promoting violence and hatred for us around the world.

At this time, it is naive to contemplate "Why they" hate us so much. We have to search for the answer to that question, and answer the question of behavior. We have a problem of ignoring people and keeping them isolated in the name of protecting their right to privacy. As a result, many are suffering from loneliness and developing abnormally. We often ignore the ominous signs of distress. In this case, Cho abnormally was noticed by Professors Carolyn Rude and Lucinda Roy, both current and former chairwomen of the university's English department.

Although a Virginia District court found Cho an "imminent danger to others," no precautions were taken, for fear of intruding on his privacy or his freedom of expression. Now imagine what price we are paying for protecting our so-called right to protect. The time has come when we have to look beyond the superficial causes of such tragic incidents as mental instability, gun culture, and advancement of psychological attitude. In reality, we have to come out of our egocentric attitude of rich and powerful society, members of a superior race, race, or culture.

We have to see everyone on this planet as human beings. We have to stop claiming such as a superior and, as a subordinate and our culture over others. We have to realize that there is no such thing as physical race against each other's physical and cultural superiority or inferiority at any time and era.

Also, we should not ask anybody such questions as "Where are you from?" looking at their distinctive physical features, or make remarks such as, "Welcome to civilization" (I was greeted with this remark by a professor of a prestigious university when I arrived here in 1979).

We are all from this planet. We are all fellow human beings! If somebody gets angry, frustrated or depressed, we have to extend our helping hands toward him or her, instead of calling that person "evil" or "enriched." Shooting will stop then and there.

—*Qazi N. Uddin lives in Hanover.*

Opinion

Editor: Marianne Ratcliff, 437-0250.   Thursday, May 31, 2007   FC

B8

What about human fights?

Re: your April 12 article, "Senate OKs Gallegly bill on staged animal fights":

It is good to know our lawmakers are making it illegal to stage animal fights. President Bush will sign this measure soon. Many people do not like this age-old tradition of some cultures because it constitutes cruelty to animals.

The Humane Society of the United States has rightly stated, "Staged animal fighting is barbaric and often linked with other serious crimes, such as illegal gambling, drug trafficking and acts of human violence."

While I agree, I cannot but wonder: Why should we, as a civilized society, allow staged human fights in Las Vegas, which not only are barbaric but also promote acts of human violence? These cruel and barbaric entertainments were prevalent in the ancient Roman Empire, when, in staged fights, gladiators were allowed to kill one another to satisfy the bloodthirst of kings, queens and spectators.

No doubt, it is utterly inhuman to derive pleasure out of such spectacles — spectacles in which a human being is mercilessly beating up another human being to be glorified by the onlookers or the sponsors of the event. This is definitely a manifestation of a crude, barbaric, evil, primitive and unsophisticated state of human mind from which we have been able to remove ourselves over the span of 3,000 years and build this wonderful civilization.

Ironically, we are concerned about cruelty to animals, but not concerned about cruelty to our fellow human beings.

It is ridiculous to claim we are civilized human beings and, therefore, cannot tolerate cruelty to animals, while we allow human beings to beat up each other mercilessly.

It is about time to ban such savagery in the name of entertainment or sport.

— Qazi N. Uddin,
Ventura

PULSE

Watching TV facilitates learning

By Qazi N. Uddin

To ask "What are the benefits of watching or not watching TV?" is similar to asking "What are the benefits of reading or not reading books?"

Obviously, no one questions the benefits of reading books, but, amazingly, people do question the benefits of watching TV.

TV has earned a bad reputation since a majority of TV program producers abuse it by broadcasting pornographic, obscene and disgusting materials in the name of providing entertainment.

Of course, it's no different with books. However, nobody says, "Don't read books." We suggest reading good books, not bad ones. Why don't we do the same thing when we deal with TV? The Star Pulse page question should not be about 'benefit or lack of benefit of watching TV.' Rather, it should address what we watch.

TV is one of the most wonderful gifts of this civilization. I consider advancement in science and technology a blessing. Many inventions and discoveries have been able to improve our lives. Acquisition of knowledge and understanding brought scientists to many difficult problems and helped promote harmonious relationships among various nations around the world.

There is no denying the fact we can acquire knowledge without TV. We can improve our lives and develop good relationships. However, we should not ignore the fact that there are three kinds of learners. Some people are kinaesthetic learners, some are auditory and some are visual. TV provides a wonderful opportunity for visual learners to acquire knowledge quickly. In addition, we can take advantage of kinaesthetic, auditory and visual learning styles simultaneously to facilitate learning.

No one will object to the convenience of using TV as a learning tool. However, in the name of providing entertainment, some producers cater to a group of immature viewers by inciting their programming with violence, crime and explicit sex.

We are genuinely concerned that unsupervised viewing of such materials is detrimental to our children and ultimately may promote crime and violence.

So, we should concentrate on what to do about it, instead of wondering about the benefit of not watching TV at all. The reason we have not been able to do anything about it so far is that there are people who believe there is such a thing as "adult entertainment."

So, we adults are entitled to view obscene and vulgar programs and children are not. The assumption is that adults age and easily prevented by TV programs. They can make intelligent decisions. Some also use "freedom of expression" to protect "adult entertainment."

However, the study of social science indicates that, in some cultures, children are not maturing. They remain children for the most part of their lives. Unfortunately, the United States is one of those cultures.

Social psychology found out that many people influenced by their permissive societies may grow up chronologically but not mentally.

If we fail to control our urge to view obscene and explicit social contexts, it is expected we did not grow up mentally. That means we are not grow up mentally, by which we mean responsible. Therefore, there is no such thing as "adult entertainment." We are, in fact, jeopardizing our children's future.

It is now evident that we should get together to vulnerably object to glorification of violence, sex and crime in TV programming. Only then, we won't have to confront such an absurd question as "What are the benefits of not watching TV?"

— Qazi N. Uddin lives in Ventura.

COMMENTARY

Americans need to treat driving as though it were their job

By Qazi N. Uddin

The tragic death of Beth Doan on July 21 in Yemen, caused by a Hilux-truck driver, shocked me profoundly because I could not afford to buy a car, but because even those with bad cars had drives. Although I did not have a car, I had many opportunities to ride cars owned by friends and relatives. They all had their drivers. I rarely saw any car owners driving their own cars.

Ironically, Bangladesh is one of the poorest countries in the world. However, we will always find a few rich people who are able to buy cars and hire drivers. What I am talking about is this. We used to ride trains and buses for long distances and rickshaws and baby taxies for short distances. The

World country) and lived there for 34 years. Never did I have to drive in that country, not because I could not afford to buy a car, but because even those with bad cars had drives. Although I did not have a car, I had many opportunities to ride cars owned by friends and relatives. They all had their drivers. I rarely saw any car owners driving their own cars.

Many people make a living by driving rickshaws, baby taxis buses and trains. They are well trained and concentrated because driving is their job, and they have to do a good job to keep their jobs. These drivers don't have to make eye contact with passengers, engage in conversation, answer cell phones, apply makeup fail mak[e]d, speed up to run a red light. Because their only job is driving, they keep

majority of the middle class and poor in Bangladesh either walk or ride, they don't have to drive. There are drivers to operate those means of transportation mentioned above. Those drivers are professionals. Driving is considered a profession.

their eyes on the road and think and their destination.

Unfortunately for perhaps understandably, we all become drivers in the United States. However, we are not professional drivers. We are students, teachers, doctors, nurses, engineers, secretaries, clerks, lawyers, managers and journalists. We have so many things on our minds other than driving.

On the way to my work for teaching, I always mentally prepare my lesson plans and find myself unnecessarily waiting in a green light and get a rude awakening by a loud honk and speed up, alas, to run a yellow light again!

Therefore, my suggestion to

all American drivers is that we should stop thinking of ourselves as individuals and devote ourselves into two separate entities, one is a driver and the other is whatever specific profession we belong to.

That means we have to develop two entirely different personalities — one for driving and the other for our professions. That is, when I drive, I have to think of myself as a professional driver, not as a teacher, lawyer, doctor, nurse, engineer or anyone else.

Driving should not take a back seat and become rising, if we honestly and sincerely want to minimize such tragic accidents.

— Qazi N. Uddin lives in Yemen.

»YOUR LETTERS

Disagree, but don't hate

Re: Richard Larsen's Oct. 9 essay, "From polarized to hating":

Finally, an essay making a clear distinction between "hate" and "difference of opinion." Larsen made it very clear that, if I have a difference of opinion with someone, that does not necessarily mean I hate that person.

I have been trying to instill this idea in people all my life. Dec. 8, 1994, I wrote a letter to The Star regarding illegal immigrants and urged everyone not to express their hatred indiscriminately: "It is not my intention to encourage or justify illegal immigration. For the time being, it would be nice to stop using the word 'criminals' when we refer to illegal aliens. We should not express any hatred toward fellow human beings by calling them criminals." I was mercilessly attacked following my letter's publication. My opponents reminded me that all illegal immigrants are criminals, and criminals should be termed criminals, and I should not express any sympathy for them.

Larsen has rightly observed, "The masters of hate led people to believe that illegal immigrants are to blame for the rise in crime .... They did this by simply labeling every illegal immigrant in this nation a criminal because they crossed the border illegally." It is a very good feeling to see that, what I was thinking 13-years ago, Larsen has almost the same thing to say at the present time.

All reasonable and critical thinkers must have differences of opinion. They should be allowed to express them without being labeled as haters. Larsen is right. Fear of "them" generates hatred.

Most of the problems regarding human relations we face now in this world are the result of hatred toward fellow human beings. Criticism or having a difference of opinion has nothing to do with hatred.

— Qazi N. Uddin,
Ventura

"IT'S THE SAME EVERY SEASON... I'VE MORE TOMATOES, ZUCCHINIS AND PRESIDENTIAL CANDIDATES THAN I KNOW WHAT TO DO WITH!"

243

Alone in a world of sympathizers

Bangladesh disaster stirs little empathy

By Qazi N. Uddin

I have been living in Ventura since 1987. Well, you can live in a place for a long time and announce to the world that you enjoy your privacy and don't like to be bothered. I am not one of them.

I consider myself an outgoing person. I participate in local cultural and social events and, being a college instructor, it is hardly possible for me to live a secluded life. I cannot shout, "Leave me alone," because I have a family to take care of that includes my wife and two daughters.

My daughters received their educations locally at Anacapa middle and Buena high schools before receiving their M.D. and Ph.D. My wife works for the Ventura County Human Services Agency. As for myself, I made it to the front page of The Star and the Los Angeles Times for my outstanding contribution (so the news features state) toward educating disadvantaged students.

The point I am trying to make here is I have become a part and parcel of this community. I have never lived that long in any one place, even in my native country, Bangladesh.

However, I still have a feeling that I am living here by myself alone. Why? Because I have a very peculiar background. I lived in Bangladesh for 34 years before I decided to escape. I don't feel good about using the word "escape" here, but that was the real feeling at that time. When you live in a country that long, where you were born and brought up, you cannot shake off some feelings and emotions related to that country, be it horrible or pleasant.

Sympathy versus empathy

So, it is natural for me to feel sad when a disaster hits Bangladesh. Besides, I left my extended family members and friends, along with my language, culture and society. When I see that my people back there are still suffering, I feel really depressed. In such a state of mind, people need empathy, not sympathy. Naturally, when a natural calamity of huge proportions hits Bangladesh, my American friends express their sympathy.

Since I can see the difference between sympathy and empathy, I never feel that my friends are saying, "We are with you, you are not alone." I always wonder if the locals could create such a feeling among foreigners when they are in distress as, "Don't worry, we are all in it together," what a beautiful world this would be.

Sympathizing with someone's misfortune is feeling sorry for him or her. Feeling sorry does not really mean feeling the pain and suffering someone is experiencing. Unfortunately, in this world we live in now, there is little room for feeling empathy for people when they live far away. When disaster hits home, we become a little more concerned, try to understand the nature of that tragedy and develop empathy.

On the other hand, for people farther removed, we believe nothing can be done other than to say sorry and, in rare instances, send some money to help. The reason people don't feel empathy when they are far from the actual place of occurrence is that they think nothing can be done against the fury of the nature. It is, after all, a natural disaster!

This is why it is important to realize that nature also

My presence in Ventura can create awareness among locals to think beyond local problems. If my presence here can bring Bangladesh's problem to Ventura, then Venturans will become universal human beings. This world awareness can start here and spread...

discriminates even when a disaster takes place in the middle of the night in the frigid waters of the Atlantic Ocean. Does anyone remember that when the Titanic sank, more than 60 percent of those holding first-class tickets survived, only 36 percent of the second-class passengers were saved, and only 20 percent of those on the lower decks?

Unique position

When I was in Bangladesh, I was literally on the lower deck of this world! No wonder it felt like escaping when I was able to see the Statue of Liberty! During my stay in the coastal city of Chittagong in Bangladesh, cyclones hit twice. In 1966, 25,000 people were killed and in 1970, 40,000. During the second one, I narrowly escaped death when the roof over my head twisted like cardboard, and I, along with my family members, had to duck under beds. Then, in 1991, when I was here in Ventura, a killer cyclone hit again and took away 128,780 lives with it.

What was the response of the civilized world? Feel sorry and send some money, if you can. Obviously, I did not like that response. This is not what I am talking about. This sympathy will help the survivors be ready to die during the next cyclone. This is why I feel the burden of an entire country is on my shoulders alone. I am the only one here who is feeling the pain and suffering. Civilization demands that we feel the pain and suffering for people in distress, regardless of whether they are far or near, and that we participate in minimizing that suffering.

Help needed to save lives

When we identify a pattern of cyclone or any other form of disaster in a particular location in this world, we could do some investigation to come up with plans and programs to save lives. What Bangladesh needs are many cyclone shelters built on offshore islands and low-lying coastal areas. It needs to develop means of communication and transportation for evacuation, so people can be saved from tidal waves. Unfortunately, Bangladesh is so poor, it does not have the resources to do it alone.

My presence in Ventura can create awareness among locals to think beyond local problems. If my presence here can bring Bangladesh's problem to Ventura, then Venturans will become universal human beings. This world awareness can start here and gradually spread all over the world when people all over the world are going to think internationally, not locally. This is when this world will be a very different place to live, when no one ever will feel isolated and alone.

— Qazi N. Uddin lives in Ventura.

Thursday, Aug. 28, 2008   WC   The Star

PRESIDENTIAL CANDIDATES

Repair America's image

My understanding is that unless you own some rental properties for business purposes, you don't need more than one home to live a comfortable life. Rich people may own some vacation homes in various resort locations for pleasure or recreation; however, that should not be considered a necessity, but, obviously, a luxury.

If you can afford and decide to live a lavish and luxurious lifestyle, you are entitled to live it in a capitalistic society. However, you should have the honesty and mental strength to admit you prefer to live a private and lavish life, not only by owning seven or eight homes, but also by owning a private jet and a yacht, in addition to having a private beach along with some limousines. However, you cannot claim you need them.

This is very disappointing that a person like John McCain, who is aspiring to be president, does not have that mental strength to admit he is one of those who crave a luxurious lifestyle.

If it is true he does not even know how many homes he owns, he is not fit to be our president. We cannot afford to present to the world a president with an extravagant lifestyle who does not even have the courage to admit it.

America is engaged in two messy wars in foreign lands and in an abstract war on terrorism.

To be able to win, America desperately needs a president who can inspire respect around the world through dedication and sacrifice. At this time, becoming president is a big responsibility, not a matter of joke.

This is the time for a president to re-establish America's image as a compassionate leader with regard, respect and concern for those who are striving to provide a roof over their heads.

— Qazi N. Uddin,
Ventura

E.O. GREEN SCHOOL SHOOTING

Americans can learn from others

By Qazi N. Uddin

When investigators of a tragic school shooting say they are baffled, it annoys me too much. To announce that this is an isolated incident that defies all explanations is to shun all kinds of responsibilities and to express a feeling that "we give up."

To accept the truth is to hold something or someone accountable, which the authorities are reluctant to do. Because the truth might offend someone, we say this is a bizarre incident. The newspaper headline goes like this, "Illinois gunman's rampage baffles police, colleagues." The question surfaces, why should it baffle police and colleagues when everyone knew that Steven Kazmierczak — who killed five and wounded 18 at Northern Illinois University on Feb. 14 — had a mental illness?

He was in a mental-health center for some time and he had an interest in guns. On top of everything, the Federal Bureau of Alcohol, Tobacco, Firearms and Explosives knew that Kazmierczak bought four guns from a federally licensed dealer. Ironically, Kazmierczak bought his guns from the same dealer who sold guns to Virginia Tech shooter, Seung-Hui Cho, who killed 33 students. After all these, you are saying it baffles you? Give me a break!

Another most irritating thing that has become a norm is to use the very trite expression, "searching for an answer," when a shooting occurs on campus. It is to pretend that the answer is not so obvious.

My feeling is that everyone knows the answer, but no one wants to face the reality. So, the authorities, journalists, social scientists, intellectuals and politicians all want to hide under such a pretext, "We are searching for an answer."

Well, if we continue searching for an answer, although we "know" it, soon, we have to surrender this civilization to the whims and caprices of a few mentally ill people.

I have been addressing this question of campus shooting in The Star since 1968 after Jonesboro. Since then, I answered questions regarding Columbine and Virginia Tech. Now, I am answering questions again after Oxnard, Louisiana and Illinois. My answer is: We have to follow the examples of other cultures where they do not have any campus shooting.

Yes, there are still some highly sophisticated cultures where campus shootings do not exist, where people have profound respect for education and educational institutions, where parents stay together to raise their children, parents' top priorities are safety, well-being and education of their children. Where citizens do not carry guns and do not go to their constitutions to claim the right to bear arms. A few gun owners are considered uncivilized and uncultured.

I grew up and lived in one of those cultures (Bangladesh) for 34 years. Now, I have lived another 22 years in the United States. So I know what I am talking about. There was no incident of campus shooting during my stay and no news of campus shooting from there during my long absence.

Likewise, most of the Southeast Asian countries, such as, India, Myanmar, Vietnam, Philippines, Malaysia and Indonesia can claim that they have no such thing as campus shooting. People in these countries have not fallen in love with guns either. They hate guns, not because they can't afford to buy one. They believe "a pen is mightier than a sword." We are not talking about poor countries. Even people in Japan and Canada hate guns. No wonder they also don't have any campus shooting!

Therefore, the time has come for the United States to wake up and accept the truth that it has something to learn from these countries, instead of neglecting these countries as underdeveloped and uncivilized. Learn something from them about their attitude toward family life, education and management of anger and frustration, to minimize violence and create a healthy society. In addition, get rid of your love affairs with guns. It is only then campus shooting will stop, and the United States will be able to regain its prestige in the civilized world.

— Qazi N. Uddin lives in Ventura.

»YOUR LETTERS

Religious rule unconstitutional

Re: Richard Larsen's April 22 essay, "Misreading U.S. society":

I have always admired Larsen for his straightforward approach to issues that concern us all, regardless of whom he criticizes, the pope or the president. Once again, he is right on the mark: "People throughout history have challenged any authority who turns dogma into autocratic rule."

This is precisely the point. All religions have the right to proclaim supremacy or superiority. They may as well announce they have the right solution to all problems humans encounter. However, they should not be entrusted with authority to impose their ideas on others.

This is exactly why our Founding Fathers heralded in our Constitution the separation of church and state. The government of any democratic country should not take part in advising or forcing people into strict adherence to the rules and regulations of any particular religion.

History bears testimony to the fact that, whenever religious fundamentalists took control of the government of a country, people vehemently opposed that government, even though they belonged to the same religion. Having faith in a religion is one thing; being dictated by fundamentalists is another.

This is why religious fundamentalists should not have political power. If governmental power and authority are necessary to force people to become religious, then where is the power of religion itself? We are not against religion or religious leaders. A religion should be able to attract people, not intimidate them. Asking for authority and governmental power is intimidation.

All major religions have provided us with wonderful ideas that formulated our moral and ethical values.

In a democratic society, a government should be "of the people, by the people and for the people," not "of the religion, by the religion and for the religion."

— Qazi N. Uddin,
Ventura

WILLIAM L. HAMMAKER: A CENTURY OF PEACE

A universal human being

By Qazi N. Uddin

There is no telling when, how and why a friendship develops. This is one of the many mysteries of life that we human beings experience. We rarely contemplate on such mysteries to learn from them. We just accept the fact that someone is a best friend and attribute the reason to being similar in thoughts and in likes and dislikes; to having same interests or same age. Amazingly, this is not always true. Psychologists found out that opposites do attract, and they also believe there is no such thing as altruistic friendship. We develop friendship to achieve some objectives. However, some friends defy all such explanations. My friend W.L. "Bill" Hammaker is one of them.

Although I consider myself a friendly person, that does not mean I always crave friendship whenever I see an opportunity. I have my pride and prejudice like everyone else. So, one day, when I received a phone call from a stranger just to tell me he enjoyed reading my article in The Star, I was delighted. I didn't envision the possibility of an enduring friendship emerging.

Normally, someone calls me about my articles with an angry tone. Enjoyed my article! My readers rarely take the trouble of picking up the phone to tell me that. But there was a difference that time. It was W.L. "Bill" Hammaker. Not only did he praise my article, he also invited me to join the celebration of his 96th birthday party on June 5, 2007. I gladly accepted. At that time, I had no clue that a new friendship had just begun.

When I arrived at the party, I felt like a fish out of water, I simply didn't belong there. A 99-year-old man surrounded by his family, friends and admirers. That appeared like a different world to me. So, my wife and I tried to avoid attention. However, that was not possible. Bill dragged me to the limelight, bragging about his new "writer" friend. I was

really embarrassed. However, immediately the world around me changed. Bill made me feel at home.

If it ended there, I would not be able to claim that I have a centenarian friend. Bill continued calling me every now and then to talk about issues that concern us all, and, of course, when he saw one of my articles in The Star. During our conversations, I came to know him better. He told me of his philosophy of life, his passion and his association with the international organization Fellowship of Reconciliation, which he joined more than seven decades ago. He recalled giving a speech for peace and against war at Johns Hopkins University in 1936. He told me about coming to Ventura County in 1945 and serving as the director of the Ventura County YMCA for 23 years. He served the Rotary Club of Ventura East as president in 1963.

A few weeks ago, he called to remind me he will, officially be a centenarian today, June 5, and will have a party June 11. I must not miss it. At that precise moment, I sat down to contemplate on the reason for this centenarian's fascination for an ordinary person like me.

I don't consider myself so visible that a person of Bill's age and stature will crave my friendship. Besides, I am only 65 and he is now 100. So, my thought process brought me to a wonderful realization.

This is perhaps the secret of longevity of human life. Some people live longer because they live in a different world. Apparently, they live with us, but they don't think like us. Our world is our country; their world is the whole universe. The richness, the abundance and the diversity of this universe attract them. They know how to break their own boundaries, limitations, monotones and reach out to others, to seek out a new dimension, a new meaning of their existence. I think of them as ageless, timeless and limitless human beings. They just don't seek

William L. Hammaker of Camarillo, photographed last month in h backyard, turns 100 today.

Bill is one of those who has no superiority complex, no boundaries. He wants to reach out to every single human being on this planet. He belongs to a country of diverse human beings and that inspires him to live for 100 years and beyond, so he can meet and hug everyone. Long live Mr. Hammaker.

out their own, they seek out others. They learned how to embrace the entire human race, not to confine them to any particular country, race, religion, or ethnicity. They are universal human beings.

As a person, I may be very insignificant to those who developed a superiority complex. Those who look at my distinctive physical features and think of me as "other," as inferior, might lose all interest in me.

They shorten their visions and

their expectations become short. How can they live longer with shorter expectations? Bill is one of those who has no superiority complex, no boundaries. He wan to reach out to every single hum being on this planet. He belongs a country of diverse human bein and that inspires him to live for years and beyond, so he can mee and hug everyone. Long live Mr. Hammaker.

— Qazi N. Uddin lives in Ventura

Contact Us | Site Map | Archives | Alerts | Subscribe to the paper

Home   News   Sports   Business   Arts & Living   Opinion   Obituaries

Pulse | Letters to the Editor | Forums | Brian Dennert   Marie Lakin   Jason Love   Greenberg's Cartoons   Richard Larsen   Let

Blog: LettersToTheEditor

search |

About tl

Home › Blogs › LettersToTheEditor

Letters to the
by our editor's
published.

Surfing isn't real reading

on July 30, 2008 10:31 AM |

Re: Richard Larsen's July 28 essay, "Will the Net kill reading?":

Twelve years ago, I wrote a letter to The Star emphasizing the importance of reading in which I
opined, "Reading inspires thinking, and thinking generates writing."

It is a very good feeling to find Larsen expressing the same kind of concern: "Literacy includes the
ability to make sense of what is read and to put it into context." This is precisely what the process
of thinking does for an avid reader.

No matter how much we lament the inability of our young generation to write a coherent essay and
how much money we spend on teaching composition, the situation is not going to improve if we
continue downplaying the importance of reading and "shun books in favor of Web surfing" as the
essay's secondary headline put it.

Reading informative and objective writings helps us to gather information, but creative and
imaginative writings that are found in narratives and subjective writings help us to think critically
and analyze and organize our thoughts to be able to express ourselves in writing. There are some
basic skills this civilization has been able to acquire, the importance of which will never diminish.
Reading is one of them. Of course, one may ask, reading of what? And the answer is reading of
creative and subjective writing — not that much of informative and objective writing that we can get
by surfing the Web.

There is a big difference between surfing the Web and reading news analyses in editorials,
columns and opinion sections. Larsen aptly states, "Being Web-savvy may help people navigate
the Internet, but literacy is what helps people advance civilization." So, to make a sweeping
generalization that reading is not important in this age of electronics supercommunication is not
only thoughtless, but also dangerous.

— Qazi N. Uddin, Ventura

Search

| Search |

About thi

This page cor
by Andrew Ho
July 30, 2008

Fundraisers &
previous entry

Burying the g
entry in this bl

249

Don't count on humans

on September 22, 2008 12:51 PM | Permalink

It appears that we can't depend on human beings anymore to be responsible, duty-bound and careful in doing their jobs. In the future, we'll have to transfer these qualities to sophisticated machines that will presumably do a better job than we human beings do. Preferably, such a job as mass transportation of human beings to short- or long-distance destinations should be handed to conductorless machines so lives could be saved.

It's no wonder U.S. Rep. Elton Gallegly and two other congressmen from California in the wake of Chatsworth disaster have filed legislation that would require railroads to install "positive train control" systems. Why not? When we human beings are becoming more and more irresponsible and cannot control our urge to indulge in text messaging and showing a very negative poor judgment at our job, then machines should take positive control over human's negative behavior.

It would be very prudent for human beings to design a personal means of transportation that would be driveless, accident preventive and pedestrian sensitive. Our universities have already developed smart computer programs to teach our new generations, and we hear that soon computers will replace our physicians and provide accurate diagnoses of our illnesses. In grocery stores' checkout stands, we won't need any human help any more -- this has already started in some places -- and soon in restaurants, dinner plates will arrive on conveyor belts

Therefore, it appears that every disaster has a silver lining! Our congressmen can immediately think of some positive control system technology instead of advising us to control our behavior and exhibit some positive attitude when we are on duty. No one is realizing that no matter how many new technologies we develop, we shall never be able to come up with a substitute for human beings' sense of duty and responsibility.

-- Qazi N. Uddin, Ventura

BARACK OBAMA

4 changes already happened

By Qazi N. Uddin

It appears that some people have not yet been able to realize the importance of Barack Obama's victory in this election. Those who are not willing to see anything significant happening pretty soon or in the near future, it is not difficult to understand their attitude. They are either pessimists or racists. Pessimists have no racial prejudices. They are simply negative people. They can't envision any bright future, regardless of any major changes in their environment. On the other hand, racists didn't like Obama's presidential candidacy to start with, considering his racial background.

However, our problem with these two groups of people is that they have already started denouncing Obama's success and spreading negativity that nothing will change. Whoever becomes the president, the "same old, same old" will happen, or Obama will bring "socialism" to the United States.

These people have failed to recognize the four very important changes that have already taken place with Obama's victory. First of all, we don't have to use Lincoln's "government of the people..." any more to claim that the United States is a democratic country. This election has established this fact beyond the shadow of any doubt.

Second, this election reinvigorated the concept of "success from the scratch." From now on, no one will have any excuse for their personal failures. That is, they cannot say that they are being discriminated against.

The need for affirmative action will diminish! Obama's victory has brought it to the forefront that even any of us gathered from Kenya can become president of the United States. So, don't blame others for your misfortunes or failures.

Third, this election has definitely established this fact around the world that this is a not a racist country any more. The majority of the people of the United States is colorblind.

The world has developed a tremendous respect for the American people. The world now believes that when the time comes to elect their leader, Americans don't look at the color of someone's skin.

Finally and most importantly, this election will be recorded in the history as recognition of the importance of global awareness by the citizens of the United States. They want to restore their image that has been terribly damaged by the action of the previous governments.

—Qazi N. Uddin lives in Ventura.

Voters denigrated

Re: Harvey Paskowitz's Nov. 6 letter, "Congratulate the media".

So, Paskowitz believes The Star and the media helped Barack Obama get elected. How insulting to the millions of voters across this great land who made their decision from their belief that the Republican Party has let us down for eight years.

I guess Paskowitz should buy a radio and turn on local station KVTA 1520 AM if he wants to hear "outright lies, unsubstantiated rumors, half-truths." Just take a listen to those on-air "personalities."

If Paskowitz needs his "Republican fix," that's the place to go.

— Gary J. Grayson,
Ventura

PULSE ... is a place for ideas to ... inform, to per- ... en to entertain. ... ou are invited to ... r mind, to read the ... of knowledgeable, ... il, involved Ventura ... esidents, to help ... pulse of our commu-

Nobel Laureate proves rewards of selflessness

By Qazi N. Uddin

A Nobel Laureate for peace was in the backyard of my Venture home on Memorial Day.

He was addressing a gathering of around 200, explaining his projects aimed at eradicating poverty from the world. Since then, I have been inundated with queries as to how a person of such stature landed in my backyard.

It is very rare for a Nobel Laureate to be found addressing a spellbound audience of ordinary people in the backyard of an ordinary person's home. However, in this case, a world-famous person decided to stand underneath a tent in the backyard of his friend's home to deliver a speech open to all.

It is a normal tendency of human beings to try to establish relationships with world-famous personalities whenever they see an opportunity. So, if I feel tempted to claim I have a Nobel Laureate friend, I cannot be blamed for that. However, the problem associated with making such claims is that it always leads to self-glorification.

Therefore, I have decided not to concentrate on myself, but to elaborate on the qualities and achievements of an individual with whom I grew up, went to the same school and worked at the same institution. My intention is to introduce a person who had a humble beginning in an impoverished country, yet, was able to attract the attention of the world and, eventually, win a Nobel Prize. I am talking about Dr. Muhammad Yunus of Bangladesh who won the Nobel Prize for peace in 2006.

I first came to know about Yunus in 1960 when I was a college student in Bangladesh. He excelled in almost all extracurricular activities, winning awards, writing in debates, journals, participating in debates, cultural shows and sports. He, along with his two brothers, was always on top of everything.

Seed of greatness

After he won the Nobel Prize, I started reconstructing that period of my life with him only to be amazed by discovering the seed of his hidden greatness. My recollection brought me to the realisation that he was a very different person. While self-improvement was always my goal, he was concerned about the well-being of people around him and getting involved in such activities as raising funds for the cyclone victims in Bangladesh.

In 1963, after teaching in several colleges, I found an opportunity to start a college in a community called Hathazari, Incidentally, that was Yunus' hometown. While I was busy raising funds and constructing a new building for the college, Yunus was studying in the United States for his doctorate. He returned in 1972 with a doctorate in economics and started teaching at Chittagong University, which was located in Hathazari.

However, Yunus was not only teaching. He started working with the villagers, establishing in 1974 his "Nabajug Tebhaga Samiti" (New Age Three Share's Association). Its purpose was to help the landless farmers cultivate the lands they were working and get one share out of three of the crop in return. Later, in

1977, he established his "Grameen Probkalpo" (Village Project), and I believe he then conceived his soon-to-become-world-famous "Grameen Bank" (Village Bank), which is based on his concept of microcredit.

My intention here is not to explain in detail his concepts of microcredit, by which he was able to eradicate poverty from many rural people's lives in Bangladesh and help liberate village countries, and help liberate village women from the grip of misery, but to draw attention to the fact that, at that time he was working selflessly, he was not aspiring for fame. Rather, his detractors were criticising him for changing the traditional way of women's lives in Bangladesh. Undaunted, he kept up the good work.

In the meantime, I found a job at the University of Chittagong in 1976. Yunus was there in the Department of Economics. This is how we became co-workers. In 1979, I left Chittagong University to receive higher education in the United States. The difference between Yunus and me was that he decided to return to his country after his studies in the United States and immediately started teaching and working for the poor villagers; on the other hand, I decided to stay here for my own benefit.

Thinking about others

The purpose of writing this, therefore, is to emphasise the fact that always striving for personal glorification and personal achievement will not help the cause of establishing world peace. In our personal lives, we should always think about how to help people, instead of being self-centered. Likewise, for a community, society or country, it is not a good idea to think about self-interest. We should think globally, not locally, the same as we should think not only about ourselves, but also about others.

This kind of thinking made Dr. Muhammad Yunus a very different kind of human being. That is why when I invited him to come to my home after his speaking engagement at OSU Channel Islands, he did not hesitate.

— Qazi N. Uddin lives in Ventura.

India Partition not the result of jihad

By Quazi N. Uddin

Re Sunil Dutta's Aug. 18 commentary, "Pakistan's jihadi politics rooted in India Partition".

In fact, Pakistan's jihadi politics has nothing to do with India Partition. Partition was the result of British imperialist rulers' "divide and rule policy." It is unfortunate that some Indian intellectuals living in the United States provide the Western world distorted facts with the sole ambition of demeaning Islam, Muslims and Muslim countries. We have enough problems already regarding misrepresentation of Islam. Such distorted explanation of "jihad politics" in the Muslim countries only strengthens the misconception that Islam is a religion of violence.

It is hard to believe the writer thinks Pakistan was secured from the British by a Muslim leader, Mohammed Ali Jinnah, who exploited Islam to gain political power. It is true that the enmity between India and Pakistan started since their very beginnings in 1947 as independent countries. However, the emergence of Pakistan was not related to Jinnah's exploitation of Islam, and Pakistan's politics was not shaped either by its subsequent alliance with the Islamic jihadists.

Here is the true history of the creation of Pakistan and India as I have witnessed it being born in undivided India under British colonial rulers. I lived in British India and East Pakistan (now Bangladesh) for a total of 34 years, so I know what I am talking about.

The British ruled India for about 200 years. Before that, India was under Muslim rulers for 700 years. The British came to India as traders and, with the help of a local "traitor" named Mirzafar, invaded the capital of the Muslim rulers in 1757. In India and Pakistan, the words "traitor" and "Mirzafar" have become synonymous.

After capturing India, the British rulers decided to crush, as usual, Muslims, depriving them of all sorts of patronages and privileges to prevent them from gaining strength, so they wouldn't be able to fight back. On the other hand, they sought cooperation from Hindus and promoted their causes. This fact has been aptly established by the historians as the "divide and rule policy" of the British administration.

Indeed, the British rulers pitted Hindus and Muslims against each other by instigating communal riots, with the ambition to rule India forever.

On the other hand, the Muslim rulers were not Islamic fanatics. Although they ruled India for 700

However, the emergence of Pakistan was not related to Jinnah's exploitation of Islam, and Pakistan's politics was not shaped either by its subsequent alliance with the Islamic jihadists.

years, it was not their intention to turn India into a Muslim country. India still is a Hindu majority country, which bears testimony to the fact that the Muslim rulers did not try to convert Hindus through intimidation.

If they tried, 700 years was enough time to do that.

Besides, there was no single instance of Hindu-Muslim riots in India during those 700 years. Riots between Hindus and Muslims started as soon as the British took over the administration of India. So, India's Muslim rulers were not Islamic-jihadists. However, Dr. Dutta never mentioned that fact in his commentary. He squarely blamed Jinnah for taking advantage of Islamic sentiments to create Pakistan.

Dr. Dutta forgot to mention that if was Jinnah who called for Hindu-Muslim unity to achieve independence of India. Therefore, he was called the "Pioneer of

Hindu-Muslim Unity" in India. Eventually, Jinnah had to accept the British decision to divide India on the basis of Hindu and Muslim majority areas. However, it is too naïve to believe the British just wanted to create Pakistan (a Muslim country) because Jinnah wanted to.

If the Indians had not started freedom fighting, which the British called "terrorism," and subsequently Gandhi did not come up with his noncooperation and nonviolent movement, I doubt very much whether the British would have left India in 1947. However, before they left, they decided to give Indians a Parthian shot and divided the country.

So, India's Partition and the creation of Pakistan were not the result of Islamic jihad, as Dr. Dutta wants his Western readers to believe. It was not Pakistan's fault that a Hindu king of Kashmir (Muslim majority) decided to join India during Partition and Afghanistan cannot control its Islamic militants. It is absurd to attribute Pakistan's current problem with religious fanatics to its Islamic roots.

— Quazi N. Uddin, Ph.D., Ross in Pankow.

Jihad, terror not the same

By Qazi N. Uddin

Re: Bill O'Reilly's Nov. 14 column, "Fort Hood is not a tragedy, it's terrorism":

O'Reilly believes that Maj. Nidal Malik Hasan is a jihadist and, therefore, he is a terrorist. According to O'Reilly's understanding, "jihad" and "terror" are synonymous. From such a misconception, he is blaming President Barack Obama for not declaring the Ford Hood shooting an act of terror by a Muslim jihadist.

However, if O'Reilly did some research, he would have no problem finding that "jihad" and "terror" are two completely different things. In fact, "jihad" is just the opposite word for "terror." To say that all jihadists are terrorists is to say that everything cold is also hot. The Arabic word jihad has many connotations, such as to strive, to struggle, to exert, to fight, and to make effort for individual and spiritual accomplishment and refinement.

Does it have any military connotation? Yes, Quran suggests believers have the rights to defend themselves by going to organized war (not terrorism) for self-defense at times when they believe their existence is threatened, which some people, subsequently, termed "holy war." Christianity also has such a holy war, called crusade. However, we all know the days of jihad or crusade to signify religious holy war are over. So, when a disgruntled or mentally unstable person cries "jihad" or "crusade," he or she does not automatically become a

Besides, jihad, or crusade, is not supposed to be carried out by individuals. In the Middle Ages, at the dawn of the spread of new religions, such military adventures were carried out by organized countries to save their territory or to drive out nonbelievers from adjacent territories, anticipating threats from them. So, to believe that an individual killed 13 people in the U.S. to save or glorify his religion is ridiculous.

On the other hand, terrorism is a political term. Creating terror is the only weapon of less-powerful people against the most powerful. Less-powerful people cannot fight a regular war to win. They know it's impossible, so they want to terrorize a most-powerful person or country by inflicting maximum pain and suffering.

Islam and every major religion strongly denounce terrorism. During imperialism, many British colonies started terrorizing British army and personnel to achieve independence. British called them terrorists, but, in their own countries, they were known as freedom fighters. Even in the U.S., when George Washington and his supporters started terrorizing the British army, he was called a terrorist by the British.

So, the origin and development of terrorism are associated with political grievances of a group of people. In fact, terrorism is a relative term. Someone's terrorist is someone else's freedom fighter. Terrorism has nothing to do

with religion. Islam and other major religions do not endorse terrorizing people to convert them.

Prophet Mohammad in his final address in a gathering of Hajj (annual pilgrimage to Mecca) in the field of Arafat, announced: "Everyone is entitled to his or her religion. Do not fight over religion. The right path is clearly separated from the wrong path."

It is a fact of life that whether someone practices his religion or not, a person grows up with his own religion and culture. So, when a Christian gets angry or surprised, he or she might cry out loud, "Jesus." It's very natural.

On the other hand, when a Muslim becomes disgruntled or mentally unstable, that person might shout, "Allah hu Akbar" (God is great).

It is sad that O'Reilly does not understand this fact of life. Therefore, he constructed this logical fallacy: "And then yelling, 'Allah Akbar' (God is great), while gunning down innocent people, the math is on the blackboard. Maj. Nidal Malik Hasan is a terrorist; he murdered 13 people in the name of jihad."

With such faulty logic, he blamed President Obama for not immediately declaring this tragedy an act of terror.

— Qazi N. Uddin lives in Ventura.

Addressing the government's role in teen pregnancy

by Qazi N. Uddin

We all agree that teenage pregnancy is a menace to our society. From all consideration, it is very detrimental for a teenage mother's and her child's way of life. Teenage pregnancy, which is known as "taboo-having-babies," has disturbing; first as soon as a teenage pregnancy is revealed, the teenager involved loses all kinds of support and sympathy; first of all from her own parents and then from the rest of the people known to her.

That is why a pregnant teenager might suffer from depression. This depression persists after she opts for abortion. Adoption or keeping her baby on her own. The prospect of the father, being responsible aspect of the father, being responsible for, generates a sense of desperation, and the decision to raise the baby develop anxiety, hopelessness.

In such a miserable situation, a pregnant teenager cannot concentrate on running her career objectives, still becoming a productive member of the society. She acquires a new stigma of the single-teen-mother," which is not really glorified in the real world outside of Hollywood. This is the most natural outcome of being-pregnant as a teenager.

So what should we do? We human beings were able to develop such wonderful concepts of regulating our days a family life. This is marriage and starting this sustainable civilization how we created this sustainable civilization

However, during the last 50 years in the United States, we decided to deviate from that path, and some of our intellectuals started writing books entitled "Good Riddance" to denounce the traditional family life. Our film industries decided to promote and glorify having babies out of wedlock and single parenting. In addition, our society has become very lenient and permissive toward premarital and immature

the role of a Good Samaritan. It has designed plans and programs to rescue our pregnant teenagers. The state of California, through its Social Services Agency, designed a program known as "Minor Consent Services," which is defined as such: "Minor Consent Services are certain 'sensitive services' covered under Medi-Cal for which a child may apply without parental consent."

Does it occur to anyone in our government that in its effort to control teenage pregnancy, it is in fact promoting immature sexual activity, it is in fact promoting the fear of getting pregnant?

sexual relations among our young generation. As a consequence, we are witnessing a surge in all kinds of indiscriminate sexual behaviors resulting in AIDS, STDs and teenage pregnancy.

However, dose indiscriminate sex may culminate in unwanted pregnancy regardless of precautionary measures and distribution of condoms among teenagers, society remains passive and unsympathetic toward the plight of the baby mothers and their children. So our benevolent government wanted to play

Basically, it is telling our teenage girls, "If you are sexually active, your parents do not need to know that. You can come to us. We will provide you with birth control pills and condoms." The intention of our government is obvious: control teenage pregnancy. However, despite such precautionary measures, pregnancy does occur. So the government again came up with a plan to tell our teenage girls, "If you get pregnant, don't worry about it. You still can come to us. We will help you to get an

abortion. What if you don't want an abortion? We will help you to give up your baby for adoption. You want to keep your baby? No problem. You still can come to us and we will provide you with pregnancy-related services until your baby is born and you are under 21 years of age. Then you are on your own. You have to find your way in this wonderful world without being prepared to face it." Of course, the last sentence is mine. The government is not announcing it to a pregnant teenager. What a wonderful social service! And what a wonderful way to eliminate teenage pregnancy!

Does it occur to anyone in our government that in its effort to control teenage pregnancy, it is in fact promoting immature sexual activity, it is in fact removing the fear of getting pregnant? The assumption on the part of our government in that teenagers will have sex no matter when, and immune the family and society out there are very involved about teenage pregnancy; it is our sacred duty to do something about it. Of course, we have to use your tax money to be able to do that!

How did we end up in such a big mess? The answer is very simple. When parents are off the hook (they don't have to know whether their teenagers are sexually active), when disintegration of traditional family life has been glorified as "Good Riddance," when society becomes permissive toward deviant human behavior, then the big government should step in with its innovative ideas.

Qazi N. Uddin is a resident of Ventura.